HIDDEN IN PLAIN SIGHT

Also by the author

Brand Leadership:
The Next Level of the Brand Revolution
  with David A. Aaker

Erich Joachimsthaler

HIDDEN IN PLAIN SIGHT

How to Find and Execute Your Company's Next Big Growth Strategy

Harvard Business School Press

Boston, Massachusetts

Library of Congress Cataloging-in-Publication Data

Joachimsthaler, Erich, 1956–
   Hidden in plain sight : how to find and execute your company's next big growth
strategy / Erich Joachimsthaler.
      p. cm.
   Includes bibliographical references and index.
   ISBN-13: 978-1-4221-0165-0 (hardcover : alk. paper)
   ISBN-10: 1-4221-0165-7
   1. New products. 2. Consumers' preferences. 3. Consumers—Research.
I. Title.
   HF5415.153.J63 2007
   658.4'06—dc22

                                                            2007006551

To Daniela, Sara, Sophie, and Julian

Contents

Part III Strategies for Realizing Customer Advantage

Preface and Acknowledgments

"Why didn't we think of that?"

We live in a world of innovation overdrive, overloaded by consumer choice and excruciatingly tough commercial realities, realities that include the rapid commoditization of markets, technology shifts, margin pressures, and relentless fragmentation of consumer and business markets. Real and organic revenue growth trickles down to a mere percentage point or two.

Companies with any talent seek to achieve new growth and reinvent their core business model. They generate innumerable ideas, strategies, and new or improved products or services by the day. Ideas layer upon ideas; success often begets success.

The problem is that growth naturally brings with it the need for changed organization, hierarchy, structure, processes, systems, and policies that also can inch the company further from the very people the company has been serving. A kind of smokescreen develops that makes it very difficult to see the biggest opportunities for innovation and growth even though they are right there, hidden in plain sight.

How difficult? Try forgetting the business you're in, for a moment, and inserting yourself into the daily routines of the people you'd like to serve. Forget your product or technology. Forget your service. Forget your brand. Consider these people's daily activities and goals—try to imagine the contexts in which they live or work, to fully see the dynamic and complex ecosystem of their lives or work processes. Can you see the contours, depth, and structure of this system? Can you do it without instinctively placing your product in the scene or distorting your observations to fit your company's offerings?

It's not easy, right? That's why you are dismayed when a rival company or a start-up comes out with a wildly successful new innovative concept or idea that your company could have introduced. "Why didn't we think of that?" you ask. "We have the smarts, we have the resources. We should have thought of that. How did we miss it?"

That's why this book is not about refining marketing research, or becoming customercentric, or guiding customers to plumb their psyches, or co-creating value with customers, or integrating customers into your value chain, or positioning more distinctly, or sharpening your new product development process. It does not press any of these traditional hot buttons. Instead, it lays out a new model of strategic innovation for achieving profitable business growth. It will help you to:

- "Resee" your customers in entirely new ways and discover the biggest opportunities for growth that are right in front of you

- Define entirely new opportunity spaces by imagining potentially new innovations—from strategies, business models, and comprehensive portfolios of new products and services to marketing tactics and branding programs—that cut through the clutter to the delight of your own managers and dismay of your competitors

- Devise and execute a strategy for profitable growth that will fit into people's behavioral routines and transform their experiences with your company or your company's products and services.

"Thank goodness, we thought of that!"

Only with untainted eyes can your company's managers spot or envision the innovations that will really engage consumers or customers, transform their experiences, and, in so doing, can reinvent your company and deliver new growth. Imagine the intoxication of working on what truly hits the spot with people—consumers and customers alike—and that creates lasting advantage for your company as well.

For the last twenty-five years, I have investigated why some innovations, business models, business strategies, and marketing and branding tactics hit the mark, and why others do not. I have worked with industrial companies, consumer goods companies, retailers, financial services firms, media-and entertainment companies, telecommunications providers, health-care institutions, and many others. Before that, as an academic, I conducted studies in the same areas. Throughout my research and experience, one idea has surfaced consistently, no matter the type or size of organization, no matter whether serving industrial customers or consumers: the biggest, best, brightest, and most successful opportunities for innovation and growth are right here, in front of us, and we often can't see them or don't act on them.

These opportunities are yours for the spotting and the taking. But to see them and profit from them, you must first abandon some of the tried and proven conventions of innovation, marketing, and strategy formulation; you must discard some of today's common assumptions and management practices and adopt a fresh new way of planning and executing your strategies today and your innovation and growth strategies of tomorrow. It is my hope that this book will show you how.

Acknowledgments

In this book I have synthesized many years of experiences working inside companies, as well as best practices and extant research on strategy, marketing, innovation, and building strong brands and businesses. I had the privilege of working very closely with several companies on their tough challenges and issues. These experiences have shaped major portions of this book. I thank the many executives who gave me the benefit of the doubt, who trusted me and confided in me and also extended that trust to the people who work with me.

I have drawn on many streams of thinking, managerial practices, and developments in academia and industry. I have benefited greatly working with some of best minds in the marketing world: David A. Aaker and Kevin Lane Keller, with whom I have shared a long journey of intellectual and professional development. In addition, I have drawn extensively from the works of other academics and their research in strategy, innovation, and marketing. Over many years, I have had a close professional relationship with many colleagues at Harvard Business School and IESE Business School, and others in several executive programs who have helped greatly in the development of this book.

An important source of advancement of the book has been my colleagues at Vivaldi Partners. They have provided me with a constant source of ideas, insights, and lessons. They helped me along when my own thinking required clarity and structure. It is very hard to overemphasize their importance in this project. I would like to thank Markus Pfeiffer, who contributed significantly at every stage of this writing project and to every stage in the history of the company to date. Nick Hahn worked with me on several major applications in the consumer goods world and has contributed in important ways. Agathe Blanchon-Ehrsam is one of the foremost thinkers and creators of the methodologies used to study the behaviors of consumers. I would also like to thank: Hartmut Heinrich, who helped from a media-and-entertainment and technology industry perspective; James Cerruti, from the financial services perspective in the United States; and Mark Esser, from a financial services perspective in Europe. Sandro Principe contributed to some key developments in the quantification of innovation and growth opportunities, and German Yunes provided many innovative thoughts and experiences on activation in Latin America. Many other friends and colleagues have contributed over the years; and I want to thank particularly: Enshalla Anderson, Juergen Benkovich, Samantha Cescau, Jack Lee, June Lee Risser (Reckitt Benkiser), Laurie Giandomenico (EffectiveBrands), Silke Meixner, Adam Schorr, Andrea Wolf, and Markus Zinnbauer.

Several academics, professionals and thought leaders are an integral part of our work on innovation and growth strategies. I have greatly benefited from their thinking and want to give a big thanks to: David Arnold, David Collis, Grant McCracken, Anthony Freeling, Ronnie Goodstein, Paddy Miller, Barry Nalebuff, Eric Noel, Dwight Riskey, Majken Schultz, and Glen Woroch.

Several researchers, consultants, and colleagues contributed on key chapters of the book. My warmest thanks to Kateri Benoit, Jack Lee, Anthony Leung, Georgina Miller, Bethany Otuteye, Tammy Tan, David Tran, and Delfina Zweifel. The book never would have come to fruition without the encouragement of Alfonso Gimenez, Jan-Christoph Koestring, and Federico Riege.

Over the course of the past years, I have greatly benefited from working with several very talented writers who helped in significant ways to get the manuscript to conclusion. Regina Maruca has helped write and rewrite many drafts, and Steve Fenichell has worked with me on writing most of the case studies. Both Regina and Steve also have been invaluable sparring partners and challengers of my thinking throughout the writing of the book. I would like to also thank my agent, Esmond Harmsworth.

I want to thank Kirsten Sandberg, who really pushed the manuscript in quality and content in very profound ways, and I deeply thank her colleagues at Harvard Business School Press, who have worked very professionally in seeing this project through its various stages.

—Erich Joachimsthaler
New York City
November 2006

Part I

Hidden Opportunities to Innovate and Grow

Chapter One

Looking from the Outside In

I N EARLY SPRING 2005, senior Sony executives were shocked to see Sir Howard Stringer, then the chief of Sony's U.S. operations, listening to an Apple iPod while riding an elevator in the company's U.S. headquarters. The *New York Times* summarized Sir Howard's cheekiness as a "visible if unstated rebuke to the technologists [at Sony] for falling behind the curve in downloadable music by concentrating on various proprietary formats for storing and playing music."[1] Other media outlets, academics, and analysts agreed. When the board gave the chairman's post to Sir Howard instead of Ken Kutaragi, Sony's senior technologist, whose managerial responsibilities diminished, those views seemed justified.

They were not. As we see it, that was not Sir Howard's message. By myopically seeking to place blame, most analysts and other observers missed a greater point: Sony—for all its sophisticated customer research tools, marketing methods, and analytic capabilities—had failed to identify and exploit a huge opportunity to provide a product that people not only welcomed and purchased but thoroughly enjoyed, reveled in, had fun with. The technologists' skill and focus were side issues.

In other words, Sony did nothing wrong but rather there was something vitally important that the company didn't do. To our minds, Sir Howard's wearing his iPod at work made an example of what people were doing every day then, and that's what matters most. They were changing the way they were buying, listening, storing, and discarding music. They were changing their behaviors and the products and services they used during their daily routines around music. Sony—at least that time around—failed to see and act on the opportunities these changes presented for the company.

If Blinded by Success, Then Blind to Innovation

Sony is a great example of a highly successful company whose successes have necessitated making its operations efficient and effective through adopting structures, processes, systems and policies that eventually come between the company and the people who might be its biggest opportunities for growth. Marketplace winners still emerge, though inconsistently, and the company can still grow and reap a profit. But the barrier becomes painfully apparent when the company increasingly finds itself watching a competitor hit the sweet spot with a new product, service, or business model just waiting to happen. "Why didn't we see it? It was right there in front of us, hidden in plain sight!"

We have been studying companies' connections and disconnections with consumers for more than twenty-five years and have worked inside a huge number of them. We have researched innovation practices with organizations ranging from the Allianz Group to Zara, from GE to Unilever, and from BMW to Frito-Lay. Across all of this research, a common theme has emerged and intensified: if a company is to truly hit the spot with innovation time and again with any consistency, and wishes to achieve profitable growth and create an advantage, it must do three things. First, it must understand the people it is trying to serve as the individuals they are—apart from any connection or interaction with the company. That is, it must be able to temporarily forget and let go of its current business, strategies, products, and brands as it observes how people (not just customers and potential customers) go about their daily routines. It must understand their behaviors in context, and develop a deep, inner conviction of the changing outer world—an objective view of how changes in people's ecosystem of life affect that behavior.

Second, it must know how to go beyond its own perimeters of products, markets, and competencies; let go of and challenge the assumptions, common practices, and golden rules of doing business still held today; and go beyond what it has learned from consumers. Only then can it conceive of entirely new opportunities by innovating across those people's behaviors— as Apple has done across the changing ways of how consumers buy and listen to music. It must know how to define the spaces of greatest opportunity that nobody has yet even imagined.

Third, it must see itself "from the outside in" and formulate strategies around people's behaviors, not just seek to satisfy consumer needs and wants or customer requirements. It must execute activation plans that engage consumers and seamlessly fit all kinds of innovations into peoples' and consumers' behaviors—or a customer company's work processes—so that the people absorb and assimilate them. It must create transformational life experiences, not just communicate features and benefits. Only then can companies spot and consistently and successfully bring to market winning innovations, achieve profitable new growth, and reinvent their business for the future.

This is not easy. But it need not be terribly difficult. The right instinct already exists in most companies. We are, after all, customers and consumers— *people*—ourselves.[2] As our examples will show, managers must learn to protect and direct that instinct to lead, and embed it in the organization, despite, and along with, the nature and ever-growing complexities of business.

Our goal for companies is the pursuit of what we call *customer advantage*, which occurs at the intersection of opportunities for innovation, major trends and market discontinuities, people's changing behaviors and experiences in life or work, and competitive success. To pursue customer advantage, we offer a framework called the *demand-first innovation and growth*, or DIG, model. We call the model *demand-first* because it provides companies with an unbiased, untainted view and an outside-in perspective of the demand opportunities before their own offerings are taken into consideration. This model should help companies:

- Understand the comprehensiveness and complexity of the changing ecosystem of demand and identify the biggest opportunities for innovation and growth that go beyond the linear satisfaction of needs and wants through new products and services

- Apply that knowledge to create entirely new opportunity spaces by seeing and expanding upon what cannot be seen by consumers and by innovating across their behaviors and daily routines

- Rethink the essential strategies of a company's core business, products or portfolios, and actions with the objective of designing transformational experiences that change people's behaviors and that create new ways of activating strategies that are radical departures from conventional practices

- Establish processes to ensure that—whatever their market position, size, or organizational complexity—companies never again lose sight of why and for whom they exist

As you will see as you read and implement the ideas in this book, the implications of this new model for innovation and growth for businesses are profound and will change how you think about strategy, marketing, innovation, and growth. You can benefit by implementing only parts of the DIG model. If you implement the entire model, then you will capture the ecosystem of consumer demand before your competitors or potential rivals do, whether you serve consumers in Idaho or Bangalore or sell industrial chemicals to a local manufacturing plant or a global enterprise. Your business will have a systematic and repeatable process for capturing the opportunities for innovation and growth today and in the future, and a chance to profit substantially from creating the future.

Hidden in Plain Sight

What's really going on when a company finds itself asking, "Why didn't we think of that?" Put simply, the company has lost the ability to see, *really see*, the opportunities presented by the changing consumption or usage behaviors of people it is trying to serve. The company cannot spot or recognize and pursue the abundant opportunities that exist in plain sight. This happens in several ways.

First, routine processes (including the kinds of strategic and operational practices that are necessary to manage an organization across multiple product lines and/or in far-flung divisions) can fragment a company's view of customers. Different divisions or business units focus on different aspects of what the company considers its market. Customers become a demographic or psychographic "segment." The company ceases to consider the whole consumption and usage behaviors of people in the context in which they live, work, and play.

Second, these pursuits quickly limit the company's outlook under the guise of retaining intrinsic knowledge and value or sticking to one's knitting. Consider how often a company (yours?) chooses to pursue and repeat a market research study so that it can continue investigating a trend line. A company may similarly invest in a certain market because that direction has proved, in the past, to offer good growth opportunities. Or a company might allocate resources to large and successful divisions because those divisions have track records that mitigate risk.

Solid business cases can be made for all these maneuvers. But, insidiously, they move the company just slightly more away from the people at the receiving and using, living and enjoying end of things. Even when and if a rogue designer or engineer conceives of a product or service that could be the next big venue for growth, too often the innovation is either swept into the rubric of an existing corporate strength, or it is damned with faint praise, and given some encouragement and funding but not enough to give it a fair shot in the market.

Third, the company (in keeping with the tradition of the last fifty years or so of marketing and business) persists in believing that the key to growth lies in identifying and satisfying customers' needs and wants, or in providing solutions for the tasks or jobs it knows that customers must take on and must get done. The problem is that defining opportunities in terms of needs and wants—even unmet, latent or unarticulated needs—is too narrow and simplistic a perspective. It misses the point, fails to anticipate the future, and tends to short-change the innovation and growth process. Managers become fixated on attributes and improvements of the feature set, and fail to generate a comprehensive understanding of the complicated, multidimensional daily experiences that people are living or working around. Whether it is a high-level and complex industrial purchase transaction or a simple emotional consumer purchase, managers never fully understand the real motivational forces of consumption and purchase: the desires, urges, hopes, seductions, fantasies, and dreams that overpower, tease, titillate, arouse, and take control of our behaviors—the forces that people surrender to.[3]

Consider this snippet from an article by journalist Dennis Kneale, published in *Forbes* magazine's November 14, 2005, issue:

> [M]y shiny new iPod Nano is as sleek and sexy as a little black dress. It packs a startling amount of sound and a thousand songs into a case so slight you forget it's there, thumping away at the end of a snarl of thin, white wire and Milk Dud earplugs. For me, it was love at first hype.
>
> But this is fickle attraction. Each time Apple issues a new model, the one in your pocket suddenly looks dumpier, older, conjuring up a gadget geek's most dreaded feeling: I'm so dated. In the handheld world we are what we reap—we pick products for how they make us feel about ourselves. On a recent subway ride to work, as my iPod Shuffle (150 songs) on a lanyard around my neck played a random set, I looked up and got a jolt of envy and shame: There was the new Nano, tiny and gleaming—and playing in the hands of another rider. Days later my Nano upgrade was complete, my Shuffle shelved and my envy replaced with pity for those with the iPods of old.[4]

The opportunity with this customer has nothing to do with improving the attribute or feature set of an MP3 player, or serving a daily task, or fulfilling a need or want for listening to music "on the go" that wasn't already addressed twenty-five years ago by the Walkman. It just isn't about that.

What really matters here is that this person's daily behaviors—the activities of riding the subway to get to work or just to get across town, the social-cultural context of life in the big city, the ways and forms of expressing himself, his feelings about himself, and how the iPod adds to and fits into that whole—have changed over the last years. He says it himself. But most companies miss it. Instead, they continue seeking needs to fill and holes to plug, providing "more or better" of the same old same old. How else can you explain a chip company's putting ever more silicon on a microchip to squeeze out ever more megahertz, making the tiny device faster and faster—when a computer's functionality depends less on megahertz and more on the software it must run. What if the "cheaper, faster, cleaner, stronger, sexier" arms race that so unimaginatively underpins so much of modern marketing and innovation practices were revealed to be a bankrupt enterprise? What if, as the rakish Rhett Butler famously declared in *Gone With The Wind*, customers quite frankly "don't give a damn" about whether the product comes equipped with a Memory Stick or a popsicle stick, just as long as it easily plays downloaded digital files? The company obsesses over serving customers, or winning the product innovation game, but misses what matters to people altogether.

And that's why it's time to look beyond the tried and proven "need-fulfillment" paradigm. Supermarkets are stuffed with forty thousand products (stock-keeping units, or SKUs), while the average person needs 150 SKUs to satisfy 85 percent of her "needs." The same goes for other categories. By itself, the need-fulfillment paradigm that underlies so many business practices—from customer orientation, service quality, and customer relationship management (CRM) to value chain integration—has outlived its useful life.

Fourth, the company's knowledge of customers becomes infused with an *inside-out* perspective. That is, the organization's employees consider all information before them in light of their own products, processes, and capabilities. Even companies that seek to learn about customers' experiences under the umbrella of customer orientation or customer focus most often do so with the knowledge of their own products and services firmly in mind. Their incentives force them to lose their objectivity. The company's managers begin defining their problems—and opportunities—in their own terms.

In this context, opportunities for innovation and growth are often overlooked or never even discovered. All that customer research, brand equity, market share, success, and momentum combine with strategies, processes, and organizational structures to conceal or distort opportunities that would otherwise be *right there*. If this clutter were cleared away, the opportunities would be clear and abundant. As William Blake wrote in *The Marriage of Heaven and Hell*, "if the doors of perception were cleansed, everything would appear to man as it is: infinite."[5]

Unbiased Perspective: Or How Not to Go Native When Going Native

Your company may be successful. It may be having a banner year. You may be on the cutting edge of technology; your go-to-market strategy may be superlative; you may be committed to letting your employees be creative and free to innovate; you may be conducting detailed research into the ways in which your products and services are used or experienced. But your best practices, processes, and structures, while fueling your success, may also be setting up that smoke screen that will foil you down the road.

You need an ability to retain an unbiased perspective as you immerse yourself into people's consumption and use behaviors, their lives, and understand how people live, what they do, when and why, with the 1,440 minutes they have each day. Think of Jane Goodall. Goodall was a breakthrough scientist because she studied the behaviors of humanity's closest relative by immersing herself into the lives of chimpanzees and living alongside them—not merely by observing them—and by rejecting or subduing any insights based on preconceived notions or existing theories of their behaviors and the drivers behind them. At the time, her colleagues thought she was "doing it all wrong."[6] Today, of course, the lasting value of her work is widely known.

Ask yourself: Do you really know your area of greatest opportunity in the complex and changing ecosystem of people's lives? How do needs and wants interact with the behaviors or activities and goals of daily life? Where do consumers find passions, fantasies, and urges? How do these passions change from one social-cultural context to another? Do you really know how this system evolves? Are you *absorbing* firsthand knowledge about how your customers' needs and wants intersect with their daily routines and consumption or use behaviors? Can you say with confidence that your best opportunities (if you see them) don't get lost in your organization? Or are you merely *deciphering* information and considering it from the perspective of what you already know you must offer and the trends you are supporting with your pipeline? Are you, in fact, optimizing the status quo?

Or forget all those questions and ask yourself just one: can you be sure that your biggest opportunities for innovation and growth are not hidden from you in plain sight?

The Clutter of Current Processes and Practices

How specifically can a company's own highly successful practices and policies inadvertently distance it from customers? In the words of David Maister, Charles Green and Rob Galford, coauthors of *The Trusted Advisor*, "Name it and claim it."[7] You must appreciate why the clutter exists, to understand how to get around it. Consider the following common practices and goals.

Differentiating Products from Competitors' Offerings

This standard aspiration has long been an undeniably important and valuable mainstay of strategy. The awesome power of sustainable competitive advantage has been proved time and again. But competitive strategy is fundamentally about doing things differently from other companies (or even doing different things) within a given market.[8] Competitive advantage invites competitors to steadily chip away at even the most marginal advantage and adroitly copy any differences. Differentiation rarely expands or transforms existing market boundaries or categories. For some companies, the time and resources expended on developing strategies and tactics promoting differentiation provide a most convenient excuse for limiting the exploration of new and uncharted territory. So much time is devoted to adding extra features or services to existing products that create only marginal differences, that the company becomes mired in a culture where top managers feel they cannot spare the resources to look beyond current core offerings.

Segmenting the Marketplace to Identify Customers or Consumers

Segmenting the market is another standard operating procedure, often highly successful within given limits. But the very act of segmentation can exclude potentially profitable customers and consumers by focusing exclusively on an existing customer set or demographic. Segmentation may also steer companies the wrong way with regard to understanding how their products are received and used by customers when managers assume that the customers' world is structured in the same way as data is aggregated.[9] Even when the data is valid, companies may behave as though the data is telling the whole story, which all too frequently it is not.

Growth Through Mergers and Acquisitions

Generally, the rationale behind growing an entity by acquiring another is centered on achieving efficiencies of cost, scale, or scope. The underlying premise is that greater market share equals greater profitability because companies benefit from the realization of efficiencies. While numerous executives and scholars have cast serious doubt on this belief, Wall Street still generally supports the approach, with the unfortunate result that many companies continue to attempt to grow and increase profits through acquisition, with varying degrees of success and failure.[10] Again, even in successful mergers and acquisitions, managers don't focus on the all-important organic growth, and entire avenues of opportunity tend to be overlooked in the wake of these imperfect unions, because companies typically focus on making the marriage work within the boundaries of markets already defined by investors and managers.

Developing New Products and Extending Brands

Extending a brand into an adjacent market or category has become a very popular approach to achieving growth. In fact, nearly three-fourths of all newly introduced products in recent years have been brand extensions—mostly incremental extensions. Many of these products, however, fail to meet expectations for growth.[11]

Even more problematic, recent research we conducted with Chris Koestring demonstrates that in fact the "standard prescriptions" used in managing brand extensions often do not filter out less optimal brand extension opportunities. Those same prescriptions frequently block managers' views of more radical new products that could be successfully launched at not only existing but new customers. If the managers who brought the insulin pen from Bang & Olufsen Medicom to market had applied current and conventional wisdom about brand extension to their work, that product might never have come to fruition, or would have been buried as an "accessory" deep within another product line, and as a result would very likely not have received the positioning it needed to break out and succeed. Here's another example: if the managers who helped Virgin sprawl from selling used records to bridal services to airlines and music stores had applied conventional brand extension wisdom to this organic process, the very face of that company would likely be different (and possibly far less well known) today.[12]

Listening to Customers or Consumers

This may well be the business mantra of our time. It is a staple of a broad range of approaches—co-creating value with customers, CRM, customer centricity, vertical customer integration, and supply chain management. But listening, in practice, all too often fails to reveal the next product or service that prompts customers to say, "I can't imagine what we did before we had this." As Henry Ford once acidly noted, "If I had asked customers what they wanted, they would have told me they wanted a faster horse."[13] Even the most efficiently run focus groups and customer surveys are contrived circumstances, tending to elicit results that don't translate nearly as well as they should into the real lives of the people who do (or might do) business with your company.

Even companies engaged in one of the latest and most popular iterations of customer research—"listening," "observing," "ethnographic," or "observational" research practices—designed to enhance understanding of customer experiences often fall short when it comes to suggesting how to put the information gathered to the firm's best advantage. All too often, marvelous insights gained about what the people who buy particular products do, and how they live, become quickly absorbed into a corporate mind-set already well furnished with knowledge of existing product lines, innovations in the works, and competitors' market positions.

Most critically, the link between customer experience and existing company context is never broken—managers never let go of their own context of products, services, and capabilities. In practice, as opposed to theory, most companies' best attempts to learn from customers' experiences result in incremental improvements in the customers' experience with that company—at the point of purchase or with ongoing service relationships. The landscape is established (and its limits inherently set) before any genuine innovation takes place in the market.

Most of these practices are valuable to a point; the rationale behind them is clear. But all of them share a common weakness: these endeavors are conducted from the *inside out*. That is, they are undertaken with a point of view that originates deep inside the established bandwidth of the organization. As a result, they never truly break into the realm of understanding customers and consumers as people, or understanding their behaviors. Lacking or missing this greater context, managers often overlook or never sense or discover viable and unique opportunities for growth.

The Pursuit of Customer Advantage

Harvard marketing guru Ted Levitt once gamely observed that customers don't want quarter-inch drills; they would really prefer to buy quarter-inch holes.[14] He advised companies not to focus on products but rather to concentrate on developing specific solutions to specific problems or tangible benefits. Do not talk about the size of the drill bit, the thinking went, but about the flawless hole that the drill bit makes in Sheetrock.

Such an approach, advanced at the time, is actually limiting today. Customers today don't care about buying the drill or even the hole (the solution or benefit); they want to decorate their home by putting up pictures or enriching their lives through personal expression on the domestic front. What they really want is to experience the sense of accomplishment that comes from enhancing daily life through pursuing a home improvement project. All those pesky details—hole sizes, drill sizes, and so on—are factors they would prefer not to spend much time thinking about.

Achieving customer advantage means understanding *total demand* as an area, like an ecosystem of dynamically changing and interacting customer needs, wants, fantasies, desires, and urges as well as specific everyday life concerns, projects, activities, and tasks in context. The various elements of the area form a dynamic and complex whole, a *demandscape*, which, in turn, interacts with other demandscapes.

Customer advantage reflects a capacity to let go of customers and leverage a deep understanding of how people absorb or assimilate products and services into their daily routines. The goal of customer advantage is to identify and develop innovations—products and services, new business models, go-to-market models, marketing programs, and service configurations— that fit into customers' lives and let them choose, are relevant for the everyday challenges customers face, and create transformational customer experiences. Customer advantage seeks to fit in and change how customers go about their tasks, projects, and activities in their daily lives or workflow processes either by interjecting a product, brand, solution, or service in new ways within customers' regular routines or by helping customers expand the range of their activities in ways that feel intuitive, enriching, and desirable.

The NetFlix Example

Netflix, the movie rental business founded in 1999, provides a good, simple example of what customer advantage looks like.[15] Cofounder and CEO Reed Hastings saw the hassle that people go through to return movies (possibly they have children in the car, possibly it's raining, possibly they don't really have the time to swing by the movie rental store) and the frustration they feel when they must pay a late fee (because they forgot the due date, or they were just out of time on the day they had to return the movie, or they hadn't yet been able to sit down and enjoy the movie). He himself was charged a $40 late fee for returning the movie *Apollo 13* past its due date. That may have been the ultimate catalyst; he then set out to make the routine of renting and watching movies better and more rewarding. His company took an existing product (movies to view at home), a simple Web site for selection, and an existing service (regular mail delivery) and molded them and enhanced them to provide a new offering that people accepted and assimilated readily into their lives, with relief.

Importantly, Netflix is not simply about getting movies in regular intervals through the mail with no late fees for returns past the due date, or the logistics of purchase and delivery; although that is the initial attraction for many customers. Netflix's opportunities are much bigger—almost infinite. The potential for creating true customer advantage stands out in bold relief.

Consider: through its Cinewatch system, Netflix captures how needs and wants change over time for each of its 6 million subscribers. It urges its customers to participate in a rating exercise; the average user rates more than two hundred films, and Netflix crunches customers' rental history and film ratings to predict what they will like. So each time a customer visits the Web site, his or her experience is truly tailored; as the customer provides more feedback, the company recommends more movies. What's more, each member of a household can have his or her own "profile," so that recommendations are truly personalized.

Great features for the customers, but that's really the tip of the iceberg. The information that Netflix gathers regarding customer likes and dislikes helps Netflix decide whether to buy and how much to pay for DVD rights and whether to sponsor movies and documentaries, even independent ones that would otherwise never be produced. Potentially, as the company bypasses Hollywood for content, it could sit on the top of the entire industry of entertainment and filmmaking, influencing filmmakers, producers, and agents, as the ultimate authority of what people want, desire, and fancy to see. For example, after reviewing and analyzing its customer ratings of other movies, Netflix invested in the documentary *Born into Brothels* when no studio would touch it. Netflix staffers then recommended the movie, and some five hundred thousand customers eventually rented it. *Born into Brothels* went on to win the Oscar for best documentary.

Ultimately, Netflix can do for movies what IKEA has done for design and furniture. It can democratize filmmaking, help young filmmakers, and potentially disrupt the entire movie business, in its quest to please the people it got into business to please. This is capturing the ecosystem of demand at its fullest.

The question, of course, is whether Netflix executives will understand what its opportunity is—what is inside and what is outside of its opportunity space? Will it create the innovations that it must to define the perimeters of this opportunity space, or will it wither away as a sophisticated mail-order service company? As the company becomes the next billion-dollar dot-com, can it also create the series of innovations that will capture the ecosystem of consumer demand and bring it to market? Will that next innovation fit into customers' everyday lives and be assimilated just as the original DVD rental service has been? Can the company do it again? And again? And again?

The Sony Example

For some companies, the one "aha" that launches the enterprise is "it." For others, the ability to observe customers with an unbiased perspective rises and falls on the influence of one or another top executive. For a third group, if the company grows large enough on its original idea, it can afford to employ and encourage a bank of entrepreneurial customer-minded thinkers, so that future innovations bubble up, and the processes and policies of successful companies can take hold, simultaneously supporting and limiting the company, as we've discussed.

Sony is an example of both of those last points. Cofounder Akio Morita was widely known in Japan as "the master of watching."[16] The Walkman had its origin in observation. Morita noticed how the daily routines of young people changed around pursuits of fitness and other leisure activities and transformed their habits and behavioral routines. Morita saw a huge opportunity space beyond the living room: young people walking, running, and driving and transforming these behavioral experiences. He saw a strategy beyond segmenting the market from standard to high-quality stereo equipment for sophisticated listeners and challenged the convention to position around different quality levels. The launch proceeded using an unconventional and unorthodox activation program targeted to young consumers: getting them to sample the product by walking with it through the Ginza. And for more than five decades at Sony's helm, Morita and his partner Masaru Ibuka created a paradise not just for *engineers* but also for *customers*, marred only by some notable misadventures (Betamax, for example) in which the company's sheer size and success created an inside-out perspective and the accompanying smoke screen between company and customer.

The goal, then, is having the pursuit of customer advantage embedded in the fabric of the organization. This will ensure that innovation is not just a one-off proposition. It will also ensure that a company's newfound ability to spot (or conceive of) opportunities does not stem from a static point of view.

The Starbucks Example

What does the pursuit of customer advantage look like when it is ingrained in this way? Starbucks, at least as of this writing, is a good example. The Starbucks story has been told, almost too many times, in the media, and in academic publications. Its essential, early facts are well known: Howard Schultz, during a trip to Italy, saw how the café *was part of customers' everyday lives*. He imagined a space in the lives of Americans where such a business could fit (a "third place"—not home and not work— that would be welcomed and absorbed into people's regular existence). He then returned to the United States and transformed the Starbucks coffee company into the successful chain of cafés we know today.

That "original" Starbucks history is by itself a great illustration of the pursuit of customer advantage. Think about it; no one in New York City, for example, needed a new place to buy good-quality coffee, pay $3.93 for a caffe latte, or spend fifteen to twenty, even forty minutes a day mostly waiting in line among public workers, students, tourists, or office employees. Yet New Yorkers have flocked to Starbucks in droves—about eighteen times a month, on average, per customer.[17]

But what is critical here is how the company has continued its pursuit and how the activities of the firm have together created the third place— not as much in terms of content (the coffee, the ambience, the service) but in terms of the initial insight of Schultz in Italy: the human condition and sense of community, how the café was part of people's lives. Consider how Starbucks located new stores using an unorthodox retail strategy.

Schultz chose not to rapidly establish several hundred Starbucks stores around the country using the typical franchise arrangement. Such a strategy would have ensured accelerated growth through opening storefronts wherever real estate happened to become available and consumers lived. However, such a strategy would have never created an authentic third place. To truly change how people lived their daily lives around coffee, Starbucks needed to densely locate its stores where people live, work, and play—even if the competition in these areas was already most intense and "demand" ostensibly already satisfied. This counterintuitive approach required Starbucks to locate several stores competing directly with each other, paradoxically to the benefit of all. Or consider how Starbucks built its brand.

The most natural brand extension for a food service establishment is to broaden the menu. Starbucks did some of that very successfully, but much more important in defining the perimeters of its opportunity space, the third place, was its expansion into music and movie production, sponsorship, and distribution. It even founded its own music label. Its music efforts, now in place since 1994, have helped new bands like Antigone Rising, a band that initially enjoyed little traditional music industry support on radio. Its album sold more than 70,000 copies, a vast volume for a comparatively obscure act. In 2004, Starbucks sold 775,000 copies of *Genius Loves Company* by Ray Charles, who died in June of 2004. Charles's work won eight Grammys in 2005.

Or consider how Starbucks adapted to changes in the ecosystem of demand. Around 2002, Starbucks tested the Hear Music Coffeehouse in Santa Monica, California, equipped with "media bars" at which customers can easily burn their own CDs using tracks stored in the café's library of over two hundred thousand songs. It equipped most of its U.S. stores with T-Mobile WiFi HotSpots so that customers can download music, surf the Internet, and do whatever they need or want to online. With these initiatives, Starbucks changed its stores to fit the broader set of everyday life activities, goals, and priorities of its customers.

While other food service retailers are busy adding fruit salad to their menus to keep up with the changing times in American health and wellness trends, Starbucks activates its strategic blueprint, creates the third place, and increasingly captures more of the ecosystem of consumer demand—what matters to consumers: a place to relax, to listen to music, to socialize, to work, to shop, to unwind, to talk.

The Front-and-Center Motivator

Essentially, the pursuit of customer advantage requires a company to rescind its focus on competitive advantage as the front-and-center motivator. In theory, this can be daunting; in practice, it frees the company to innovate much more creatively and meaningfully and see the big opportunities in plain sight. It also provides a strong rationale for the company's raison d'être. With the pursuit of customer advantage as an underlying philosophy, a company is not nearly as susceptible to "silver bullet" change efforts, or to the dangers that accompany the "keeping up with the Joneses" syndrome, or the pursuit of adding features to products or services—the "featuritis" disease. Yes, it remains important to scrutinize competitors' offerings; no, their actions no longer drive the company's reactions.

With the pursuit of customer advantage embedded in the fabric of the company, in fact, the business gravitates naturally toward the ongoing creation of new and vibrant growth areas or platforms that remain relevant by capturing the changes in the ecosystem of demand. That is, they evolve as customers evolve, and they retain the all-important ability to respond and be relevant in customers' lives. These areas of growth can be developed by a company through:

- *Positioning existing or new products or services at natural intersections of customers' consumption and use behaviors.* In chapter 3, we'll explore the case of Frito-Lay, which illustrates how an existing product successfully and easily moved into new consumption episodes in customers' everyday lives. In chapter 8 MasterCard's case illustrates how the company relocated the purpose of its brand in people's lives.

- *Changing or enhancing customers' daily routines and creating transformative experiences around activities, projects, and tasks in new and welcome ways.* GE Healthcare, described in chapter 5, provides a good example of how its anesthesia delivery unit changed the serial realities that doctors and anesthesiologists face in the operating room. Procter & Gamble (P&G) enhanced people's household routines through Swiffer or McClean AutoDry products. These companies have both created new—and, as of this writing, enormously large—markets from a host of familiar product roots.[18]

- *Delivering on previously unleashed or unarticulated desires, dreams, fantasies, and urges in the social-cultural context of people's lives.* As we've said, there is so much more to the pursuit of customer advantage than fulfilling needs as articulated by customers. The cases of Axe, described in chapter 6, BMW in chapter 7, and MasterCard in chapter 8, illustrate how the pursuit of customer advantage can also incite passion for an aspect of people's lives that previously did not inspire such a level of emotion.

In the brief positioning statement on the inside front cover of the J. Peterman catalog, there is a line that reads, "People want things that make their lives the way they wish they were." This line captures the essence of customer advantage.

The Seven Beyonds

For those unwilling to adopt an outside-in perspective, the future likely holds a fairly linear projection toward certain demise and a predictable downward path into commodity hell. The path begins with steadily rising costs generated by attempts to differentiate from competitors' offerings. Higher costs necessarily entail lower profits; lower profits mean lower investments in differentiation; less differentiation means fewer customers; fewer customers mean lower profit; and so on down the stairs to commodity hell.

Adopting the DIG model offers a way to break out of this cycle of doom. This is so because looking at customers in their lives and seeing the world in which they live from outside your company's bandwidth provides a unique viewpoint about your business—it is a way to see what cannot be seen in plain sight or to do away with the smoke screen, a way to create future breakthrough growth and reinvent the company's business. Put another way, the model allows a company to see the marketplace from a broader vantage point we call the *seven beyonds*.

1. Beyond Existing Customers

To many firms, there exist just two types of people in the world: current customers and potential customers. To many firms, there exist only two paths to growth: turn the latter into the former and get the former to buy even more goods and services, preferably at a higher price. The most popular way companies attempt to do that is by collecting copious amounts of information about existing customers. Most marketing research very precisely measures and quantifies customer "preferences," for example. The problem is that existing customers are a finite bunch. Companies measure (or define) preference at a very superficial level, at which preference is subject to excessive change or no change at all.

One of the reasons for the natural fixation of executives on current customers is that they are more willing subjects for marketing research. Because they are interested in the quality of the products and the services they buy, they tend to make excellent and cooperative subjects for surveys. Moreover, most marketing research requires that subjects know about the brand or product in the first place, or customers would give answers to questions they know nothing about. But what about all those people who don't yet know or purchase your brand?

The pursuit of customer advantage provides an opportunity to gain deep, useful insights from unserved customers or noncustomers because the starting point of the research is different: the *behavior of people* in the context of their lives, not just customers and certainly not just existing customers. By understanding all potentially relevant aspects and dimensions of peoples' lives, one can more readily evaluate how brands and products enrich their lives. Such insights provide the best opportunities for creating new customers.

2. Beyond Existing Brands

At some point in recent decades, the idea of a brand portfolio made its way into the playbook of marketing executives.[19] The basic concept, of course, is that brands should be viewed as a team, not unlike a soccer team, in which the portfolio is sent out to the field to compete against other teams. For the team to begin winning more games, there must be defined roles among the players or brands, the relationships between which must be clearly established with well-defined ground rules, known as portfolio guidelines. While this analogy is intriguing, customers don't care about it. They don't see the portfolio in total, anyway; at best, they see part of it. A customer advantage perspective helps see current brands, products and services, and the entire portfolio with respect to how customers see them and how well the collection or team fits into customers' everyday lives and to what extent it adds value.

3. Beyond the Category

Once upon a time, products or services could be neatly classified into a category. The classification was useful because there was a time when customers compared one brand or product with competing alternatives within a category. There was competition among brands and competition among products. But this time is gone. Today, the category as a unit of analysis is blurring. Sure, people do buy toothpaste and very readily recognize competing brands as a "category." But factor in gum, mints, and mouthwash and the context of daily life, and you see how the boundaries become vague.

And consider: Kodak competes with Hewlett-Packard head-on, while the companies used to operate in different categories or industries—one in the photographic business, the other in the printer business. (By the way, where do you look when you want to know the time? At a watch? A cell phone? The dashboard of your car?) Which brings us to the next beyond.

4. Beyond the Industry

Industry boundaries also have blurred. As Gary Hamel has said, "We live in a world where industry boundaries are like borders in the Balkans." [20] Is the Palm Pilot a telephone, an organizer, a handheld computer, or an e-mail system? Where does competition for the Palm Pilot come from? Is it more likely Nokia or Sony or Gateway than Research In Motion's (RIM) Black-Berry or plain old paper? How many things does *your* phone do?

From a customer advantage outside-in point of view, the question is not "Who are you competing with?" but "What is it that you want to accomplish in terms of customer advantage? What is it that you will do to embed yourself into customers' everyday lives?"

5. Beyond Silos and Functions

Companies that are organized around functions continue to miss out on great opportunities because of the barriers inherent in the structure. (This despite great strides in communications across functions in recent years!) Just consider how Levi Strauss missed out on the changing trends in the apparel business in more than ten years. Salespeople may not communicate anecdotal but valuable and insightful customer information to the marketers, so brands do not reach their potential. The marketing department may not be aware of unique manufacturing or distribution capabilities that could provide the basis for valuable differentiation. The chief executive officer is kept informed but stays in the dark: he or she is often served up the information he or she would like to hear. Growth strategies are often crafted to meet projected finance models instead of being based on real market opportunities. A functional organization serves the function, not the customer. Most top managers *know* all this, and yet it persists. Its very momentum prohibits change.

Introducing a demand-first outside-in perspective helps functions unite by giving them a common perspective. If this view is shared across the entire organization, functional barriers become increasingly porous. Every mind is working on improving the value proposition, and new opportunities to add value travel more freely across the entire organization.

6. Beyond the Boundaries of the Strategic Business Unit

Even at the strategic business unit (SBU) level, the perspective, while much broader, may still be too narrow. In chapter 2, we introduce the case of Procter & Gamble, which was able to create entire new categories, such as at-home teeth whitening, by bringing together people from its fabric- and home-care divisions, its oral-care division, and corporate R&D. GE provides another example. GE is at its best in identifying organic growth opportunities when it leverages its businesses across SBUs on behalf of customers. One example of this is the horizontal organization of market leaders at GE. A couple of years ago, GE appointed market leaders for each of its business units with no vertical line responsibilities but the charge to identify and develop opportunities across the GE organization—from the outside-in perspective and beyond functional or product group silos. In chapter 5, we introduce this case study.

7. Beyond Habitual Domains

New opportunities, ideas, and innovations come from people who can cross-pollinate ideas from other areas. It is necessary, therefore, to look beyond your discipline and expand your habitual domain. If you are a marketer, look at the creation of customer advantage from the perspective of the operations manager. If you are in business, look at how medicine, biology, or the social sciences solve the same problem. Get anthropologists, linguists, engineers, psychologists, sociologists, artists, product designers, or business analysts to view the opportunities from the outside in.

So what lies around the corner for your company? Absent the pursuit of customer advantage, we could probably make a fairly intelligent guess: your chances of realizing profitable organic growth will be as hard as getting blood out of a stone. But when you begin to lift the smoke screen or cleanse the doors of perception, you can see the opportunities that are hidden in plain sight—and you can see them as they are: infinite. What's more, the resulting new avenues of opportunity so completely *fit* the customers and provide transformative experiences that other companies will find it difficult, if not impossible, to follow suit.

When a company replaces the pursuit of *competitive advantage* with the pursuit of *customer advantage* as a guiding principle for the enterprise, the new focus does not mean that it must necessarily undergo a complete reorganization, either in its structure or in its practices. In fact, the new focus may not even require a company to scrap the strategies it has already been successfully using to promote and expand existing product lines. Instead, those activities are temporarily deemphasized to permit the elasticity required to see the opportunities in plain sight, to identify new opportunity spaces and to find and execute strategies and actions that create new growth and help to reinvent the core business model.

In the next chapter, we will examine the demand-first innovation and growth model piece by piece and offer a case study of one company that has successfully adapted the pursuit of customer advantage.

Chapter Two

Capturing the Ecosystem of Demand

T HE PARTICULARS of understanding the ecosystem of demand, and of being able to use that knowledge effectively, vary from company to company. That's why the bulk of this book is devoted to exploring the demand-first innovation and growth (DIG) model (see figure 2-1)— the means by which an organization can pursue customer advantage—in detail and through the experiences of a variety of companies. For now, it is important only to understand the big picture. The model offers a systematic and repeatable process that helps companies embed the pursuit of customer advantage deeply inside their organizations. It consists of three interlinked parts: the *demand landscape*, the *opportunity space*, and the *strategic blueprint*. Reduced to its essentials, the model calls for companies to:

1. *Create a demand landscape* through an enhanced understanding of how people behave and live their lives, pursue work processes and how they consume, apart from the company's existing product offerings or capabilities

2. *Reframe the opportunity space* by applying an innovative routine of structured-thinking lenses to identify opportunities that customers can't begin to tell about

3. *Formulate a strategic blueprint* so that the company can pursue these new opportunities effectively, and make it relevant in the social-cultural context of the daily experiences of people. The strategic blueprint also serves to root the ecosystem perspective on demand deeply within the organization so that the direct connection to customers' lives is never distorted or lost

A company *must* use all three parts of the DIG model to find and execute its next innovation and growth strategy. Most companies today conduct very good customer research; insights from ethnographic research abound;

FIGURE 2-1

The demand-first innovation and growth model

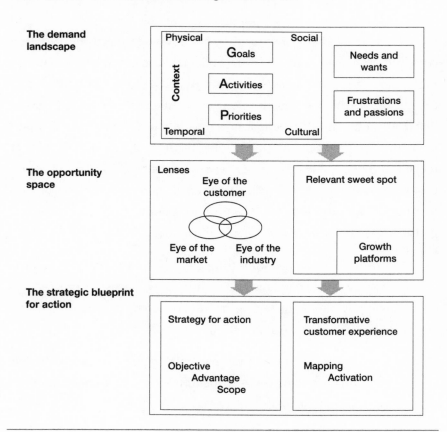

many have a solid understanding of the demand landscape that surrounds them. Many, however, do not bother looking for the real opportunity space on that landscape; some gain some insights from consumers or customers, but many do not know how to quantify these opportunities or translate their insights into actions and results.

Still others do *not* conduct solid customer research and instead go after opportunities from a traditional perspective, often launching technologically superior products that completely miss the boat on connecting with, or fitting into, or becoming part of customers' daily lives. As a result, companies miss identifying and capturing the full spectrum of opportunities for innovation and growth that exists along the entire value-generating process, from consumer insight, to technological development, to marketing and action and the major subprocesses.

The biggest failures occur when the DIG model is focused only on a piece of the major business processes of a firm, when it becomes part of a functional silo or specialty. It is not good enough to say the new products group or R&D is in charge of developing new products, and marketing is in charge of advertising, communications, and selling. Then, the model will reinforce the fragmentation and divisionalization that often resides inside organizations rather than alleviating it. Resources need to be allocated top down, performance goals need to be set and made explicit, and the model needs to be implemented so that it is a systematic and repeatable process, definitively defined and directed by people with the will and the skill to take it throughout a company.

We will drill down another level into the DIG model later on in this chapter. First, let us offer a glimpse into what one company has accomplished by putting an unbiased outside-in approach front and center.

Procter & Gamble (P&G) has been an exemplar of how a deliberate outside-in perspective can foster innovation and growth by helping employees spot—and build on—the kinds of relevant opportunities that are generally hidden in plain sight.

As you read through this case, it is important to keep in mind the three pieces of the DIG model and how they must work together. P&G did not use the terminology we have developed for the model. But the behaviors are clearly there. Digging deeper into customers' everyday lives (rather than studying purchasing behaviors or even consumption from a product-oriented perspective) completely refreshes a company's view of the "pull" from customers by providing a look at the ecosystem of demand. Thinking more broadly and inventively about how that pull might be achieved reveals new opportunities through the development of ecosystem-driven growth platforms. And acting more deliberately to convert these opportunities into results leads to new connections and engagement with customers and, ultimately, customer advantage.

Procter & Gamble

When Procter & Gamble CEO A. G. Lafley took over the reins of the Cincinnati-based customer goods giant in the summer of 2000, the most recent chapter of the venerable company's 167-year-old history rated as anything but a robust growth story. Under Lafley's predecessor, the Dutch-born Durg Jager, revenue growth in its core brands was negative, costs had soared, profits flattened, and P&G's once-rock-solid blue-chip shares had slackened by 43 percent over the previous seventeen months—a period that, perhaps predictably, precisely coincided with the length of Jager's tenure.[1]

Of particular concern to anxious P&G investors had been the company's failure to gain significant growth in its core brands—Tide, Pampers, and Crest—against the onslaught of aggressive and innovative competitors. Both Pampers and Crest had yielded long-standing category leadership positions to Kimberly-Clark and Colgate-Palmolive, respectively; Kimberly-Clark's Huggies had overtaken Pampers by bringing to market a superior version of toddler training pants. Colgate had deftly outflanked Crest by introducing a compelling new line of teeth-whitening and breath-freshening toothpastes.

At the turn of the twenty-first century, the proud pioneer of brand management during the Depression under CEO Neil McElroy seemed to be stumbling in ways that struck observers as strikingly similar to the bevy of ills afflicting a number of other legendary customer powerhouses, from Coca-Cola to Unilever to Kraft.[2] All were engaged in a Darwinian struggle to spark innovation and foster organic growth—revenue from core businesses excluding gains from acquisitions—while operating in a dramatically different customer environment from any that had historically preceded it. As A. G. Lafley ably summarized the situation, a wholesale transfer of power from the manufacturer and the retailer to the customer lay at the core of this seismic shift.

The problem was figuring out how to respond.

Lafley started out by doing many of the same things most CEOs do when embarking on a substantial corporate turnaround: he swung the axe to $1.7 billion in costs in a companywide restructuring while presiding over the acquisitions of hair-care icons Wella and Clairol, in addition to the January 2005 $67 billion merger with Gillette, by far the largest acquisition in the history of the company.

Yet by all accounts, Lafley deliberately concentrated the lion's share of his executive efforts not on operational streamlining or headline-grabbing acquisitions but on rejuvenating the company's core businesses and dramatically ramping up P&G's sluggish product pipeline. "Organic growth is the most precious kind of growth," Lafley insisted, outlining the fundamentals of a philosophy that placed maximum emphasis on fomenting sustainable top-line growth even at temporary cost to bottom-line results. "Organic growth is more valuable because it comes from your core competencies. It's like a muscle. If you use it, it gets stronger."[3]

As the former head of P&G in Asia and North America as well as its beauty-care business, Lafley was no stranger to innovation, having successfully overseen a major expansion of the Olay brand with the introduction of two revolutionary skin-care products, Olay Daily Facials Foaming Massage Cloths and Olay Total Effects. He had successfully launched Liquid Tide and Tide with Bleach, and championed the debut of the firm's single significant e-commerce venture, Reflect.com.

Yet when he chose to tackle the far more daunting challenge of spurring significant growth in a company that counted thirteen brands in its portfolio with annual sales in excess of $1 billion, Lafley focused on spurring innovation *by initiating a radical transformation of a notoriously stodgy and hidebound corporate culture and mind-set.* Possibly the most prominent and pervasive among the unexamined orthodoxies with which the P&G culture remained riddled was the comforting notion that all worthwhile inventions and products must have originated inside P&G's own labs. A corollary to the same notion was that the offerings must have likewise been lovingly shepherded from concept to prototype by P&G's in-house technical staff. All that quickly changed.

"We invented 'Not Invented Here' here," jibed Jeffrey Weedman, vice president in charge of global licensing and external business development, in response to Lafley's ambitious agenda to generate half of the company's new product concepts from outside the company.[4] Noting bluntly that P&G was "as likely to find an invention in a garbage can as in our labs," Lafley overrode mounting internal concerns that "open source" innovation would lead to the wholesale outsourcing of R&D at the firm.[5] He championed research that reached beyond the company's existing bailiwick. He explicitly encouraged practices that promoted, together with his chief marketing officer (CMO), Jim Stengel, a new level of cross-leveraging of the best ideas and successes across the company as well as a new level of business and marketing accountability; in part, this included restructuring performance measures. And he proceeded to roll out a string of breakthrough new products, a surprisingly large number of which plainly relied on intellectual property licensed from outside the firm.[6] Among the novel P&G offerings to proudly bear the "Not Invented Here" label are:

- *Olay SK-II Regenerist.* An age-retarding face cream designed to capitalize on baby boomers' mounting infatuation with the miracle of Botox, infused with a wound-healing peptide molecule licensed from France's Sederma Labs.

- *Crest SpinBrush.* An inexpensive battery-powered electric toothbrush acquired from independent inventor John Osher in 2001, which quickly racked up $160 million in sales to become North America's best-selling toothbrush. The same imported technology has spawned yet another new product, Tide StainBrush, an electric stain-removing brush.

- *Mr. Clean Magic Eraser.* Jointly developed in partnership with BASF, derived from an obscure wall-cleaning product spotted by the wife of a P&G executive in Japan. This product was based on the formidable erasing properties of a foam product developed by German chemical colossus BASF, which by coincidence just happened to be a major P&G supplier.

- *Glad Press'n Seal.* A polymer food wrap developed jointly with Clorox, a company that directly competes with P&G's Pur water purification brand with its Brita unit. The adhesive-film technology used in Press'n Seal derives from a proprietary film developed by P&G as the essential material in Crest Whitestrips, yet another new product launch spurred by a then-novel partnership among three P&G divisions.

Importantly, these successful products originated well outside the perimeters or walls of Procter & Gamble. What matters, however, is that it was not only technology that was sourced from the outside. More importantly, the products created the momentum P&G needed to break through the traditional boundaries of the markets in which they reside. The process of opening up the company's thinking about innovation and consumers allowed the creation of new ways for delivery of established brands; it made the organization porous; it permitted brands to cross categories and in some cases articulate such new categories as odor elimination, daily facials, and at-home teeth whitening.

The development of Crest Whitestrips vividly illustrates the point. Although the product of P&G's internal R&D process, this entirely novel dental-care product reflects Lafley's signature strategy of nurturing innovation by increasing communication among previously disconnected and distant business units. "With Crest Whitestrips," P&G's Chief Tech Officer, Gilbert Cloyd, recalled, "we had people from our oral-care area who obviously knew something about whitening teeth, and we had people in our corporate research and development organization who developed some novel film technology. Then we actually brought in some people from our fabric and home-care area, who were experts in bleach."[7] The result was not merely the addition of a new product to P&G's product lineup or a traditional brand extension for Crest but the creation of a new category, which jibed perfectly with the conceptual broadening of the Crest brand into home dental cosmetics, a line of popular products to which P&G recently added Crest Night Effects paint-on whitening gel.

As *BusinessWeek* noted with a tone of respect verging on awe, "Rather than define itself by its products or the confines of a category, P&G has expanded its mandate to become a solver of every problem in the home."[8] Rather than concentrate, as Colgate-Palmolive had done, on refining specific product attributes, P&G had recalibrated its opportunity space for the Crest brand from "dental care" to "oral care," a seemingly simple yet profound semantic shift that opened up room in the space inhabited by Crest for such significant innovations as the Crest SpinBrush Pro electric toothbrush and Crest Whitestrips.

In this new scenario, the-product-formerly-known-as-toothpaste emerged to fit naturally into a broader time and space in customers' everyday lives as any product or service that provides them with "a healthy, beautiful smile"—the new opportunity space expanded from Crest, the toothpaste.

In that same spirit, Mr. Clean, which had previously been firmly positioned as a brand targeted at women cleaning the kitchens of their houses, now moved out into the driveway and the garage, in the form of Mr. Clean AutoDry and AutoDry Pro-Series, a home car-care product that resembles a plastic iron equipped with a garden water hose, providing a classic case of customer advantage for the company in the form of a solution for men who both love their cars and want their Saturday mornings back. Other P&G products were also developed to flesh out that solution and, with it, the total customer experience. The Swiffer AutoDuster, Febreze Auto Fabric Refresher, Mr. Clean Magic Eraser Wheel & Tire and mops, brooms, and wipe-ups, for example, help "complete" an integrated system of products, services, capabilities, and tools that doesn't just meet one customer "need" (getting rid of a spot or cleaning without abrasives) but addresses the bigger area of the ecosystem of demand and results in retrieving Saturday morning from the doldrums of daily chores.[9]

The company's single biggest brand, Pampers, with sales in excess of $5 billion, stepped up to the plate as well, reframing from diapers to baby care to a wider range of parenting products. Tide went from being "just a detergent" to becoming an expert on fabric care.[10] Such audacious reframing, expanding and broadening of the opportunity space for long-established brands permitted the enlargement of the boundaries that these brands had previously drawn solely from a product perspective.

Unbiased Insight and Strategy, Simultaneously

"You begin with an understanding of where you fit into her life and everything goes from there," said P&G chief marketing officer Jim Stengel, speaking of the company's renewed focus on innovation and growth from the demand-first perspective.[11]

That comment just about nails it with regard to the ecosystem of demand and the opportunities therein. It also alludes to the strategy that must accompany and follow the deep understanding of the ecosystem of demand as captured in the demand landscape.

What is the "everything," at P&G? It is simultaneously the creation not simply of products but innovations along the entire spectrum from consumer insight to technology development to marketing that lead to the creation of new and evolving categories, businesses, or platforms of growth, and strategies that allow the company to support their forward movement.

In the "old" P&G, the conventional wisdom said, "Concentrate on the efficacy of one brand over another." In the new P&G, the focus has shifted. Do parents really care about the comparative dryness of their babies' bottoms? Or rather do they care about the development of their children? The outside-in perspective has led Pampers to a host of highly contextually relevant consumer initiatives that move the company far beyond its traditional success model—among them, e-mailing mothers directly, tracking key stages in their babies' development, and offering guidance along the way.

Similarly, Mr. Clean AutoDry was launched through the Internet first, followed by a direct-response campaign, enhanced by buzz marketing efforts to generate word-of-mouth communications, instead of following the typical TV model of marketing. Tampax, a feminine hygiene brand, uses 250,000 girls, called "connectors," and 500,000 moms recruited by the P&G Tremor unit to spread favorable word of mouth.

The list goes on. For information about personal hygiene or anything that might matter to girls in certain stages of life, Procter & Gamble provides

Beinggirl.com, a Web site "for girls by girls." Charmin bath tissue, as opposed to simply touting the brand's superior feature set of softer, stronger, and longer lasting, transforms the most unpleasant experience of visiting public restrooms like those at country fairs, music or sporting events, or New York's Times Square into a "Charminized" comfortably clean experience.

These efforts all illustrate a broader shift in how Procter & Gamble activates its strategies, away from the mass-marketing model and thirty-second TV spots and toward new ways of connecting with and engaging its customers and becoming and staying relevant in their lives. Importantly, this means reallocating spending toward more push in the store and activating around those things that matter to customers—the activities, projects, tasks, stuff, or routines they live around daily.

How exactly does P&G find out what matters to consumers? "We are relatively light users of focus groups," Lafley maintains. "We prefer understanding real-world experiences. We would rather do shop-along or shopper simulations to get close to the real shopping experience. We like to get inside the homes and get involved in the usage experience."[12] Contending "you don't really learn anything insightful" from conventional consumer research and focus groups, Stengel has spearheaded the adoption of a new set of research tools and techniques. He has strongly encouraged his marketing staff to not merely adopt a customer's point of view but physically and mentally *place themselves inside peoples' lives* and, wherever possible, inside their homes. Closely monitoring how consumers wash their clothes, clean their floors, and care for their infants is not the be-all and end-all at P&G. The company has developed a kit of tools that has served as a useful anthropological prelude to asking even more probing questions about the deeper sources of customers' satisfactions, pleasures, and frustrations.

Market and Financial Results

Tangible evidence of P&G's determination to adroitly manage this momentous shift from an inside-out to an outside-in vantage point can be discerned in the firm's impressive market performance and financial results. Relative to the 2000 results, where P&G lost market share in seven of nine of its core brands, by 2004 nineteen of P&G's twenty largest brands improved market shares. Overall core volume rose 12 percent in the last quarter, and organic growth tripled from 2000.[13] A recent survey ranked P&G first by retailers in six of eight categories: clearest strategy, brands most important to retailers, most innovative, most helpful customer information, best supply chain management, and best category management and customer marketing at retail.[14]

In the summer of 2000, as P&G hit its low point, the company's *enterprise value* (market capitalization plus net debt) stood at approximately $85 billion. By 2005, its enterprise value had soared to $157 billion. Intriguingly, the cash flow generated by the company's multiple enterprises remained remarkably unchanged over the period, rising from approximately $5 billion in 2000 to $5.6 billion in 2005. The stability of this particular factor indicates that of the $72 billion rise in enterprise value achieved over the four-year period, an overwhelming 93 percent of the increase must be ascribed to *investors' expectation of future gains* to be realized from the company's robust growth initiatives. A comparatively insignificant 7 percent of the rise in enterprise value can be ascribed to benefits gained from cost cutting and other operational efficiencies.[15]

Put another way, P&G shareholders earned $72 billion over a period of four years by investing in a company that deliberately and systematically adopted a "customer advantage" perspective over a "product first" or "company first" perspective, not just in the province of marketing but throughout its far-flung business units. Add to that momentum the acquisition of Gillette, and the opportunity space for further organic growth and shareholder value becomes even greater.

The Demand-First Innovation and Growth Model

Why is a model necessary? Why must methodologies, tools, and processes be explicitly embedded inside an organization and reflected in performance expectations and measurements? The answer is this: without an explicit approach to formulating strategy that illuminates and defines the advantage and scope, and a plan of action that specifies the necessary effort to capture the relevant part of the ecosystem of customer demand, a company will never realize that it is missing any opportunities. On the flip side, when an understanding of the ecosystem drives innovation and the business agenda, and when an organization's processes have been properly aligned, the chances are significantly higher for sustainable, replicable, predictable growth.

Earlier in this chapter, we skimmed through the three parts of the model; here, we dig a little deeper.

1. Creating the Demand Landscape

"If you want to see heaven, you have to die yourself."
—Punjabi proverb

Rather than segmenting customers according to age, lifestyle, and regional and social characteristics, creating a demand landscape begins with mapping the behavior of consumers and segmenting their time or moments and episodes spent on activities, projects, and daily tasks, and studying the situational context in which these occur (see figure 2-2). The assumption is that the best predictor of behavior is behavior. Forget for a moment their psyches or any of the demographic or economic attributes you've assigned to them through previous research. And try to forget your company's existing offerings. Ask first: What do these people *do* each day? What things are on their to-do lists? You might find that they take the kids to day camp or visit a school counselor. You might find that they meet a friend for drinks after work or go to the gym.

There is an enormous richness and depth of this understanding of behavior when put into the context of peoples' lives—the physical, social, cultural, and temporal context. It creates a powerful departure point for the strategist to probe unarticulated, unexpressed, and incipient needs and wants or passionate urges and intense desires that people have or can have in relationship to products and services. Shifting the lens on the actual behavior in the immediate context and away from the subject provides a radically new and different view. Entirely new portraits and parts of the demand are revealed. For example, completely new and unknown patterns of desires, hopes, and passions can emerge from studying consumption fantasies in relationship to the behavioral context of life—the interactive

FIGURE 2-2

The general structure of the demand landscape

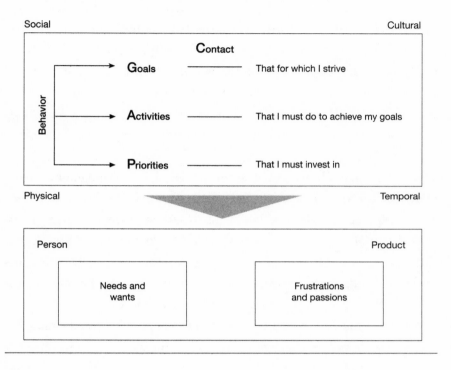

nature and the dynamics of the ecosystem of consumer demand come to the fore.[16]

Consider the following series of numbers. The first series is six and three. The second series is twelve and six. The first number of the third series is fourteen. What is the second number in that series?

Most people would guess that it's seven. It is not. The answer is eight. Why? Because the number fourteen has eight letters. (Similarly, the number six has three letters, and the number twelve has six letters.)

It's not enough to grasp a pattern; you have to first break your assumptions about what the pattern might be and then strive to understand the logic or process that truly explains what's going on.

The first step is to deeply understand the ecosystem of demand's inner recesses and secret places, and the opportunities for innovation and growth that can be potentially mapped on the demand landscape, apart from your assumptions about company, products, technologies, or capabilities.

The demand landscape maps the intersection of behavior (activities, projects, tasks, and to-dos driven by goals, needs, urges, sensations, hopes, and desires in the social-cultural context) with the capacity of an innovation to fit in and embed itself in the way in which people operate every day.[17] The main insight governing the construction or mapping of the demand landscape is that people cannot tell us what they do not know and have not experienced.[18] It is far more important to experience and watch what they do.

Many different observational, anthropological, and ethnographic methods or self-reports can be used effectively to gather the data required to create a comprehensive demand landscape. Nokia employees spend a month in the offices of mobile phone users. Microsoft shadows office workers around their use of the Microsoft Office Suite. GE Healthcare observes physicians in the operating room to better understand the way anesthesiologists interact with the operating team during major procedures.

All reflect the same aspiration: to immerse themselves into the daily life experiences of people's behaviors, to observe them as they move through their days, and then to classify those behaviors in a way that the company can begin to gain useful insight from them.

The classifications we use are *goals*, *activities*, and *priorities*. They are the basic building blocks.

- A *goal*, by definition, describes "that for which I strive."[19] All activities are performed with the purpose of achieving a specific goal or goals. The activity of clothes rinsing, for example, is likely to be associated with the specific goal of reducing the smell of the "laundry room" in my dress shirts. As compared to the more well-known needs, wants, or values, goals are more concrete, usually expressed within a context of time and place.

- *Activities* embrace all the actions, behaviors, tasks, or jobs that people engage in. They are defined as that which I must do to achieve the goals. Some activities may seem, at least superficially, trivial, superfluous, nonpurposive, and only remotely goal oriented: spending time by myself in the park during lunchtime, taking a break to relax, going to the movies, taking a vacation in Italy for two weeks.

A brand like Tide might derive considerable benefit from gaining such extremely comprehensive knowledge of the specific activities engaged in by customers associated with attempts to purchase, care for, and discard clothes. An in-depth analysis of these activities would reveal that customers engage in at least six different activities with regard to wearing and caring for clothes: wearing, washing, rinsing, drying, ironing, and storing. How do customers deal, or in some cases fail to deal, with the "dirty pile" problem?

- *Priorities* are a prime measure of the relative engagement and involvement customers have with various activities and goals in their everyday lives, from the amount of time they allocate to an effort to the amount of money they spend. Again, at this stage, the research is all about what they do, not what they say. In economic terms, priorities qualify as the "revealed preferences" of people and customers. While survey results may suggest that most Americans believe it is important to eat well and to exercise frequently, an objective examination of the behavioral data available shows that Americans actually assign a higher priority to eating pleasure than to health or nutrition. Doughnuts and ice cream are available almost everywhere, and American waistlines are expanding.

The goals, activities, and priorities that are attached to moments and episodes and daily tasks and projects represent a new kind of segment; we call them *demand clusters*. With these in view, a company can take the next step: to layer in the *context*.[20] What is the context in which these behaviors—demand clusters—manifest themselves? In what setting do they take place? How does context or culture drive meaning?

Just about every form of customer behavior is fundamentally context or culture dependent. Let's say that I prefer to drink Beck's beer. This statement is correct when framed within a particular context. Yet let's say that, as a practical matter, I am more likely to order a Beck's beer in the baseball stadium (*physical* context) with my son on a weekend afternoon in the summer (*temporal* context) while attending the game with some family friends (*social* context), and that when shopping for a beer to drink at home, I might prefer a Heineken or a Corona. The strategist needs to understand the different dimensions of context and culture in order to more clearly grasp the specific role of the brands, products, and services as they intersect with those contexts.

With the context firmly in place, a company can then begin to examine customers' needs and wants. These areas may seem like familiar territory to a company, but the reality for most companies is that they represent new research ground when the contexts of customers' everyday lives have been established with some specificity.

Each activity in which a customer engages has associated with it a whole host of needs. Oscar Mayer, for example, learned long ago that a powerful and thus-far unsatisfied need for ready-to-eat meal solutions that are fun for children had arisen from the changing social context, in which parents pursuing two jobs and demanding careers had less time available to prepare a healthy lunch for children before school. This insight led to the launch of Lunchables.[21]

Fortunately for Howard Schultz and Starbucks, while very few Americans couldn't possibly have expressed the fact that they *wanted* to spend up to $4 for a premium cup of coffee, if served up in an appropriate setting (physical and social context, the third place), the incipient "want" was there all along, behaviorally and context dependent but hidden, to many Americans, in plain sight.

Drilling down even deeper, a company can now begin to explore customers' *passions and pains*. In order to see further, you have to dig deeper. It is necessary to explore the full contours of the ecosystem of customer demand.

Beyond basic needs and wants lie more passionate quests to fulfill desires, pleasures, and cravings. Attaining a deep understanding of the behaviors of customers in context helps explore these powerful forces in our lives. As Gian Longinotti-Buitoni noted in *Selling Dreams*, "Dreams are shaped by culture."[22] Ultimately, we cannot appeal to customers effectively unless we tap into their dreams, urges, and fantasies.

People as a rule do not seek products or services. Products or services are merely means to get things done or to spend time their way, to enjoy and experience life. The moments and episodes of experiences are where we find pleasure. Hence it is extremely important to explore people's quests beyond needs and wants. What about grace, elegance, meaning, originality, and fun? What are the serial realities in our daily experiences that invoke these emotions? It is here where we find there is substance in style, design, and aesthetics.[23]

Customers' pain also provides great opportunities for initial insights. Identifying specific moments and episodes of activities or goals, things that one needs to achieve, the jobs one needs to get done also reveals the pains, frustrations, and hassles people have in their lives.[24] In 2005, the *New York Times* documented a wide variety of ways in which irate customers are expressing their increasing frustration with a customer landscape seemingly littered with obstacles and challenges, as opposed to more convenient solutions to problems. Some crafty customers, the paper reported, are inserting absurdly heavy weights into solicitation envelopes for which the recipient must pay postage on delivery. Others are creating clever strategies to foil persistent telemarketers. Others are tearing out dozens of blown-in subscription cards from magazines, placing them in envelopes, and sending them in to subscription referral agencies. Still others strategize endlessly to figure out ways to circumvent voice mail and synthetic call-center "personae" so that they can actually speak to a living, breathing customer service representative.[25]

With all these elements understood, a company can truly begin to understand the ecosystem of demand and start to draw up the demand landscape.

2. Reframing the Opportunity Space

"Perspective is worth fifty IQ points."
—Alan Kay[26]

The second piece of the demand-first innovation and growth model calls for the company to subject the demand landscape to the same scrutiny that an explorer might use to gaze at a map of the territory she intends to explore. Conceptual lenses and structured innovative-thinking tools that deliberately force perspectives from different angles—as opposed to conventional brainstorming—help create a vision of what customers themselves cannot see and conventional market research does not uncover.

To put this piece of the model in place, strategists need to step away from their desks and their office parks to examine their map from twelve lenses grouped into three distinct outside-in perspectives: the customer perspective, the market perspective, and the industry perspective. Critically, while they do so, the focus must be on solving an everyday problem or a whole-life problem of people or on deeper understanding of a specific episode or moment around a daily life experience, rather than on inventing and ideating around an existing or even a developing product or service, as so often is done.

As a result of this creative, but also structured and systematic, exploration and scrutiny, the company can reframe, expand, and recalibrate the area of greatest opportunity, or total opportunity space. This accomplishment, in turn, helps the company see past the insights provided by the customer and the "opportunities" that customers have described. It helps cleanse the doors of perception and lift the smoke screen. It illuminates new possibilities for innovation and growth, and it allows the company to see opportunities in context in much the same way that a blue picture in a dark blue frame appears lighter or a red picture appears lighter red in a darker frame.

After exploring the savanna, it is then, finally, time to critically examine existing capabilities, products and services, and brands offered to customers. Broadly, the question to ask at this stage is, What is the relevant sweet spot? Put another way, Where does the brand have permission to play in the demand landscape from a customer's perspective?

Can P&G become an oral-care expert from a customer's perspective, or do customers consider Crest simply a very fine toothpaste? Will people trust Richard Branson and Virgin to send them to the moon as space tourists? The goal here is finding the relevant sweet spot—and, in turn, structuring it into a platform for growth.

Reframing the opportunity space is designed to broaden the thinking to the maximum range of opportunities where the product or brand can be rendered relevant in the context of customers' lives—to see the glass half full rather than half empty, and to see what cannot be seen through mere inspection with the eye, and to see what customers cannot see.

This process is accomplished by means of a structured-thinking and problem-solving regime that stands in stark contrast to conventional free-association techniques rendered in a nonconfrontational, nonjudgmental setting, better known as brainstorming. In the DIG universe, a broad and often diverse team of executives from different functions is guided through a process premised upon the notion that while customers can tell us what they know, only the company can infer from the demand landscape what offerings might profitably tap into unarticulated and often murkily or dimly understood the ecosystem of demand.

Brainstorming techniques will be used in the third and final stage of the DIG process to ideate specific product or service concepts. While the demand landscape is obviously limited by the information that a company has been able to gather on customer behavior, activities, goals, needs, and wants, systematic and innovative structured thinking enlarges the boundaries and deepens our understanding of that landscape. This is equivalent to an astronomer mounting a wide-angle lens to have an extended field of sharpness.

The goal is to define the total potential opportunity space that captures from the relevant ecosystem those unarticulated, incipient, and unexperienced needs, those ways to deal with the frustrations and pains of peoples' experiences or define those innovations that tickle the fancies of people during the consumption and use experience.

Consider how to view the total opportunity space for the iPod. One view is to look at it from the standpoint of Apple as a brand and a company of imagination, creativity, fun, and an attitude of thinking differently. Another view is to look at it from the standpoint of Apple as a product. Here the iPod is an accessory for its computers that has a higher degree of usability and that satisfies consumer needs through a unique combination of speed, design, price, and features.

Another way to view the opportunity space is to look at how the Apple brand intersects with the activities and things consumers do daily; the behaviors and tasks that matter to them; where they find peace, magic, and fun, such as listening to music, watching a movie or a video, or taking pictures of friends and family. When the opportunities are viewed not simply from a brand or product perspective but from this more complex vantage point of the ecosystem of consumer demand, the Apple total opportunity space expands not just by the iPod but also by iTunes to include not merely a vital music business but also a growing and amazing number of other opportunities of relevance in our digital lives overall. When Apple recently began exploring the possibility of offering video clips over a new video-enabled iPod, it seemed only natural, although it promised to further broaden Apple's opportunity space from computers to music, to videos, to films, and maybe all the way to managing all sorts of tasks digitally in our everyday life.

And what about the Iams brand? After acquiring the maker of super-premium dog and cat food about five years ago, Procter & Gamble first expanded distribution beyond exclusive pet stores, which doubled world-wide sales and tripled profits. In the United Kingdom, that move alone shook up the entire pet-care sector. But beyond the broadening of distribution lies also P&G's new approach to thinking about its total opportunity space. What about the other important behaviors around pet ownership, which lead to the possibility of Iams-branded magnetic resonance imaging (MRIs) for dogs and cats—and Iams-branded insurance?[27] On the horizon could be Iams-branded grooming parlors, bedding, pet clothing, and travel accessories.

GE has redefined and significantly expanded its total opportunity space beyond just what customers see by positioning itself as providing an immeasurably wide range of solutions. An integrated marketing effort, the "ecomagination" initiative was designed to formulate imaginative solutions to such dire global hassles and challenges as global climate change and the imminent decline of fossil fuels, and to meet customer challenges. This initiative cuts across several businesses, from energy to engines.[28] With an outside-in perspective, every company and brand has the potential to change the game.

The key point about reframing the opportunity space is not simply to have a larger vision of the potential opportunities for innovation and growth but to structure the demand in meaningful groups relevant from the activities of the consumer or the customer perspective. These groups we call *demand-first growth platforms*. Demand-first growth platforms guide how the firm captures the relevant ecosystem of customer demand over time, and focus the innovation and growth agenda—from product, to strategy, to design, to marketing and activation across channels and markets.

3. Formulating the Strategic Blueprint for Action

If you don't know where you're going, any place will do.
—*Alice's Adventures in Wonderland*

The third and final part of the DIG model is the strategic blueprint for action. The strategic blueprint sets and defines the strategy and actions and activities necessary to pursue the new opportunities the company has in its sights. Importantly, when the blueprint is formulated from a demand-first perspective, it does not simply specify the activities the firm needs to pursue to achieve *competitive* advantage. It also defines those activities necessary to meaningfully activate the demand-first growth platforms in the social-cultural context of consumers' everyday lives—hence, to create customer advantage.

The demand-first perspective often challenges many of the company's fundamental aspects of strategy, organizational principles, systems, and processes and also leads to often radical new approaches and mechanisms to implementation and execution. At its very core, it calls for reexamination of the fundamental questions of strategy: What business are you in? What do you stand for? How do you capture value? How do you win? The strategic blueprint for action summarizes and captures these important implications and consequences for strategy, implementation, and activation.

Draw up a demand landscape, apply structured thinking to explore this landscape, and reframe the opportunity space. What do you see? From a demand-first perspective, you don't see The Home Depot in the business of selling hardware and home improvement products or installation services, and you don't really look at Sony as a consumer electronics manufacturer. You don't look at Henkel and Unilever as merely successful marketers of detergent and other chemicals or consumer products.

Consider, if Henkel or Unilever were to think of their detergent businesses and the Persil brand in this way, they would miss the current enormous opportunities they have in the changing landscape of home consumption, use and daily behaviors inside homes (as mapped in the demand landscape), as well as the technological changes taking place primarily in Asia, where new washing machines no longer wash with detergent (so-called non-detergent-based solutions for laundry) and come with autodosing solutions for laundry chemicals (as explored in the section on reframing the opportunity space). These stellar companies could end up like Cunard, which was the dominant shipping company at the beginning of the last century, when it shipped Europeans to America, but today only commands a fraction of the transportation business.

How do you win? In the face of the ephemeral ever-changing ecosystem of demand, in the face of new technologies, does differentiation determine advantage? From a demand-first perspective, what matters is how you blend in or fit into the serial realities of customers' lives and how consumers absorb and assimilate an innovative product or service and make it part of consumption. Instead of differentiation, the blueprint forces a company to think in terms of not only how to stand out (from competitors) but how to fit in (to people's lives) and how to realize customer advantage.

Differentiation is achieved through positioning. Positioning from a traditional strategy perspective is about a single point, an attribute or a dimension or set of attributes relative to competitors within a category, also called *value curves*.[29] We argue that it is necessary to replace this traditional and simplistic notion by positioning around an area, the relevant area of the ecosystem of customer demand. Rather than positioning on a dimension of quality or set of dimensions (for example, Lexus has the highest J.D. Power quality ratings, or Avis is better because it tries harder), positioning becomes a multidimensional exercise to capture a relevant area of the ecosystem of customer demand.[30]

An entirely new model of branding emerges. The traditional model of branding as we know it today is flipped on its head. Rather than starting with a product and adding functional, emotional and self-expressive benefit, the starting point becomes an idea of how to fit into consumers' everyday lives, and the product and services will follow. In chapters 7 and 8, we go into more depth in these areas of brand positioning and brand portfolio management as a means to capture bigger opportunity spaces and attempt a synthesis. Equally, existing notions of brand portfolio strategy need to be thought of in a new way. It will require thinking of portfolio strategy in terms of how to capture the relevant part of the ecosystem of consumer demand, rather than merely in terms of organizing and structuring the portfolio of existing and future products or services into a coherent strategy.

The strategic blueprint for action changes the fundamentals of market structure and segmentation. Market structure is usually defined along product, geography, or customer dimensions. Segmentation is the practice of dividing customers into groups or clusters of similarity.[31] In the DIG model, instead, the primary dimension of market structuring or segmentation is the behavior or consumption of people in the social-cultural context as it is revealed in the ecosystem of demand. Either there is no need for segmentation because it only artificially fragments the market, or it abandons simple product segmentation—such as premium or standard versus budget hotel services—or simple person or consumer segmentation, such as lifestyle, psychographic, or demographic segmentation. Instead, demand-first segmentation must take into consideration the behavior aspects that define daily life experiences by focusing on moments, episodes, and other serial realities that describe behavior. Such segmentation is more encompassing and more context-relevant, and changes the unit of analysis altogether. This increases significantly the ability of segmentation to predict behaviors and makes it more valuable.[32]

From a demand-first perspective, each element of the company's strategy needs to be reviewed. In chapter 6, we capture these dimensions in terms of the review and assessment of the strategic objectives of the firm, the source of advantage, and the scope, or "sandbox," in which the company competes.

The actions in the strategic blueprint need to be precisely defined so that the company realizes the advantage. Whereas it used to be sufficient to define the set of activities that lead to a sustainable competitive advantage, it is now necessary to define these activities also in terms of the extent to which they activate effectively and meaningfully the demand-first growth platforms. This follows from the fact that growth platforms are derived from the total opportunity space, and this opportunity space is in turn determined from the demand landscape. This landscape has been mapped according to the activities, goals, and priorities of people's daily experiences.

The demand-first perspective leads to a radical departure from current innovation management practices. Rather than innovation around new products or services, technologies, or business models, innovation needs to take place across behaviors of consumers or customers and meet the confines of the demand-first growth platforms—all activities need to focus innovations from product to business model on the behaviors so that the link to usage, consumption, and behaviors in the social-cultural context of consumers' everyday lives is never broken. So, our advice to Steve Jobs is to innovate around the behaviors or platform of managing people's music rather than around finding ways to create the most competitive and most beautiful MP3 player—which would be equivalent to innovating around the product-attribute trap. By creating innovations that focus on relevant behavior patterns and clearly defined demand-first growth platforms, the company makes innovation context specific and part of the culture, which leads to the achievement of valuable customer advantage.

Thinking in terms of the demand-first growth platforms further enhances the potential impact of innovation and growth opportunities in a myriad of other ways. All activation and implementation efforts are also driven by the growth platforms. This ensures that all efforts and activities—such as defining the channels of distribution, launching new products and extensions, setting the pricing schedule, developing a brand-building program, and finding an integrated communications mix—are decided on to maximize the impact on capturing the area of most relevance to the firm in the evolving ecosystem of demand.

Therefore, the strategic blueprint for action defines and articulates totally new ways of formulating strategy, and challenges existing going-to-market efforts and innovative and new activities of the firm to achieve competitive advantage. While the DIG model does not require a company to disengage from all the good work it is already doing regarding existing products and markets, some companies will see the opportunities for creating organizational change and reinvention, and some will even see an opportunity for changing the entire culture of the business. In an interview with *Fast Company*, A. G. Lafley describes how difficult the culture shift has been at Procter & Gamble. "Remember, one of the disciples had to put his hand in the bloody wounds to believe. We have some doubting Thomases."[33] Former State Street CEO Marshall Carter, whose story is told in chapter 6, regards getting his entire leadership team to accept this strategic change as his most important leadership challenge.

Cordis: A Short Case in Point

The Florida-based medical device manufacturer Cordis provides an illustrative business-to-business example of some key elements of the DIG model in action. Through a useful methodology known as outcome-based interviewing, Cordis drew a partial demand landscape and then used it as a springboard for defining and launching new products and solutions.[34]

In 1993, Cordis had less than 1 percent share of the U.S. domestic market for angioplasty balloons, surgical devices employed to open the arteries of patients with advanced cardiac disease. With the express goal of increasing its penetration of the market for these devices, Cordis conducted a series of in-depth interviews with a comparatively small sample of cardiac surgeons, a number of whom performed frequent angioplasty insertions, and a number of whom performed the procedure comparatively infrequently but perhaps could be induced to do it more often if certain presumed frustrations and hassles were removed.

Initially, the moderators conducting the interviews asked the surgeons to provide them with ideas about how to improve the product with regard to a series of clearly defined attributes: stiffer, thinner, lighter, smoother, coated, guided with a wire? Nurses, when queried, volunteered that they would like the product to be "more brightly packaged" so they could more readily identify it on a shelf in the supply closet.

Then Cordis decided to refine the interview process and add greater depth and dimensionality to the data gathered by asking the surgeons to break down the angioplasty balloon insertion procedure into a sequence of activities and tasks—making the insertion, opening the artery, placing the device at the lesion in the artery, and removing the device. Each of these distinct activities was logically associated with the attainment of a specific goal or "desired outcome." Cordis researchers identified nearly fifty of these goals, including minimizing the recurrence of blood blockage, minimizing the amount of force required to cross the lesion with the balloon, and moving the balloon more rapidly through tortuous vessels.

Cordis further analyzed these goals across an operating team comprising doctors, nurses, and lab personnel, all of whom brought a different "customer perspective" to the specific needs that they experienced during the operating procedure. When the company examined the specific use of its current angioplasty product, it identified a number of growth platforms. Cordis defined these growth platforms by segmenting cardiac surgeons not by age, income level, psychographic or demographic factors, term of practice, or location, but rather by *goals* and *activities*. Certain surgeons, for example, vastly preferred a device that permitted the procedure to be completed more quickly. Others indicated a preference for a device that was easier to manipulate inside the chest cavity. Each of these preferences opened for Cordis a new avenue of possibility for innovation.

Having garnered this data, the company went on to research, develop, manufacture, and seek FDA approval for a dozen new angioplasty balloons, each tailored to the achievement of a specific desired goal related to an activity of the angioplasty balloon insertion procedure. Armed with this innovative portfolio of products, Cordis boosted its U.S. market share of this surgical device category in less than two years from 1 to 10 percent.

A demand-first perspective would have added value to the development and marketing effort of Cordis. It could have focused investments in R&D, helped focus on key surgical procedures that are dominant or frequent in the physicians' daily lives, and led to systematic and effective development through better understanding of the potential opportunity space.

A Riff on the Social Shift Behind the DIG Model

As A. G. Lafley said, we live in the age of consumers, and the implications of this social shift not only are truly profound but are only in the early stages of realization.

The DIG model attempts not merely to recognize this shift but to derive value from it. In this new era, in order to understand the potential opportunities offered to companies, we really cannot start with our own products or even with the products in our development pipelines. We can use them for focus, maybe, but we have to start by first understanding how people spend the 1,440 minutes in their lives every day, and attempt to capture the full contours of the ecosystem of demand. For all practical purposes, we have to divide up those 1,440 minutes into episodes and moments of activities, tasks, pleasures and fantasies, and things to do that make up the day, whether it is a walk in the park, a trip to the beach, or a bite from a fresh apple. We have to analyze these behaviors and define the consumption and use context by grouping or aggregating activities into moments, into "day parts" or "day shares" (as Starbucks has done), or maybe even into "life shares." The $64,000 question becomes then the 1,440-minutes question.

Yet *day share* or *life share* (not to be confused with lifestyle) is not a competitive concept, because it is simply a measure of the total amount of space (in terms of time, effort, and priorities) your product or service potentially can command of customers' available minutes, the competition for which might be not a competitive product or service but any other activity that the consumer considers engaging in at the time. This is a telling point, and perhaps also one of the hardest to digest, because use of the DIG model is motivated not by traditional "competition" but by customers themselves. The irony is the circular nature of the approach; the outcomes of using the model are often measured in terms of performance vis-à-vis other companies.

The question today must not be, "How can I sell this product successfully in the market made up of preteen girls?" but instead, something on the order of "What is it that I need to do to fit into an eleven-year-old girl's life and gain a maximum share of her 1,440 minutes?"

How do we find out the answer? Certainly not by asking the eleven-year-old directly but rather by seeking to gain an understanding of how she lives that life—through observation, through mapping her life and activities, projects, tasks, and everyday matters, moments and episodes of pleasure and frustration; probing deeply into her goals, needs, and things that she most fervently hopes to accomplish, the things that she does to get there, all the ways that she has figured out to get on with her life and derive pleasure from the same 1,440 minutes we all spend every day.

Marketers spend infinite amounts of time studying how customers purchase products and how to make it easier for them to part with their money. But the shortcomings of this approach, even without our understanding of the shifting balance of power, are most clearly obvious. For Sara's 1,440 minutes of life in a day, it really doesn't take that much time to shop and purchase with mom, download a song, or buy a video on demand. (In over twenty-five studies involving more than 875 adults and recording more than 525,000 activities, my colleagues and I found that purchase as compared to consumption activities accounted for less than 15 percent of adults' average daily lives—the rest of the time is spent "living.")

So what goes on during that "living" time? Perhaps the answer for a company looking to become more relevant in eleven-year-old Sara's life may not be another product, or even a better product, a cooler product, or a cheaper product. Maybe it is giving her that product—yes, literally *giving* her the product; Google, Rhapsody, Club Penguin, iTunes, kiddonet.com, Skype for talking live to her friend, and AIM for instant messaging account for an important share of her life—and they have become strong brands! The answer to gaining a greater share in this girl's life, to be invited in, or better fitting in, may be a technology innovation, or a business model innovation, or a marketing innovation, or even no innovation at all.

In this world, innovation is no longer defined by a set of features, breakthrough, disruptive, or incremental innovations. And competition need not come from another company that makes and sells the same kind of product with the same sorts of features as others. (A genuine innovation may in fact involve *removing* a set of features or shifting away from a product entirely.)

Beverage industry analysts may write volumes extolling and predicting the endless seesaw swing of market share between archrivals Coca-Cola and PepsiCo for ownership of the beverage occasion. But the genuine landscape faced by both companies involves not so much competition with each other, or even competition with other beverage companies, but rather competition from a broad range of sources beyond the boundaries of the beverage industry, from foods to sports to music to movies, or parents spending quality time with their kids, or kids spending quality time with their friends. The real landscape they face is not the competitive landscape but the demand landscape.

Ask: what does the ecosystem of demand tell us? While beverage companies typically expend vast marketing resources in attempting to capture ever-more-slender slices of market share from each other by asking their agency partners to come up with a "big idea," perhaps a more productive set of questions to be asked would revolve around determining the moments and episodes of the ecosystem of demand that come together to create a "beverage occasion" in a person's life, and how conceivably Coke, Pepsi, or Dr Pepper might fit into that life.

To approach this juncture requires more than simply identifying needs and wants and understanding customers. It requires more than understanding the lives of people or lifestyles through observation, shadowing, or other ethnographic or anthropology-inspired research. Achieving success demands thinking deeper, harder, differently, and longer into the central question of how life can be transformed and improved—not just how behavior can be predicted from attitudes but how behavior can be sustainably changed. It requires thinking beyond the opportunities created by identifying needs and wants—satisfied and unsatisfied needs, articulated and unarticulated needs, today's or *incipient* needs in the social-cultural context.

Ultimately, this shift of perspective takes the whole idea of collaborating with customers to another level. It is about searching for products and services for customers rather than the other way around.[35] It is about defining innovation in people's daily experiences and life terms. It represents a change of the dominant paradigm of business and marketing today. Not that this paradigm is obsolete in all cases, but it certainly is in many.

Part II of this book explores each element of the DIG model in turn through detailed case studies. It is difficult to separate the elements of the model in practice (as we've said, they must work in tandem). So the cases include all elements, though they emphasize the particular one being discussed to illustrate the richness of the DIG model. Frito-Lay's approach to creating a demand landscape begins in the next chapter.

Each company's approach to the demand-first innovation and growth model will also be unique; thus, Frito-Lay's particular choices regarding research methods and analysis may not be right for your company. We'll provide a step-by-step guide to each element of the model, following the illustrative case studies. We'll also discuss a variety of options for research and analysis.

Part II

Demand-First Innovation and Growth Model

Chapter Three

Creating the Demand Landscape

A S 2003 CAME TO A CLOSE, the Frito-Lay division of PepsiCo, the largest snack manufacturer in the United States, had quite a lot to smile about. The Plano, Texas–based organization was the hallowed home of several billion-dollar brands (Lay's, Doritos, Tostitos, Quaker, Cheetos, Ruffles, and Fritos). It was also the unchallenged market leader in half of the world's top ten snack chip markets.

In the United States, the company controlled a commanding 65 percent share of the $15 billion salty snacks segment. And with 2004 revenues poised to grow 5.6 percent to $9.6 billion (up from $8.6 billion in 2003), Frito-Lay had also handily bested snack and cereal rivals Kellogg, Hershey, General Mills, and Kraft in the competition to gain a greater share of the $37 billion "macrosnacks" market, a broader category that also included such portable taste treats as candy, cookies, pastries, and ice cream. At year-end 2003, Frito-Lay owned 15 percent of that larger space and was hungrily gunning for more.[1]

One of the reasons for the company's success was its superior ability to stay on top of high-profile customer trends—for example, the quest for health and wellness. Earlier that year, the company had announced the removal of artery-clogging trans fats from Doritos, Tostitos, and Cheetos, brands now capable of joining Lay's, Ruffles, Fritos, and Rold Gold pretzels in a trans-fat-free brand portfolio. Frito-Lay also introduced its first line of natural snacks, marketed under the Natural name and logo, while PepsiCo publicly pledged to purge its product line of any brand that failed to use "essentially healthy ingredients or offer improved health benefits," under its Smart Spot initiative.[2] While most of the salty snack manufacturers in the United States use a blend of frying oils—corn, cottonseed, or sunflower oil—in 2006 Frito-Lay announced that it was switching to 100 percent sunflower oil for all its products.

So what did the company have to complain about, with brand extensions and profits popping, revenues soaring, market share rising, and the company contributing nearly half of parent company PepsiCo's profits, all going straight to the bottom line?

One concern that plagues all successful large companies is the fact that their very size and success make maintaining high rates of top-line growth a challenge. Additionally, there was the question of new growth and opportunities. Where did Frito-Lay intend to go and to grow, and how did it plan to get there from here?

The Unit Volume Issue

Consider, for example, the challenges facing Carlos Veraza, Frito-Lay's then newly appointed vice president for marketing for the immediate consumption (IC) channel.[3]

Coming off a stint as a senior marketing executive in the company's Mexican division, Veraza was not intimately familiar with the IC arena. But the more he learned about the IC channel, the more concerned he became. As he wrote in a memo to his superiors:

> The IC channel is one of our most important relationship partners. The channel includes so-called "C-stores," including national and independent chains, small grocers, drug stores, dollar stores and "mom-and-pop" shops . . . The IC unit growth has been growing less for several years than expected, while Frito-Lay seeks to support retailers by enhancing their margins for Frito-Lay products. This situation stands in strong contrast to PepsiCo's and Frito-Lay's strong focus on and strength in "convenience," its critical mass in retail outlets, and its powerful distribution capabilities.

Summing up, he said simply, "We were not growing as fast as we should have been." In Veraza's view, the company's overwhelming strengths in production and distribution appeared to be masking potentially debilitating weaknesses (as well as unseen opportunities) in a number of critical areas. To cite just one example, he pointed to Frito-Lay's direct store delivery system, established in 1941, long before the independent Frito and Lay companies had merged and been acquired by PepsiCo. Over time, this system had fostered a corporate mind-set that was focused intently on distribution efficiency, often to the detriment of promising initiatives that might have led to driving greater customer demand for the brand.

Additionally, Veraza observed, while Frito-Lay's commanding 80 percent share of the salty snacks category might mean a great deal to marketers, what did it do for consumers? Consumers didn't see the market as categorized in that fashion, but rather considered a salty snack as merely one of a range of potential choices within the broader snacks category.

A few other disturbing trends were afoot in the IC channel as well, among them the fact that in a bid to achieve greater growth, convenience stores had diversified their product mix in recent years. Ten years before, a consumer might have confronted eight categories of goods in a convenience store, while today she might be likely to find twenty. The implications of this development for Frito-Lay were not insignificant, because the category of snacks as a whole was being squeezed as a portion of the overall convenience store product lineup.

Despite this trend, Frito-Lay marketers had achieved improvements in top- and bottom-line growth over the previous decade by doing something Veraza called "weighting up and pricing up." (Whereas ten years before, the bulk of Frito-Lay sales in convenience stores had been in 25¢ 1-ounce bags, by the turn of the twenty-first century, the bulk of its business consisted of 99¢ 4-ounce bags.) But those improvements, Veraza thought, were ultimately not sustainable.

"The top line was in great shape, and the bottom line was in great shape. But *unit* volume was declining," Veraza explained. "We were rapidly eroding our consumer base, and pretty soon, this pricing up and sizing up model was going to run out of runway."

With the erosion of the firm's unit base, the number of transactions consumers were engaged in with Frito-Lay was becoming smaller and smaller by the day, week, month, and year. Just as alarming was the fact that in contrast to a consumer marketing powerhouse like Procter & Gamble, Veraza's marketing team lacked useful hard data tracking consumer trends and preferences relating to the Frito-Lay brands, particularly when it came to convenience store purchases. "The real uncharted territory was how little we knew about the customer," Veraza explains. Compounding the problem was a strong, often unexamined bias within the Frito-Lay and PepsiCo operating organizations to conceive of initiatives consistent with and supported by the existing operating system.

The looming issue, as Veraza chose to frame it, was two pronged: "First, we knew too little about the consumer, and second we knew even less about *how* and *why* consumers consumed Frito-Lay snacks."

Unbiased Observation/Counterintuitive Discoveries

The first phase of research conducted by Veraza's team consisted of the systematic placement of security-style video cameras in selected convenience stores. But rather than examine those tapes (which ran twenty-four hours a day) for security infractions, Veraza and his colleagues spent hours monitoring them for clues to how consumers shop for and buy Frito-Lay products. Like anthropologists or sociologists, they immersed themselves in the unique commercial ecology of the convenience store, observing customers walk into the stores, walk down the aisles, walk past some products and pause before others, make a purchase or not, and walk out. Frito-Lay needed to know what was happening on the shelves and in the aisles. What they found was something of a shock to the system—a system of long-established beliefs. The data they collected, when properly analyzed, flew directly in the face of the conventional wisdom long enshrined at the firm.

In every store, Frito-Lay products were at that time exclusively stored and displayed on a specially designed wire rack known as a front-end merchandiser (FEM), which served as the unique point of sale for all Frito-Lay purchases. "From time immemorial," Veraza recalled, "the strategy had been to position the FEM six feet from the cash register, so that customers standing at the counter were never more than an arm's length from a wide range of Frito-Lay products." This massive presence came equipped with copious signage to catch a customer's attention and was visually and physically designed to take up a massive presence in the presumably fickle customer's field of vision. Yet as the in-store videotapes revealed, much to the marketers' surprise, a majority of consumers could be seen plain as day walking into the store and heading straight for a point in the shelves they appeared to know from prior visits. On more occasions than any of the monitoring marketers would have expected, customers walked by a perfectly positioned FEM without giving it a second glance, let alone a second thought. "Consumers were just flying by the FEM," Veraza noted. "You could have put dancing monkeys on that FEM and consumers wouldn't have noticed." As far as the majority of consumers were concerned, the FEM, a solemn shrine to a beloved brand, didn't exist.

The origins of the FEM as a point-of-purchase display were clearly rooted in one of the oldest, most deeply entrenched and largely untested beliefs shared by snack food marketers over the years: that nine times out of ten, the purchasing of salty snacks was an "impulse buy." Based on this questionable assumption, enormous effort and costs had been expended to appropriately design and position the FEM in the store to catch the eye of the customer. But as evidenced by the videotapes, most customers appeared to go into the store already knowing what they wanted. Grabbing a bag of Fritos, Doritos, or Lay's at a 7-Eleven store seemed to often be a more premeditated ritual or deliberate purchase than a spontaneous burst of mental and physical desire. "The whole impulse-buy idea in which we had been so heavily invested for years," Veraza and his colleagues were stunned to conclude, "was dead wrong."

The implications of this realization were profound for all the major Frito-Lay brands. As Veraza forthrightly put it, "Everything we were doing was now up for grabs. Now we had to decide, if these purchases were to some degree planned and deliberate, what did that mean for our marketing strategy?" One conclusion that could be safely drawn from even the preliminary data was that Frito-Lay's current marketing strategy was destined to go out the window.

"We had to start thinking more about *why* consumers consume our products and no longer about *how* they purchased them," Veraza explained. "As opposed to just sticking a big rack of chips in front of their faces, we had to know more about how our brands intersected with the daily life of customers."

A New Line of Inquiry

Veraza resolved to approach these issues from a dramatically different vantage point than the strictly logistical. Rather than focus obsessively on how many pounds of chips the firm put on the floor of the store, or how rapidly those boxes moved from factory to selling floor and into the shelves of the FEM, he and his team were obliged to alter their focus to seeing the marketing problem from an outside-in, as opposed to an inside-out, perspective. Of greatest concern to Carlos Veraza was plumbing the depths of the three Us: the frequency of usage of Frito-Lay products (usage), the number and identity of the customers (users), and the varying life contexts (use) in which Frito-Lay products were consumed.

As a first step in facilitating this conceptual and practical shift from a primary focus on the purchase process and purchasing behavior (*point of purchase*) to the consumption or use context (*point of purpose*), Frito-Lay, assisted by a team of consultants, evolved a methodology for exploring customers' everyday routines.[4] Frito-Lay employed outside consultants because it was critical that respondents in no way suspected that the study had been commissioned by Frito-Lay.

Veraza and his colleagues adopted a set of tools and methods that would have given conventional marketers and statisticians pause. They did not, for example, seek to assemble a "statistically significant sample" of respondents. As opposed to making *brief* contact with a statistically significant broad mass of customers, they decided to make *deep* contact with a few dozen. Instead of asking shoppers how they *felt* about the broad category of snacks (or Frito-Lay snacks in particular), they decided to find out as much as they could about how people in general interacted with snacks, and about how snacking can so often become part and parcel of the activities, goals, contexts, and priorities of people's daily lives. Veraza and his colleagues proceeded to make contact with a select group of customers to ask them in detail about those contexts and situations.

As the basis of the research, the team chose to employ a methodology known as the *diary method*. Thirty-five selected individuals were handed cameras and daily diaries and asked to record their activities, episodes, and moments, thoughts, and feelings around the "framing question" of food consumption over a thirty-day period (see figure 3-1).

And in response to outraged statisticians, they pointed out that although the absolute number of *respondents* was not statistically significant, the number of *activities* was. If, on average, each of the customers experienced or underwent twenty food-related activities per day—"I have a coffee in the morning with a pastry." "I have breakfast with my daughter before dropping her off at school. I feed her a snack after school." And if they

FIGURE 3-1

In-depth "day in the life" diaries and confessional interviews

1. Activities log
As you go through your day, please write down everything you do, especially activities related to looking for, buying, eating, and providing food (snack or meal).

Time	Activity	Goal	Importance	
6 Am	alarm goes off for Benn to get up	5	5	Where I usually eat (include people, if relevant)
6 30 Am	I get up make our shakes	18 + 13	4	
7 Am – 8 44m	left to take Benn to Class (EMD) in lewisville got back home had cereal for Becca & cream of wheat & splenda for me.	22 / 18	5 / 3	Where I usually go to buy food
9 15 – 12	laid around in bed + watched movies	30	3	Where I usually snack (include people, if relevant)
12 30	Mac + cheese for lunch me + Becca.	22	3	
1 pm	Started Chicken in crockpot for chicken salad this weekend.	33	4	Where I usually go to buy snacks
1 – 330	Cleaned house talked on computer + drank 2 glasses of ice tea	5	5	
330 - 6p	left to get Benn	22	5	

Daily life exploration of Julianne—40, married with three children, nurse

recorded those daily food-related activities for a month, the resulting data would cover 35 x 20 x 30 = 21,500 activities. Statistically significant? The naysayers had to admit that 21,500 was a huge number of data points.

In the initial interviews, Veraza and his team embedded a "framing question":

> Please tell us about the activities, projects, and tasks in which you engage oriented around the preparation and consumption of ready-to-prepare and ready-to-eat foods.

A follow-up letter to respondents outlined the procedures:

> Thank you for your interest in our customer study and for your will-ingness to participate in the upcoming journal exercise and in-depth discussion. In this package you will find all the materials you will need to prepare for the discussion: a twenty-five-day journal, an instant camera, two boxes of instant film, a blue pen, and a roll of tape. The journal contains detailed instructions about the different exercises you will be performing over the period. This journal is now your journal! Personalize it in any way that you like. Express yourself freely and add more pages if you require more space. You will need the camera for some of the journal exercises, but in addition please take pictures of anything else that appears to be interesting for your journal. We hope that the completion of your journal will be fun and that you will enjoy the creative tasks that are included. Don't forget to bring your journal to the scheduled in-depth discussion.

The journals, it turned out, illuminated a wide range of associations and at-titudes that exist around the consumption of ready-to-eat and ready-to-prepare foods. In the subsequent four-hour in-depth discussions, or "confessional conversations," which took place after Veraza and his research team reviewed every page of the journals, respondents were asked the following questions:

- Tell me more about this moment, just this particular episode in your life.

- What is so special about it?

- What happened before this episode and afterward? (This question solicited a rich portrayal of the context in which people intersected ready-to-eat food in their everyday lives).

The information that the company obtained about the context of purchase and consumption led to an even deeper exploration of consumer needs and emotions. Following a well-deserved break, the respondents were asked to fill out another brief questionnaire exploring their emotions and perceptions about a number of ready-to-eat brands. Then, finally, they were informed of the sponsor of the study and asked to respond to a final broad set of questions relating specifically to the brand and product portfolio of Frito-Lay.

Ultimately, the discussions and data were analyzed and the results compiled in a detailed map of the demand landscape, the purpose of which was to dissect consumer behavior into its component parts and tease apart the relevant dimensions in customers' lives. The result was a comparatively complete portrait of the ecosystem of customer demand.

An Ecosystem Coming into Focus

When a company sets out to create a demand landscape, it is not unusual to track several hundred or even thousands of behaviors and then cluster them into distinct categories of goals, activities, and priorities. Add to this as much information as possible about customer needs, wants, pleasures, and pains—in short, all the contextual elements that make up the dynamic and complex ecosystem of customer demand—and the result is a comprehensive consumer demand landscape. This landscape should display in rich schematic detail an ecosystem that illustrates in awesome precision how consumers go about living their lives.

It should also reveal how products, services, or brands intersect in time and space with consumers' occasions to live, play, and work, as defined by the matrix of goals, activities, and priorities that constitute the leading features of the landscape.

"I always eat potato chips with a sandwich" is a moment when the brand Frito-Lay intersects with the occasion of eating a sandwich. As more "intersection points" were identified, the landscape became increasingly robust.

One of the key insights a company can gain from its demand landscape is how different brands in the company's portfolio link to different behaviors—defined in terms of consumption episodes or contexts experienced by consumers—and how these behaviors invoke certain needs and wants, and in which contexts these behaviors are combined with complex emotions, urges, and passions.

Frito-Lay found that while some brands were more closely associated with eating a sandwich and prepared at home for consumption out of the home, others were keyed more toward socializing at home with friends. This finding, layered onto the company's more traditional understanding of consumer segments that might harbor preferences for specific brands, aided Frito-Lay in reevaluating its entire view of existing and potential consumers. An entirely new avenue and dimension of insight regarding purchase and consumption was discovered.

Take-Away Lessons

Frito-Lay discovered that the process of creating a demand landscape provided it with an opportunity to combine direct and indirect methods of research. This helped increase the reliability and validity of the data and structure existing data in new ways, thereby creating a new way of looking at customers. The starting point was important—by observing consumers first at the point of purchase (the video camera study) and later at the point of purpose (through diaries, observations, and in-depth conversations), the marketing team gained an outside-in perspective of consumers by means of unbiased immersion in their everyday lives, an experience that occasionally challenged widely held assumptions by the company. Through the mapping process, the company learned that observed and reported behavior tends to be a far more reliable barometer and indicator of consumer behavior than a more direct inquiry about needs, values, and desires, particularly if the questions are posed in relation to a specific product, service, or brand. From observed behavior, it is possible to infer what consumers truly want and desire.

The importance of the social-cultural context cannot be overemphasized. Traditional research may ask a person, "How important is health to you?"

She may answer, "very important," "not so important," or "irrelevant." But if the diary shows her working out in the gym three times a week for the past four weeks, the prominence of this activity and the importance of the health need is much more accurately assessed. Articulating a need is one thing—actually having it and doing something about it is quite another.

Examining goals, activities, and priorities in the episodes and context of everyday life, in other words, provides a richer set of reference groups than if the context is absent from the inquiry. A person might like to drink water at home in the evening, but after a great workout, that person might prefer to drink Gatorade. Within the landscape of consumer demand, context is critical.

Frito-Lay also learned the inestimable value of conducting research that is not directly linked to a given product or service. There should be nothing in a demand landscape specifically relating to specific products; rather, such research is centered on the goals, needs, and activities that people pursue, in which—incidentally—a number of products, brands, and services may play a role.

Frito-Lay's demand landscape included a range of brand values and associations but did not include a specific range of Frito-Lay products. The only basis of inquiry was to determine in which quadrant, niche, or corner in the everyday lives of people Lay's played best, independent of how Lay's was perceived in the marketplace. By asking what kind of snacks consumers like most within a given demand cluster—"I like something chocolaty or something salty while socializing with friends at home at night"—marketers could learn the identity and location of the specific brand equities of Lay's that might potentially intersect with a particular demand cluster.

Such a data summary differs markedly from more conventional consumer research. As opposed to being asked typical purchase or brand funnel questions such as, "How likely are you to buy this specific product or that one? Would you consider this brand? With this price or that? This color or that?" respondents are asked questions about the contours and texture of demand in their everyday lives. These questions reveal new and relevant information.

Step-by-Step Guide for Creating the Demand Landscape for Your Company

In chapter 2, we outlined at a "headline" level the elements needed to create a demand landscape. Here, we'll break the process into specific steps, with additional guidance on tailoring the process to your company.

Step 1: Identify activities, goals, priorities, context, needs, frustrations, and hassles.

Step 2: Group into demand clusters—use goals or activities or context as means of clustering.

Step 3: Complete demand clusters through adding existing research (saturate).

Step 4: Evaluate the demand clusters with respect to their strategic usefulness.

Step 5: Evaluate how a brand "fits into" or plays out in a demand landscape.

Step 1: Identifying the Basic Elements of the Demand Landscape

The process begins by developing a broad matrix of use and consumption situations. These situations should be described in terms of basic elements such as goals, activities, and priorities. The diary method (which Frito-Lay used) is a popular way to solicit these situations. In some cases, particularly in industrial customer applications, it can be more practical to conduct an outcome-based interviewing procedure, as discussed in the Cordis story in chapter 2, or to use noninvasive observational methods (see the GE Healthcare example in chapter 5).

The reality is, a dizzying array of methodologies is available to help companies establish the basic components of the demand landscape. We offer some thoughts on selection in the final section of this chapter. In general, though, the objective is to get a cross-section of people in the study group. One useful framework is to choose subjects along the brand-relationship continuum.[5] Another option is to choose customers along a continuum of involvement or engagement with the usage and consumption of the product or service or category. For exploring trends, a study of behaviors of fringe or edge customers relative to mainstream customers makes sense.

Once a slate of behaviors has been recorded, one-on-one discussions or interviews with respondents are typically required to explore in greater depth the contexts in which activities take place, goals are realized, and priorities are established. Such discussions can be revealing. People tend to be highly forthcoming in describing the needs, frustrations, feelings, emotions, and fears they feel at a particular moment. They tend to mentally immerse themselves in the situation (as they go through their diary, for example) much as they would do when confessing something. You should expect their level of interest and engagement in these discussions, even for low-interest products, to be similar to the enthusiastic way in which people describe a gripping scene in a movie.

Once the consumption, use moments, or episodes have been explored in depth, the company can start exploring purchase processes. For Frito-Lay, this secondary part of the interview (which covers much more "traditional" marketing research ground) began to bridge the outside-in perspective with the company's existing offerings and going-to-market effort.

Frito-Lay asked questions such as these: Had the interviewees recently bought a bag of Doritos in a convenience store? What products or brands might they have substituted for Doritos if they hadn't found their preferred flavors, bag sizes, or packaging? How did they rate those competitors according to a ten-point scale of priorities and preferences?

The answers provided information that would help the company move into the second piece of the DIG model and begin to reframe its opportunity space.

Step 2: Grouping into Meaningful Clusters on the Basis of Goals, Activities, or Context

With the basic components of the demand landscape identified (see the excerpt of the demand landscape earlier in this chapter), a company can then begin to group individual components into "demand clusters." The grouping is performed according to the similarities of the activities, through common themes emerging from the goals and taking into consideration the priorities that customers set for these goals and activities. This can be an enormous undertaking; however, it is a critical step toward understanding the ecosystem of demand. Frito-Lay, for example, took into account more than 10,327 activities, 33,333 goals, and several hundred "use" contexts. The company then created several dozen broad categories of goals and ultimately narrowed the analysis down to just 15 goals associated with several hundreds of activities around ready-to-eat and ready-to-prepare food. Examples of these goals ranged from very functional goals like "to correct poor health" to more specific emotional goals like "to treat or to indulge."

Creating this demand landscape is, from the vantage point of traditional market and customer research, terra incognita. What Frito-Lay had been seeing for years was how its products compared with competing products in the minds of the customers queried. What Frito-Lay had *never* seen was how Frito-Lay products fit into the lives of people defined over the broad range of activities and goals associated with the consumption of ready-to-eat and ready-to-prepare food.

Step 3: Saturating the Demand Landscape

After establishing the rough contours of the demand landscape, a company can then layer in its existing traditional research. Most companies possess extensive research on customers, but typically this information is buried deep inside market research reports, collected from different samples for different purposes. Still more research may be available at the industry or category level. However, none of this data can be put to a useful purpose, because it often lacks an appropriate framework and structure. Frito-Lay relied on its own extensive research, such as the proprietary iTrac research as well the syndicated World of Snacks study by Landis. The World of Snacks study, for example, provided customer information across more than 250 attributes. These attributes were mapped into the demand clusters. Landis also provided product-category-level data, such as the percentage of customers who consider potato chips to have nutritional value. Through this crossing of existing data with the demand clusters, the size of the demand in each cluster was determined. Here the purchasing information gleaned during the interviews is brought into play.

Step 4: Evaluating the Demand Clusters with Respect to Their Strategic Value

Frito-Lay used three levels of criteria to evaluate the clusters defined by activities and goals. First was the relative priority that customers place in their lives on a particular goal or activity or cluster. Second was channel fit. The question was to what extent a particular demand cluster was compatible with the IC channel, such as convenience stores, drugstores, vending, and dollar stores versus large formats. Finally was the market attractiveness—for example, the extent to which a cluster is more or less competitive with other product categories. It turned out that some highly valuable demand clusters were also highly competitive and overtargeted by alternative product offerings, such as beef jerky or cookies.

Step 5: Evaluating How the Current Brand Fits into the Demand Landscape

The idea here is to understand whether the difference in use and consumption of a particular brand is due to the product itself or to the way it has been traditionally positioned toward customers.

One of the most important insights that Frito-Lay gained from this step in the process was that each product played a different role in customers' lives as described in terms of the demand landscape. This important insight led to a further study of the role of the brand in relationship to context.

To better understand this dimension, Frito-Lay mapped the Lay's brand identity elements and attributes across the demand landscape. This analysis produced a startling finding: while the Lay's brand was positioned historically and deliberately on delivering *functional benefits*, as summarized by the notion of "irresistibility" (as brilliantly executed in the classic campaigns "Bet You Can't Eat Just One" or, in a later campaign, "America's Best Tasting Potato Chip"), and the emotional benefits and feelings of satisfying a craving (letting oneself go), Frito-Lay learned in fact that customers associated Lay's with specific use contexts, activities, and goal achievement that had more to do with emotions surrounding these contexts than with feelings concerning the potato chips themselves.

Another major insight came from learning that the activities were not necessarily significant meal occasions, such as lunch or dinner, or important activities or moments (for example, the little time I have to barbecue with friends and family); they were, if anything, moments of simple joy that often invoked inner-directed feelings, their meaning to oneself. For consumers, achieving the goal of "being comforted and reassured" inexorably invoked an image of a beacon or lighthouse—a solid, constant place where the passing of time isn't a cause for concern.

Lay's, surprisingly enough, was often seen as just such a lighthouse, offering comfort in a timeless, ever-present moment. Realizing this, Frito-Lay decided to refocus the positioning to stress "moments of simple pleasure"—a contextual, social-situational reference pointing to many activities in the chosen demand clusters.

"Comfort and reassurance" further formed the intersection of Frito-Lay with "health and wellness" because one gains comfort and reassurance in the context of all the broad range of activities people pursue to attain that goal. "I bake a pie because my mom used to. I make a special effort to make handmade mashed potatoes for my family. I am emotionally comforted because I am doing something great for my family." Health—a goal that supersedes comfort and reassurance—may be a matter of consuming wholesome foods, foods like my mother used to make, foods that aren't very processed. Or it could mean obtaining a sense of emotional well-being from the prospect of comforting, familiar food.

The intersection of health and wellness with comfort and reassurance was a place in which the Frito-Lay brands could become most relevant to people— a specific way to fit into customers' everyday lives. So yes, absolutely, Lay's was "America's best-tasting chip," but the research suggested that matching attributes and benefits to those needs was less important than linking Lay's to the many activities in customers' lives associated with achieving comfort and reassurance goals while articulating the role of Lay's in those goals.

Inclusive Research, Relevant Results

Meet Hank (see figure 3-2). Statisticians would call Hank an outlier. He gets a score on every dimension of conventional research into customer needs, wants, and motivations. He appears everywhere. And as a result, in all likelihood, he's the kind of guy who is usually eliminated from data sets as "unclassifiable." He's usually not included in analysis.

FIGURE 3-2

A day in the life of Hank

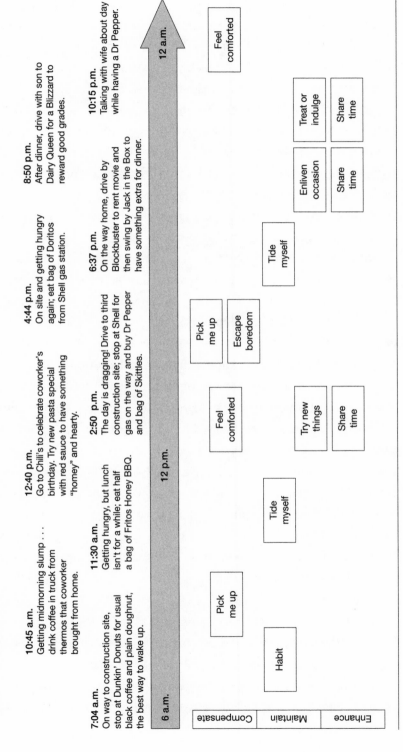

Face it: a traditional marketer would have a difficult time targeting this customer. Assigning Hank to a segment according to needs or wants is not easy —he seems to have too many different needs (like all people), sometimes to indulge or socialize, sometimes to escape boredom.

But suppose Hank is a frequent and enthusiastic customer of snack foods. Suppose he happens to experience more than the five distinct motivations for snacking traditionally classified by conventional researchers as prime motivations for eating salty snacks.

One immediate and practical result of creating a demand landscape is that it forces a company to think far deeper about the complexities and evolving nature of customer demand than it may ever have before. At Frito-Lay, even though the demand landscape only provided one slice of the complex map of the ecosystem of customer demand around food and consumption relevant for Frito-Lay, it already showed that the opportunity for Frito-Lay was far bigger than ever imagined, by simply looking at the category-typical lunch and dinner occasion. Not only was the opportunity bigger in terms of size, it was also bigger in terms of truly increasing the health and wellness of customers through transforming the experiences around food consumption by making every day simply a little more joyful.

In order to learn more about the nature of consumer demand, we need to dissect the demand landscape by observing its contours from several lenses. Frito-Lay looked at what happened temporally before and after a snacking occasion in consumers' everyday lives. Were there any systematic patterns of behavior? One insight for Frito-Lay was that while there were only a limited number of lunch and dinner occasions per person in which Lay's could be made relevant, there were a significant number of activities where a sandwich was consumed "naked," without a complement such as potato chips. The demand landscape discovered these episodes and moments in customers' everyday lives.

Frito-Lay also looked from the perspective of the overall market, looking more broadly at the landscape, and asked, How is the pattern of behavior different for an extreme consumer like Hank from the average consumer's? These and other explorations at the periphery of the consumption and use experience provide new insights into a company's total opportunity space.

At Frito-Lay, the explorations led the company to develop a strategic blueprint for action that involved not only refocusing its strategy but also rethinking its new product development, prioritizing innovations, reassessing its overall brand portfolio, and revamping the entire activation of its marketing efforts. Here are some highlights of the early efforts in activating the new direction for Lay's.

Frito-Lay's Strategic Blueprint for Action

By viewing the demand not simply in terms of customers' needs and wants, delivering America's best-tasting potato chip, and marketing the notion of irresistibility, Frito-Lay developed a much broader and deeper understanding of the opportunities for innovation and growth for Lay's. By seeing the entire ecosystem of demand and seeing how Lay's intersects with this demand, Frito-Lay saw opportunities for new products, new ways of activation, new ways of engaging with customers, and new ways of developing customer advantage that were hidden to them in plain sight.

The relevant demand opportunity for Lay's became the moments in everyday life when we take the time to focus on what really matters—the simple joys in life that make every day a little more joyful—not simply the lunch or dinner food consumption occasion. Essentially, moments of simple joy redrew the scope of the Lay's opportunity in a significant way— away from a strategy of enhancing simply lunch and dinner occasions through the best-tasting Lay's potato chips. Instead, Lay's positioning was dimensioned in a new and powerful way to capture a larger area of demand. The direction was away from an emphasis on product quality—as in the best American potato chip, irresistibility, and the feature set—and more focused on how the all-American classic Lay's brand and its inherent qualities of goodness, wholesomeness, authenticity, realness, genuineness and the values of home intersected in those moments that matter to consumers. Lay's was conceptualized as a lighthouse—a constant and dependable entity in a fast-paced world.

In order to drive activation, Frito-Lay clearly defined the Lay's moment— what it was and what it was not. For example, a typical moment in customers' everyday lives was a picnic or barbecue, a family reunion, reading a book, or simply relaxing. It was not a stressful meeting, being at a bar, going dancing, or elegant or formal events. The Lay's moments were further defined in terms of location, casting, product wardrobe, and expression. Expression was defined, for example, in terms of happy and positive, not over the top, and occasion appropriate. This contextualization of the overall strategy proved useful in terms of developing the overall activation effort, which became that of the *smile break*.

The lighthouse was a metaphor and a concept, but the smile break became the driving idea and action that reified the lighthouse in everyday life. Frito-Lay considered this its most immediate opportunity for development. A smile break might be a simple moment like "I'm typing at my laptop at work, but I take a break to go online and buy a little book for my mom." Smile breaks are moments in which people take time to do unplanned, genuine, positive things—things, in short, that make them smile. They may be in the larger scale of things of greater or lesser importance.

The next phase was to activate the smile break moments to create the Lay's brand across media (from TV, print, radio, and the Internet to sports and special events), across channels of distribution, across trademarks (Lay's Classic, Lay's Stax, Baked Lay's, or Lay's Kettle Cooked), across visibility platforms (sandwich, retail events, smile promotion, and the calendar holidays, like Fourth of July), across customer demographics, and across multiple-customer touch points, such as on packaging, in stores, on the Web, and merchandising destinations. Frito-Lay TV and print spots and outdoor advertising created by the New York–based agency BBDO keyed off the notion of the smile break by featuring genuine people, not actors, wearing smiles in a variety of settings and contexts. Internet sponsorships and packaging exhorted customers to "Get your smile on." On the packages themselves, promotions encouraged customers to take a break, pause, and read a funny little story or comic strip. In-store merchandising also featured regular people engaged in taking a variety of smile breaks. For Frito-Lay, the smile break replaced the existing marketing efforts with a behavioral proposal to—in effect—sit up and smell and taste the chips, savoring the special and magical moments in your life. All Lay's merchandising and promoting and advertising suggested a moment, a purchase occasion, or a smile break, as opposed to a hot price.

The results? Growth in the hotly contested IC store channel increased by 10 percent in the first few months of the rollout and grew 15 percent in grocery stores. Frito-Lay in general and Lay's in particular had long been losing unit growth even while retaining a dangerously high market share. Without having to tweak size or price, Lay's $3 billion business, accounting for close to a third of PepsiCo's revenues (bigger than flagship brand Pepsi), jumped 10–15 percent in a quarter. Brand equity for Lay's increased across all segments as measured by brand regard or measures such as "proud to use" and "this brand has momentum."

Within a few years of thinking differently about customers, Frito-Lay has fundamentally altered its strategy to stress enhancing the consumption moments over simply maximizing the pounds on the floor.

Selecting the Best Research Methods for Your Company

Companies setting out to adapt a DIG model have an increasingly large number of research methodologies available to them. Many of these data-gathering methods are drawn from ethnographic research used in the fields of anthropology, psychology, and sociology; most are viable and can be used effectively in different types of companies and across industries.

The problem is, of course, choosing the right ones for your company and situation. The abundance of options has, not surprisingly, created confusion around which methodology should be used when, for what effect, and for what purpose.

The framework in figure 3-3 should help companies decide which methods to use when.[6] The framework takes into account the various questions strategists might be asking themselves at different stages of the DIG process, broadly:

1. *To explore*: I know I want to innovate, but what is the customer demand landscape?

2. *To define*: I know the customer demand landscape, but where is the opportunity?

3. *To enrich*: I know where the opportunities lie; how can I leverage these so my product or brand can play a compelling role in customers' lives?

4. *To refine*: I know how I want to innovate; how do I refine or test my innovation to exactly fit into customers' lives?

The data-gathering methodologies can be categorized along two dimensions. The first dimension revolves around the breadth and scope of the research, and the second around whether the research is conducted within the context of the customers' lives or not. The intersection of these two dimensions defines the four areas. Each area highlights research methods that will help marketers gather the right data based upon where they are during the DIG process.

FIGURE 3-3

Demand-first methodologies

	Focused	Broad
In context	**Enrich** • Collaging and drawing • Confessional interviews • Consumer stories • Mind mapping • Outcome-based interviews • Real-life experimenting • Talk-through research	**Define** • Collaging and drawing • Day reconstruction method • Photo journal • Photo observation • Shadowing • Text messaging/beeper studies • Video observation • Word/concept association method • Written journals
Out of context	**Refine** • Archetypal research • Card sorting • Consumer-led problem solving • Consumer product interaction • Consumer role playing • Focus groups • Participatory design • Metaphor Elicitation Method* • Talk-through research	**Explore** • Card sorting • Collaging and drawing • Consumer hypotheses brainstorming • Consumer stories • Day reconstruction method • Metaphor Elicitation Method* • Mind mapping • Unfocus groups • Talk-through research

*Trademark of ZMET

Note: A detailed list of these methodologies with source references can be obtained upon request from the author.

Focused Versus Broad Research

The horizontal axis defines whether the scope of the research will be conducted within a narrow, functional, deep, and well-defined slice of the moments and episodes in the customer's life (e.g., eating an indulgent snack or playing a recreational sport) or, conversely, whether it will look at the entirety of a customer's life (i.e., all the goals, activities, and priorities the customer has during the day as they relate to a particular activity, like eating or drinking). The former allows the strategist to drill down into detail around the customer's activities and behavior, whereas the latter allows the marketer to uncover behavior patterns and inductive/process thinking, without any preconceived notions. Focused research is inevitably narrower in scope than broad research and is thus more outcome driven.

Too often, marketers concentrate only on focused research because the findings gathered are invariably easier to interpret and implement. However, if marketers are still at a point in the DIG process where they are only beginning to map the demand landscape, they need to apply broader research methods to capture as many customer behaviors as possible.

In-Context Versus Out-of-Context Research

The vertical axis looks at the context in which the research takes place. The context of use can be defined as where a particular customer experience related to a specific innovation area or product takes place. *In context* means within the context of the customer's life, and therefore doing the research requires marketers to immerse themselves in customers' lives. *Out-of-context* research takes place in a controlled, artificial environment, such as a laboratory or a company conference room. Whether research is carried out in the context of customers' lives or not depends on the type of information that marketers need and the degree of control they want over the outcome. These two dimensions result in four quadrants:

- *Explore—I know I want to innovate, but what is the customer demand landscape?* Strategists can use the methods within this quadrant broadly and out of context. Usually, at the start of the process, they need to understand the potential areas of customers' everyday lives through an initial overview of the potential activities, priorities, context, needs, frustrations, and hassles of customers. As a result, strategists will structure projects with open-ended, broad studies that are designed to explore the customer demand landscape in order to generate hypotheses on where the opportunities for innovation might lie. Because this work is preliminary and is starting off with the proverbial blank canvas, out-of-context methodologies, such as customer hypotheses brainstorming, may lend themselves better to quickly exploring and identifying an innovation area.

- *Define—I know the innovation area; where do the opportunities lie?* Strategists can use the methods within this quadrant broadly and in context. Once they have a better understanding of the customer demand landscape and have developed their hypotheses, marketers need to test these hypotheses and define what opportunities exist. The research here is often carried out in the context of customers' lives to get an unbiased perspective. The methodologies used in this stage need to be broad to collect a range of behaviors. Therefore, the strategists can uncover more potential opportunity gaps. However, these methods also often require more resources in terms of time, money, and marketers. Methodologies such as shadowing customers or collecting information from "A Day in the Life" customer journals provide the richest and most comprehensive information for these types of projects.

- *Enrich—I know where the opportunities lie; how can we leverage these so my product or brand can play a compelling role in customers' lives?* Marketers can use the methods within this quadrant more narrowly and in context. Once they know exactly where they want to focus, they need to enrich this knowledge with granular detail on where their product or brand can play a role within customers' lives, to enable them to complete the clustering of the behaviors into demand clusters and proceed to evaluate the demand clusters with respect to their strategic usefulness. Applying these methods narrowly and in context presupposes a good understanding of the customer demand landscape and the innovation area. Outcome-based interviews or real-life experimenting are examples of methods that can be used to collect salient customer stories and insights that will help the company develop on-target products, services, or brands.

- *Refine—I know how I want to innovate; how do I refine or test my innovation to exactly fit into customers' lives?* Strategists can use the methods within this quadrant more narrowly and out of context. Strategists who already have the initial product or brand innovation need to test, refine, and validate to ensure that the innovation fits into or plays out in a demand landscape. Customer–product interaction observations, customer-led problem-solving workshops, and role playing are all methods that will allow the company to test and receive feedback on its innovation within a controlled setting. When applied narrowly and out of context, these methods are more effective and efficient in refining specific opportunities.

Chapter 4 picks up the demand-first innovation and growth model with a customer demand landscape in hand and looks at how a company can begin to evaluate its opportunity space. Allianz, the Munich-based insurance giant, anchors this next chapter.

Reframing the Opportunity Space

I T WAS EARLY IN 2001, and Allianz, the Munich-based global insurance company was at a crossroads. The company faced some
difficult challenges as a result of the deregulation of the financial and insurance sectors. Despite being faced by an unsettling period, Allianz's aim was
to transform the organization from a traditional German insurer with operations in Europe, into an international financial services provider.

These changes however, did not occur overnight. With successful acquisitions already in place across Europe in the 1970s and 1980s, Allianz
began to really establish itself. During the 1990s, further expansion was
undertaken as the company acquired operations in eight Eastern European
countries, the United States, and also, significantly, AGF Paris. This latter
acquisition in particular paved the way for further expansion into Asia and
South America.

As the traditional market leader, with a customer market share of 29 percent in Germany, Allianz's strong position during this time was not due solely
to its past merger and acquisition strategy but also to its excellent field-
agent sales force. But the organization was also firmly entrenched in traditional approaches, particularly when it came to innovation and product
development, even as market research and competitors' actions signaled a
sea change in the way the industry would go to market in the future.

For example, one of the pillars in Allianz's competitive portfolio had
long been its extensive network of captive agents, who formed the backbone of the firm's deep and rich roots in communities large and small all

across Germany. In virtually every city, town, and village in the country, Allianz agents were highly respected members within their communities. The powerful sales force consistently demonstrated enormous effectiveness as a sales and marketing tool in the promotion and sale of new and existing products and services, research also showed customers' increasing desire to bypass the formality of predetermined personal meetings with the sales force in favor of the ease of access by local bank or direct underwriters.

Yet there were questions: Was the age of the field agent ending? If not, how would it evolve? The implications were open to extensive discussion and debate. Citicorp, for example, Allianz's larger global competitor, had been pursuing a strategy that it called a *financial services supermarket* (known in Europe as the *all-finance* or *bank-assurance* model), but results had been mixed.

Allianz decided to move ahead. "The multichannel sales and marketing model was fast approaching," explained Michael Maskus, then responsible for marketing for Allianz Germany, "and we didn't want to be left behind."[1]

A New Foundation for Strategy

A marketer with senior-level marketing and sales experience at Schering, Beiersdorf and at Johnson & Johnson, Maskus had joined Allianz in 1993. At that time, Europe was going through a period of deregulation of the financial and insurance sectors. One of Maskus's key objectives was to develop Allianz as an increasingly competitive and customer-facing organization, but it hadn't been easy to shift the company's mind-set.

"Prior to deregulation," Maskus recalled, "the insurance industry was not very competitive. Since Allianz was the leader in the insurance industry and dominated the industry associations, it was relatively unheard of at that time that competitive and market-driven solutions to industrywide problems were both required and desirable."

In fact, such complacency might never have been challenged if not for the rapid integration of the European and global economies, coupled with the opening up of the insurance and financial services industries worldwide. These exogenous changes in the marketplace prompted Allianz's top managers to realize—as Maskus put it —"that being always at the top of the heap and in the driver's seat is not necessarily a good thing. Sometimes being the market leader can result in complacency within an organization; this can also stifle innovation and prevent the growth of a creative culture."

In the meantime, Allianz also expanded its asset management business by purchasing, for example, Pimco, the U.S.-based leader in fixed income and management. Over time, Allianz became one of the leading asset management companies worldwide, with €1.2 trillion assets under management. Expansion into the banking sector was realized when Allianz acquired the Frankfurt-based Dresdner Bank, the third largest private bank in Germany, for €24 billion. This significant acquisition broadened and deepened the company's already complex product and service portfolio and expanded the customer base of more than 70 million worldwide. But the acquisition, by itself, did not create the fundamental changes needed to achieve the ultimate goal of positioning Allianz as a global financial services provider offering comprehensive solutions to all customers. What Allianz truly needed was a new focus on customers and a growth model. Under the direction of then-CEO Henning Schulte-Noelle, Maskus worked on developing a strong marketing team that could tackle the current and future opportunities of Allianz.

By 2002, Maskus, now international head of group marketing, had recruited marketers from varying backgrounds to form part of the global marketing team of Allianz. Interestingly, these new recruits, together with Maskus, were not predominantly from a financial-services background but in the marketing of consumer products.

Future CEO Michael Diekmann was also a strong believer in the customer-focused approach, and at the time of the Dresdner merger, Diekmann was in charge of Allianz's operations in North and South America. During an earlier step in his career path, he served as the first customer-relationship manager, a position in which he witnessed firsthand one of Allianz's greatest opportunities: the alignment of a fragmented face to customers. The rapidly emerging multichannel sales model, all the executives realized, offered a wealth of opportunities to engage more broadly and deeply with consumers. Formerly, it also presented a dangerous potential to worsen the already prevailing fragmentation.

Historically, Allianz had been divided into separate divisions, including property and casualty (P&C), life and asset management, and corporate insurance, each "owning" its own customer base and means of accessing that base. "Depending upon the customer," Maskus observed, "and the nature of the relationship, Allianz might have been perceived as a health insurer, a life insurance company, a property-and-casualty company, or even a bank. Each customer would see you as five different companies, while from the corporate perspective, the company could easily see one customer as five different customers."

But what if customers were assigned a single relationship manager, with whom over time they might forge a deeper and more mutually satisfactory relationship?

As the company endeavored to accomplish that task, a consensus gradually built across the upper ranks of the organization that the ultimate solution was even greater than restructuring the sales force. It lay in establishing one customer view and one voice *to* the customer. "In the past, marketing was regarded as a function to support sales," Maskus explained. "The only legitimate question to be asked with relation to marketing was, for many years, 'What is a good campaign that can result in driving product sales?' Now, the question—still aimed at marketing—became, 'How can we design products based on an in-depth customer understanding and by identifying new customer needs and requirements so that they might find an insurance product they actually desire, as opposed to one they grudgingly agreed to buy?'"

Within Allianz, momentum was mounting, with the notion that products could be developed "not solely from an actuarial point of view, but also incorporating an outsider-in market/customer perspective."

From Marketing to Market Innovation

The thought of putting the new philosophy into practice was daunting. At the same time, it was tremendously exciting. "We needed to develop a funnel to put in good ideas from the customer, and a process to evaluate the needs of the customer," Erik Heusel, the project leader for the product innovation pilot, said. "A standard process that would permit us to ask the customer not for solutions but to articulate and comprehend the new and changing needs and requirements more clearly."

Understanding that need, Allianz established a new framework that married marketing with product development. It was called, appropriately enough, *market-driven product development.*

As the framework developed, Maskus recalled, the entire marketing team sat down at one point and handed themselves a deceptively simple assignment—deceptively simple because while it was easy to state, it was difficult to execute.

The assignment was this: "Think about how to ask the customer about insurance in a more intelligent way instead of just accepting that the customer doesn't care about insurance and leaving the process at that. Go beyond asking the customer how the products should be designed, but rather do what we can to find out about customers first and then develop products and services."

The Pilot Project

Importantly, this customer-facing philosophy found the sympathetic ears of two leaders of one of the line divisions: Gerhard Gehring and Thomas Summer, from Allianz's personal liability group. Gehring and Summer put their group up as a guinea-pig project, and in spring 2004, a cross-functional team of Allianz executives assembled to bring their new perspective to bear on a fundamental problem in that area. Personal liability insurance (PLI) was one of the oldest and most historic product categories at Allianz. It was also a category in which the company—while still the market leader in Germany—was witnessing its market share gradually erode in the face of inroads by newer, lower-cost entrants.

PLI is an outgrowth of German property and tort law, which states that any damage "inadvertently done to a third party's property or . . . harm that is inadvertently done to the individual himself must be reinstated by the person who inflicted that damage or harm." The often-unwitting perpetrator bears financial responsibility for reimbursing the affected third party, regardless of cost. While in most cases ("I inadvertently smashed my friend's beloved vase") the ultimate costs may be low, in some comparatively rare situations ("The vase I accidentally smashed is a Ming dynasty original," or "A chip from the smashed vase also injured my friend's eye. Now my friend is unable to work for six months, and I have to pay compensation") or in one of the most extreme cases ("I hit my neighbor's child while I was riding my bicycle, and the child is now in the hospital, injured"), the financial consequences may mount into the millions.

PLI does not cover damages caused by automobiles (by far the likeliest route to inflicting substantial physical and material damages on others) or, as Thomas Summer explained, "dogs, horses, assorted pets, boats, houses if rented, and foreign travel." And as a result of the narrowness of the product parameters, some customers were tempted to dispense with it altogether, viewing it as an option or a luxury, as opposed to a necessity. Adding to many customers' all too frequent frustration with PLI was that when they filed a claim on the policy, they discovered to their dismay that the area for which they filed (a boating accident or an injured pet) was not covered by the policy.

Preliminary research clarified the essential facts: from the point of view of total benefits relative to cost, the Allianz offering was one of the most attractive policies on the German market. Plain price comparisons, however, drawn by consumer magazines between it and rival products made Allianz's product look unattractive and therefore when evaluated strictly on the parameters of coverage and price, without looking into the details and particulars of the benefit-cost-coverage equation.

Also, on any number of independent insurance Web sites, the various PLI products and offerings were broken down in charts using only price for the amount of coverage and duration. Intangibles such as the actual payment and claim settlement behavior, or quality of service, did not surface as metrics or choice points.

In short, a highly specialized product had been turned into a classic commodity. In an arena where purchase decisions were likely to be increasingly made on few factors other than price, the advantages previously enjoyed by the premium provider, Allianz, were being whittled down. Put another way, this profitable unit, which remained a cash cow for the firm, was losing market share apparently because customers were having a difficult time appreciating the selling proposition of the product and as a result were reducing the benefits of the product to three narrow dimensions: (1) price, (2) amount of deductible, and (3) amount of coverage.

The New PLI Proposition

The mounting price pressure provided a powerful impulse for thinking about PLI and the customer relationships associated with it in a new way. Additional motivation came from the fact that the product lacked jazz, excitement, and sparkle and had seen no genuine innovation in decades. The mission and the mandate defined by the senior advisers to the project team were clear: *build an irresistible and sustainable value proposition for PLI*. A secondary goal was to apply the lessons gained from this research to other products and categories.

The primary focus was to engineer a shift from selling insurance products to enhancing the various ways in which personal liability insurance intersected with people's lives. In the United States, for example, the aptly named Progressive Insurance had introduced an "immediate response vehicle," which had not only changed how Progressive *sold* insurance but more importantly transformed how it "owned" and "used" insurance in the event of an accident. Nobody in Germany woke up in the morning feeling bereft because they lacked Allianz PLI full coverage. So how could such a shift take place?

The first step was to create a demand landscape. To do this, the project team tapped key staffers from multiple departments in the firm to participate in a series of carefully orchestrated and designed workshops. These employees included an expert in qualitative research (including ethnographic and observational methodologies), an actuary, a host of salespeople, and several senior board-level executives. Over several months, participants also included representatives from marketing, sales, the personal liability division, market research, the private consumer business, the personal liability group, and strategic brand management, in addition to a selection of key account managers. The entire process was facilitated by a small team of advisers.

Critically, the team decided that customers' views were also a necessary input to generate the discussion of potential new opportunities. Allianz had previously commissioned a traditional brand study, focusing on tracking levels of awareness, brand equity, and brand performance, as well as monitoring shifts in popular attitudes toward the Allianz brand. The firm had in addition commissioned conventional strategic analyses, tracking across the entire portfolio of insurance products offered by Allianz versus competitors.

In this endeavor, they chose a new approach to understanding customers, which focused not on their perceptions of the brand Allianz and not on their perceptions of the PLI product, but on the activities, experiences, and goals of people in their lives: how people spend their time and how they experience the various activities and settings of their lives. (Think back to the Lay's example; the motivation at this stage was the same.)

The team selected a comparatively small sample of twenty-five consumers in three major cities (Dusseldorf, Berlin, and Munich, where Allianz is headquartered) as well as a group of customers drawn from rural areas in Bavaria and the industrial area of Ruhrgebiet. During one month, participants were encouraged to report on their daily lives through detailed descriptions. They were asked to systematically reconstruct the activities and experiences of the preceding days, weeks, and months using procedures designed to reduce recall biases.[2]

After the month of indirect observation, each participant was invited to engage in a four-hour in-depth discussion, or "confessional interview," with the outside advisers and trained facilitators. Allianz team members also participated, but their identity was not disclosed until the end. The greater part of these discussions was devoted to gaining a deeper understanding of how participants established a matrix of priorities and the relevance of these goals.

Following these in-depth interviews and interactions, the Allianz team met with their advisers to structure the data, observations, journals, and transcripts into preliminary hypotheses of clusters of the everyday behaviors recorded by participants. During this process, a set of several hundred behaviors were identified as relevant to the context of PLI and formed the contours of the demand landscape. From the stated minutia ("I need to have a coffee to get away from my office and think") to more global activities with goals attached ("I need to take a vacation on Majorca with my wife"), activities were clustered into "goal-based demand clusters."

For example, a goal might be "to plan for the future." The activities might be (1) take classes for my driver's license, (2) save money toward college, and (3) set up a bank account. The results were varied and illuminating.

What Were the Possibilities and Opportunities?

Mapping the demand landscape for PLI was merely a precursor to the hard work ahead, even though it alone provided many new insights about customer satisfaction with the PLI product, perceptions of insurance companies, and opportunities where Allianz's current product portfolio could be improved and enhanced. However, the ultimate goal was to create new and powerful product or service innovations to this staid product offering, entire new growth platforms, innovative new marketing concepts, or new business models, so that customers might *want* PLI instead of passively permitting themselves to be *sold* it.

To achieve this, Allianz needed to temporarily forget about its current product offering and to *think beyond PLI*. It was necessary to retire (mentally) the current strategies, processes, capabilities, and systems of the company as a whole. The result would be an unbiased look at PLI and Allianz from the point of view of the customer, the contours of the ecosystem of demand as manifested and brought together in the demand landscape.

Exploring the opportunities for Allianz in this way consisted of two essential steps: (1) framing the issues (for retention and growth) and (2) applying the three breakthrough innovation and growth (BIG) lenses to discover and see the opportunities on the demand landscape and to critically think through reframing the opportunity space—following the words of Oscar Wilde, who wrote, "Imagination imitates. It is the critical spirit that creates." Recall from chapter 2 that these steps, taken together, embody the second element of the DIG model.

Allianz Frames the Issue

Table 4-1 shows the simplified demand landscape across the six key product dimensions and just two demand clusters for illustration—the frame that Allianz used to explore opportunities. Each entry where the product intersects with the demand cluster demonstrates how PLI serves, or potentially serves, the needs, wants, frustrations, and passions in the everyday lives of consumers who "plan ahead for the future." This demand cluster grouped many activities in which consumers engage, such as enrolling in a cash management course at the local *Volkshochschule* (community center) or discussing with their spouses their responsibilities toward their children as they grow up. With regard to this demand cluster, the leading questions became:

1. *How* does the current product offering enable customers to "plan ahead for the future"?

2. *What* product or service helps people "plan ahead for the future"? What products are in current use? How do these products in current use relate to PLI, and what could be done with the current PLI product to better interact with other products in helping people to "plan ahead for the future"?

3. *Where* does the current product offering *not* satisfy the specific needs, wants, frustrations, or passions across the demand landscape, as described in terms of the demand cluster, with regard to "planning ahead for the future"?

However, these questions only set the context, or frame the issues. They are in themselves only an exercise in warming up the critical-thinking and problem-solving efforts. They are ways of thinking about the PLI product and how it intersects with the demand from the customers' perspective. What is needed, though, is not only thinking about the core and, more broadly, beyond the core. It is from this broader, structured thinking that many of the breakthrough opportunities, innovations, and new concepts emerge. A systematic approach toward this structured thinking is provided by the three BIG lenses.

TABLE 4-1

Framing the issues

Two goal-based demand clusters	SCOPE OF PERSONAL LIABILITY INSURANCE					
	Individuals covered	Payment mode	Purchase motivation	Coverage	Geographic reach	Distribution
Plan ahead for the future						
• Activities						
• Priorities						
• Context						
• Needs and wants						
• Frustrations and passions						
Get to know new things						
• Activities						
• Priorities						
• Context						
• Needs and wants						
• Frustrations and passions						

Allianz Applies the Three BIG Lenses

Astronomers can explore space in many ways, through several kinds of "immersions." There is continuity and life in space as seen from a distance, through a telescope. But there is also change, and even discontinuity. Thus, in order to understand the entire ecosystem, one must examine it from several perspectives.

A demand landscape provides a powerful point of departure to explore opportunities by using, figuratively speaking, a varied set of binoculars and photographic lenses. There are many dozens of ways and strategic thinking tools designed to help see the opportunities by exploring the demand landscape and to see what even customers cannot see. These tools can be roughly divided into three sets of perspectives, or breakthrough innovation and growth—BIG—"lenses."

First Lens: The Eye of the Customer

From the eye of the consumer or customer, the social-situational context in which she or he lives, managers can explore new opportunities by identifying *adjacent* or *similar* consumer goals and everyday concerns. Insights can be gleaned by exploring *related* activities, projects, and tasks, as well as *priorities* or *trade-offs*. How do customers allocate their limited resources of time, money, and effort toward accomplishing these tasks and goals?

Goal adjacencies.[3] Do some everyday goals occur in proximity to other goals on our demand landscape or beyond the constructed landscape? What is their relative importance to consumers? For Allianz, one goal adjacency revealed in the demand landscape was that some people would like to "offer assistance," possibly in the form of gifts, particularly to family members—a specific frequent goal or routine grouped in one demand cluster, adjacent to which was "to plan for the future." Why not consider some way to combine the adjacent goals of offering assistance to children and grandchildren with planning for the future? Would offering customers the option of giving an insurance policy or product as a gift—perhaps to a loved one or family member—be a palatable one, perhaps by means of a simple gift voucher or coupon?

The benefits from exploring and using goal adjacencies in other industries abound. For example, in the early 1990s, a Japanese company introduced Yakult, an odd-tasting liquid with medicinal properties, to Europe. The product, though successful in Japan, did not take off on this product attribute positioning. In 1997, Danone launched a similar drink called Actimel in Europe and Latin America, this time by exploiting two everyday consumer goal adjacencies: (1) taking something light and healthy with you on the go and (2) enhancing stamina by taking medicinal supplements that build the body's immune system. Actimel was positioned as a healthy meal, as a breakfast alternative, where Danone had not previously provided a strong offering. After Danone began focusing on these two goal adjacencies, sales took off. Revenues exceeded €600 million in five years.[4]

Related activities. Within the demand cluster of "being prepared," one activity that repeatedly surfaced for Allianz was that anxious parents were attending CPR and first aid classes. They also might own home insurance in addition to PLI. Why not combine PLI life with some sort of coaching, so that the act of buying, or the purchase experience, could in some way be transformed into a consumption experience? Could insurance coaches possibly provide advice on accident prevention and risk assessment, all examined within the broader framework of personal liability?

Priorities or trade-offs. Allianz found, not surprisingly, that customers placed a high priority on saving money while also desiring maximum coverage and getting something back from their insurance (sometimes even motivation for fraud). How could Allianz reconcile these two apparently conflicting goals? One possibility explored was to offer a product that promised some form of repayment or rebate if the product was not used or a claim was not lodged within a particular time span.

The analyzing of trade-offs creates an important feature of the demand landscape. When trade-offs in the demand landscape are identifiable, there lies an opportunity. This is sometimes called a *consumer contradiction.* IKEA and Swatch neatly solved the age-old trade-off for consumers who wanted design at affordable prices. Before IKEA and Swatch came along, design was expensive. Target, Zara, and H&M also solved the trade-off between cheap and chic. Before these retail businesses and brands existed, cheap was not chic, and chic was not cheap.

Second Lens: The Eye of the Market

Marketers often study groups of consumers or groups of products in isolation from the context of consumption or use. This type of observation can result in product improvement or lead to increased customer satisfaction in a single dimension of product performance or service. But it is also limiting.

That's why turning the market on its head, so to speak, and probing the context of products from unexpected angles can reveal important insights. For example, what if a company considered its products in absentia? What if the product or service did not exist? What would customers do; where would they turn? Similarly, what if a company considered the ancillary products and services customers call into play when they're using or purchasing a certain offering? And what if the company then also pitted customers with extremely opposing views and purchase and consumption attributes "against" one another? What might that exercise surface?

Allianz proceeded to reconsider the market in light of all three possibilities: (1) substitutes and spoilers, (2) enhancers, complementors, and enablers, and (3) segments of opposite consumers.

Substitutes and spoilers. The key question here is, How would consumers go about the particular activity in their lives if their current brand, product, or service were not available? Some products can and do easily substitute for others. One brand of beer can be substituted for another; one financial adviser can be substituted for another. Budweiser may compete with other brands during the activity of watching sports with others at home. It may compete with other spirits, wine, and water during the activity of spending a night with friends. The power of this approach comes from the exploration of substitutes in context—that is, within the contours of the demand landscape—unlike the typical exploration of substitution effects in the economics class Econ 101.

An Allianz consumer may protect herself for the future by choosing from various options, substituting home property insurance, auto insurance, life insurance, or even an investment fund. Among the important consumer dynamics Allianz analyzed with respect to substitution were alternative future protection mechanisms. The key was to determine whether different consumers with different lifestyles and needs were more prepared to substitute PLI for alternatives.

A related issue to substitution is *spoilage*: the introduction or improvement of a seemingly unrelated product or service in other consumption areas that nevertheless affects consumption or use in the area at hand. Consider the effect of the iPod connector for cars on car stereo equipment and CD changers in their car trunks. Consumers are not going to throw out their car stereo and CD changers for now. But they might change the way they use their car stereo and certainly have less need to carry a second set of CDs in their car trunks. The iPod is a spoiler, but not a substitute, for certain aspects of stereo equipment and music purchase.

So what might be the impact of popular auxiliary services on the demand for PLI? The home property division had evaluated auxiliary services such as a key service (if you lose a key, a locksmith will provide free services) or a service that protects against water damage (if a water pipe breaks, an Allianz-affiliated plumber will take care of the problem). These types of services all represented potential spoilers for PLI.

Enhancers, complementors, and enablers. These are brands, products, or services that consumers use together during a consumption episode. A good glass of wine goes well with a New York strip steak and a cheesecake dessert as a key component of the entire consumption episode, while in some countries a cup of espresso is virtually obligatory. A CD is useless in the absence of a CD player. A bag of Lay's chips enhances the sandwich consumption experience. A Kit Kat chocolate bar from Nestlé may enhance the experience but may also follow, as opposed to supplementing sandwich consumption. Enablers are less directly linked with the primary product or service but are equally complementary. The iPod is more than just a digital music player—it also enables the management of music and photo libraries.[5]

For Allianz and PLI, the oft-expressed goal of planning ahead may include such activities as saving for college or retirement or making major changes in a life stage. Some new form of PLI could be considered as a supplement to these activities and thus could be offered bundled as an enhancer of other financial products.

Segments of opposite consumers. A comparison of opposites or extremes can be an extremely helpful analytical tool to identify new opportunities. In 1998, we ran a workshop for Levi Strauss in Paris. Several days were dedicated to exploring the ability of Madonna, the singer, to consistently reinvent herself over several periods of her illustrious career. One of the workshop teams drew a map with concentric circles. At the outer circle, it placed people who live at the edge or on the fringe. In the middle circle, it placed people who consider themselves cool and fashion forward, and in the inner circle, the team placed the average or mainstream consumer. From this map, the team learned that Madonna's success had to do with picking new ideas and concepts that are already used every day on the fringe, and using her iconic status to popularize these ideas and concepts first with the cool, fashion-forward crowd, which then influences the mainstream. The workshop illustrated to us that opportunities are already among us; they are just hidden in plain sight. And simply structuring the demand landscape in terms of opposites for segments can help see opportunities for innovation that cannot be seen by the plain eye.

Another example of this technique is illustrated by the Indian company CavinKare. Its Fairever brand competed against Fair & Lovely, a Unilever brand in India that enjoys a significant share of the market for skin-lightening beauty products. While Unilever positions itself in the market as the "fairness expert" focusing on young consumers in well-developed city areas, CavinKare enjoyed enormous success marketing its product to the millions of Indians in the villages, many of whom earn as little as $4 a month—a classic case of competing against nonconsumption. How? By offering the product in tiny pouches the size of tea bags, which it sells individually for the equivalent of a few cents. According to C. K. Ranganathan, the chairman and CEO of CavinKare, the success of Fairever has to do with gaining a clear grasp of the specific demand landscape of nonconsumers in India. The company found that serving nonconsumers is not simply a matter of lowering the price or introducing a value offering. In fact, economically more challenged nonconsumers demanded the same quality offering as consumers in cities. The success model depicted in the demand landscape showed the same needs but different patterns of usage and consumption in villages and different purchase patterns, which were more frequent but smaller.[6]

Allianz engaged in this approach to research by comparing and contrasting customers living in rural areas with those living in the many urban cities in Germany. The differences between the two groups were enormous since the selling effort through the agent network differed drastically. Allianz also compared groups of consumers with different decision styles and behaviors—from the distinguished-conservative consumer, who is exceedingly knowledgeable about products and often analyzes alternative insurance options without relying on an insurance agent, to other groups of buyers with starkly opposite propensities, including the willfully "ignorant" consumer.[7]

Third Lens: The Eye of the Industry

Three important thinking modes explore opportunities from an industry perspective: (1) challenging industry *assumptions*, conventions, or the status quo by examining the gap between these conventions and basic beliefs and the behavior of consumers in their everyday lives; (2) examining changes in the *environment*, including those disruptions frequently defined as discontinuities, and evaluating how these changes impact consumers' everyday lives; and (3) exploring *alternative business models*.

Challenging industry assumptions. Challenging industry assumptions requires defining the fundamental beliefs held in an industry and then challenging these beliefs by exposing, comparing, and contrasting them with the realities of the consumers' lives described in the demand landscape.[8] The founder of Lidl & Schwartz, for example, the second-largest deep discounter in Germany, successfully challenged the established belief that *deep discount* invariably means offering only private labels and off-brands, as opposed to name brands, a perception created by the business practices of dominant deep discounter Aldi. Lidl & Schwartz was able to uncover a relevant sweet spot by introducing into its stores well-established branded products, carefully merchandised to maximize store traffic. This practice changed the perceptions of deep discount as virtually synonymous with low or indifferent quality, or even prestige, and thus broadened the market that Lidl & Schwartz was more than willing to serve.

In the insurance industry, Progressive had long been noted as a perennial challenger of assumptions. Founded in 1937 by Joseph Lewis and Jack Green in a Cleveland, Ohio, garage, Progressive had initially focused on providing automobile insurance to blue-collar workers. From this base, the firm gradually expanded its reach, so that by the mid-1950s, it had evolved into a medium-sized underwriter with a national customer base. Progressive expanded rapidly for several decades on the basis of a single central insight: customers other companies generally perceived to be high risk were not as risky as conventional wisdom dictated.

Progressive also successfully engineered a fundamental shift of perspective from "What products should we attempt to sell to customers?" to "What do consumers want to buy?" and from there to the even more productive proposition "How do consumers live their lives?" The result was a service called Immediate Response (IR), which combined a twenty-four-hour, seven-day-a-week claims service with an 800 number and a management imperative to the Progressive staff to turn around claims in hours, not days. Another initiative was a Mobile Claims Office that traveled to customers, as opposed to customers traveling to it. Yet another was ExpressQuote, a free service that promised to provide up to three competitive quotes in addition to Progressive's premiums, which Progressive maintained even after research indicated that occasionally the comparison quotes came in at a lower price point than Progressive's.

Like Progressive, Allianz decided to explore the possibility of challenging conventional channel relationships in one session where it evaluated the possibility of selling insurance in supermarkets. Could there be a product that customers could buy at a cash register as one might buy milk and soap? In Great Britain, the innovative supermarket Tesco had tested a similar product, a literal interpretation of Citicorp CEO Sandy Weill's oft-stated yet never-realized dream of establishing a "financial supermarket."

Allianz, for example, asked, "If it was possible to buy PLI for one year, would it be also possible to buy PLI insurance just for a day?" It also considered additional services that would change the entire service performance of Allianz. Could Allianz offer safety consultants and services such as how to make your home child-safe? Alternatively, the question posed was, "What if one would get rid of monetary compensation for a damage altogether? What would be the implications if one replaced the base rather than the monetary equivalent?"

The fundamental question, when challenging industry assumptions, cannot be limited to "How can we disrupt the industry or change the industry's logic?" The question has to stay centered around *relevance* in customers' lives. Disruption or changing the industry logic in and of itself is not a worthy goal. And thinking simply in terms of what buyers value is too abstract and generic. It does not yield deep enough insights, given today's complex environment. It is useful, however, to apply the frameworks of disruption and changing industry logic as analytical tools to survey a well-constructed, well-conceived, and comprehensive demand landscape.

Examining changes in the environment. The demand landscape is a rich framework to explore discontinuities. Consider, for example, a major food trend from the perspective of a retailer. The year 2002 marked the first year in which household spending on food was higher in the home than out of the home in the United States. Such an inflection point drives the growth of Whole Foods Market and Wegman's.

Consider, also, what changing trends in business markets can foreshadow. In 2005, for the first time in history, U.S. companies bought more new Internet phone connections, known as Voice over Internet Protocol, or VoIP, than conventional telephone lines.[9] When two trends grow at different rates, an opportunity is usually created, especially when it impacts the demand landscape.

Veronis Suhler Stevenson, the private equity firm, predicts that new media advertising, which includes cable and satellite television, Internet, and video game advertising, will grow by nearly 17 percent every year for the next five years, reaching $69 billion by 2009. At the same time, traditional advertising, at $858 billion today, will grow only 7.3 percent.[10] In America, 2004 consumer spending on media grew by 6.5 percent to $178 billion, and this spending has exceeded spending on advertising of about $176 billion, which grew by only 3.2 percent.[11] These major shifts suggest significant changes in how consumers can be reached. There will be significant shifts in spending by marketers to search engines like Yahoo! or Google.

Allianz explored in this context new ways of going to market and reaching its consumers. How did communication with consumers have to change as a result? What was the future role of the sales network? How could the agent network be supported by the new media? How could consumers be educated?

Exploring new business models. A highly powerful exploration is to look at alternative business model designs and how they impact the demand landscape. Would another design or business model innovation better capture the relevant ecosystem of demand that underlies the demand landscape? These are important questions. When we explore new business models, we explore the entire configuration of a company as a whole. This includes the value propositions, target customer segments, distribution channels, capabilities, collaborators and partners, cost structure, and revenue models, or how the company makes money. We are looking for patterns that would apply in another context.[12]

Procter & Gamble, for example, succeeded with Pringles in winning some market share against Frito-Lay's strong and hugely successful Lay's brand to a large extent because it applied a new business model to the market. Each component of the model was in itself inferior to those of Frito-Lay's model, from the distribution system, product design, shelf life, and packaging to manufacturing. But together, the components drastically reduced P&G's cost structure and unleashed funds that the company wisely funneled into building the Pringles brand. Frito-Lay, as described in chapter 3, did not see the opportunity right under its nose until many years later. Often, the very success of one business model creates a smoke screen that prevents a company from seeing the obvious opportunities.

At Allianz, the team constructed several radical new business models and confronted these business models with the demand landscape as constructed from the consumers' perspective. This confrontation yielded an enormous amount of discussion and several practical new concepts and opportunities.

Structured Thinking, Not Brainstorming

"Oh, so you take the demand landscape and then you brainstorm," said one manager when introduced to the concept of reframing the opportunity space and the three lenses.

While a demand landscape may well open a new line of inquiry for companies, identifying an array of new opportunities can be a freeing, even exhilarating experience. But this is not brainstorming. The process of reframing an opportunity space is about applying structured and systematic thinking to the problem, as opposed to free-flowing ideation.

This distinction may seem trivial, yet it can be critical. Brainstorming is widely regarded as a stream-of-consciousness process, with no set form or framework. There is value in brainstorming—for example, to ideate new products, to create many options, some off the wall and some not. Structured thinking, on the other hand, is keyed very closely to the demand landscape of the consumers, the ecosystem of demand, and their everyday lives. The goal is not to ideate but to *solve a particular problem*. From this perspective, our approach is more akin to TRIZ, the structured inventive-thinking and problem-solving routine.[13]

At Allianz, the team used an approach to problem solving and inventive thinking introduced by Barry Nalebuff, professor of economics at Yale School of Management, and Ian Ayres, a professor at Yale Law School. In *Why Not?* Nalebuff and Ayres framed an approach to problem solving defined by four basic questions:[14]

1. What would Croesus do?

2. Why don't you feel my pain?

3. Where else would it work?

4. Would flipping it work?

Nalebuff and Ayres wrote with affection of George Bernard Shaw's "unreasonable man." "The reasonable man adapts himself to the world, but the unreasonable man persists in trying to adapt the world to himself. Progress, therefore, all depends upon the unreasonable man." They use as an example of an "unreasonable" modern man, Howard Hughes, who, in the days before TiVo and even VCRs, bought a Las Vegas TV station so that he could indulge his insatiable appetite for old Humphrey Bogart films. They use as a classical example the rich king of Lydia, Croesus, famed in the ancient world for his boundless wealth and indulgent appetite.

Allianz asked, "What would Croesus do to solve this problem?" Would Croesus pay annual premiums for PLI, or would he simply pay for any damages he inadvertently inflicted on others out of his own presumably boundless pockets? Would Croesus be inclined to drive a hard bargain on PLI, or would he be willing to take a risk and dispense with it altogether?

If consumers' planning horizons are a month, as opposed to a year, could Allianz shift the payment mode from an annual to a monthly basis? Tesco sells insurance in supermarkets. Could Allianz forge an alliance with a supermarket chain to sell insurance products there? A company in South Africa offers customers the option of being *always* insured and is willing to sell a customer a policy *after* an event as long as it is of sufficiently prolonged duration for the premium to be paid back.

And if a key purchase driver involved "planning ahead for the future," Allianz discerned that while PLI was presently positioned primarily as insurance against relatively minor and remote risks, PLI could just as easily be positioned as protection against truly catastrophic events. At present, an advertisement for PLI features a small child toddling into a living room, crying his eyes out because he has accidentally wrecked his friend's wagon and destroyed his teddy bear. Allianz considered its marketing message to make explicit the fact that PLI offers coverage in certain cases protecting the consumer against liabilities mounting into the many millions.

An adjacent goal to planning for the future was "being prepared." Could PLI help customers send children to college? What if you paid your PLI premium every year, and if you failed to file a claim from the date your child was born until he or she turned eighteen years old, on the child's eighteenth birthday Allianz made a cash payment to the college of the child's choice?

Armed with those insights and the results from the interviews, the demand landscape, and the three lenses exercise, Allianz convened a workshop at its headquarters in Munich, where a team of executives went on a virtual insights "safari." Cross-functional breakout groups consisted of executives and managers from across a broad range of business units. By the close of the workshop, the total opportunity space for PLI had been expanded significantly. The groups had unearthed nearly forty very practical new product and service concepts and opportunities, which were then prioritized according to the following criteria:

- Concepts with low growth potential were immediately eliminated, even if they looked easy to implement.

- Concepts with high growth potential that looked difficult to implement were deferred for the time being.

- Concepts and ideas that clearly had high growth potential and would be easy to implement were placed on a front burner for urgent study.

As a result, Allianz developed some practical innovations that it could put to use immediately, but more importantly, it productively expanded the total opportunity space, not just for a particular insurance product but for an entire category. The company had created a framework for potential future innovations.

Results

Since the conclusion of the pilot project and PLI workshop, Michael Diekmann, a former customer relationship manager and now CEO, has made gaining closer connections to customers the prime focus of the group. The objective is to increase customer loyalty and retention by designing innovations to products and services that enhance and add value to customers' purchase and consumption experience, with the end goal of creating more satisfied customers.

Innovation at Allianz was historically understood in terms of actions such as implementing a new rate or tariff structure, a typical example of innovation from the product perspective. Now Allianz is looking for broader solutions that will accomplish the goal of *creating customer advantage*, from buying different offerings to staying longer to recommending Allianz to colleagues and friends.

For Thomas Summer, of the personal liability group, the most tangible benefit of the pilot project and workshop was that it provided a forum in which executives from the marketing and line sides of the business could work together to generate and execute ideas that the entire multifunctional group could then be actively engaged in seeing to fruition. "I can't tell you how many times participants in the project would come up to me and say, 'You know, we had such-and-such an idea five years ago, but it never went anywhere because there was no framework to put it into practice.'"

An Ever-Expanding Spiral

Ultimately, Allianz has put itself on a new, sustainable growth path. By 2005, the company ranked fourth among financial services firms worldwide (with Citigroup holding the lead slot) and had regained strength as the fourteenth-largest commercial enterprise in the world, according to *Fortune*'s Global 500 survey ranking, with a raft of highly profitable subsidiaries and affiliates in more than seventy countries.

But, importantly, the Allianz story is not finished. The DIG model, once it is up and running in a company, resembles a relay race set on an ever-expanding spiral course. All the elements are constantly in play, building on one another and moving the company forward. If Allianz has truly embedded the art of outside-in innovation in its organization, there will be other, even more exciting developments to report as time goes on.

The next chapter focuses on structuring the opportunity space. Essentially, this stage of the DIG model provides the discipline that renders the opportunity space useful. Now that the company has opened up the world of opportunity, it is time to reconsider what it is bringing (and can bring) to the table. It is also time to hone the innovation on the table so that it can truly meet customers "where they live." From an innovation perspective, the lesson is this: rather than innovating in product, or technology, or service, or new marketing tactic, the structuring of the opportunity space calls for innovating around a demand-first growth platform—a focus on how it transforms people's everyday lives or work. As you will see in the next chapter, this starting point for strategy, innovation, and marketing is far more meaningful and valuable for the firm than existing practices that call for innovation out of context and projecting a new design, product, or technology into consumers' everyday lives from the inside of the company out. We dedicate an entire chapter to demand-first growth platforms because of the importance of platform innovation and growth for companies. A study of ninety-three companies that joined the *Fortune* 50 since 1955 showed the single most important factor that distinguished high-growth companies from others was that high-growth companies pursued growth from a growth platform perspective.[15]

The case of GE Healthcare's Carestation follows that company's adaptation of the DIG model as a whole but highlights the issues that surround structuring the opportunity space.

Chapter Five

Structuring the Opportunity Space

O N OCTOBER 9, 2003, General Electric's Medical Systems division announced the acquisition of the Finnish health-care company Instrumentarium in a deal valued at €2 billion. The day after the transaction was completed, the same GE division announced the acquisition of an even larger fish, the U.K.-based Amersham plc, in a $9.5 billion stock exchange.[1]

At a glance, it looked as if GE had secured promising personnel and product portfolios in the general areas of advanced medical imaging, patient monitoring, anesthesia delivery, critical care, and information systems. But for CEO Jeffrey Immelt, the acquisitions meant far more; they represented something Immelt referred to explicitly as "growth platforms." These were not so much technological or product solutions to specific customer problems as they were integrated systems of methodologies, capabilities, products, components, and services that would interact seamlessly with each other and intersect with a variety of as-yet-unexplored and -unexploited niches in the everyday lives of health-care providers and patients.

The term *growth platforms* has recently become a corporate buzzword, a classic entry in the world of business jargon.[2] As such, it is subject to overuse and vulnerable to misinterpretation. So let us be clear: *growth* platforms, to us, have the following characteristics:

- A growth platform spells out how a new product, service, or set of methodologies or capabilities interacts in the moments and episodes in which people perform major projects, tasks, and goals. The goal of growth platforms is to create an integrated and transformative customer experience. A growth platform suggests a meaningful trajectory of developing customer advantage.

- All growth platforms exist in at least two dimensions: (1) a *demand side*, the way customers see the moments and episodes in which they perform the jobs, tasks, and projects in their everyday lives at work or at home, hence the term *demand-first growth platforms*; and (2) a *supply side*, or a resource and capability side, which could include dimensions of a new product or brand or capability. The intersections of these two dimensions define the role of a new product, a new brand concept, a solution, or a set of methodologies or capabilities and often are a means to uncover new opportunities for innovation and growth not visible from an individual product perspective.

- A growth platform is more than a sequence of products or services (that is a product platform). A growth platform is a means of structuring the opportunity space for products and broad sets of capabilities and methodologies. A true growth platform has more than a current generation of products and launches embedded within it; it also contains the springboard—and the guidelines—for future products and launches for years to come.

Growth platforms ensure that companies avoid the temptation to innovate for the sake of innovating, or to improve or enhance the way a customer does something just because the technology exists to offer the improvement, as opposed to innovating across behaviors of customers and creating transformative experiences. They assist companies in avoiding a myopic focus on innovation around individual products or services. Growth platforms often draw on capabilities, technologies, products, and solutions across different organizational units.

When Immelt was talking about GE's new growth platforms offered through the Instrumentarium and Amersham acquisitions, he saw a way to *structure opportunities to foster a relevant and continuous cascade of innovation.*

In the previous chapter, we introduced a way to explore new opportunities for innovation and growth from a demand-first perspective. But by themselves, opportunities do not create value—they must be executed. By themselves, they do not lead to productive change and sustainable customer advantage—they must be executed. That's why the DIG model does not stop at identifying opportunities or innovations. The DIG model goes on to use these opportunity spaces and innovations and structures, restructures and recalibrates the opportunity space (by identifying demand-first growth platforms), and formulates a strategic blueprint for action.

The story of the Carestation of GE Healthcare—a group of new capabilities, products, and services centered on anesthesiologists' challenges of developing anesthesia during various surgical procedures—illustrates the model, with an emphasis on how a company can structure its total opportunity space.

From Products to Demand-First Growth Platforms

It's important first to understand Helsinki-based Instrumentarium's approach to innovation at the time it was acquired by GE. Instrumentarium was founded at the turn of the twentieth century by a group of medical doctors to import medical instruments in bulk. By the time GE entered the picture, the company had diversified into a billion-dollar health-care conglomerate combining a significant retail optical business with subsidiaries that manufactured restaurant kitchen equipment, electronic circuits, home infant-care products, and high-end medical equipment.

Of greatest interest to GE Medical was Instrumentarium's Datex-Ohmeda medical equipment division, itself the product of a 1998 merger between Instrumentarium's Datex (short for *data experts*) division and Madison, Wisconsin–based Ohmeda. Together, Datex-Ohmeda commanded significant worldwide market share and leadership in the fast-growing realm of anesthesia monitoring and delivery equipment.

At the root of Instrumentarium and Datex-Ohmeda's success in creating high-quality medical devices for the operating room (OR) was an unusual heritage of close collaboration between the company and Helsinki University Hospital. Not only did the firm enjoy a long history of recruiting young engineers from the ranks of practicing clinicians at the hospital, it actively encouraged these individuals to maintain close links and ongoing consulting relationships with their former employer. Of the two hundred–odd engineers who worked at Datex in the early 1980s, a substantial number continued to consult part-time as clinicians at hospitals in and around Helsinki. Their primary employer strongly encouraged them to deepen their understanding of how the increasingly complex clinical tools being developed at Instrumentarium functioned in a real-world hospital and operating room environment.

In the mid-1990s, Datex had introduced the Anesthesia System 3 (AS/3) and Anesthesia Delivery Unit (ADU) product sets. These new offerings integrated Anesthesia Monitoring (AM) and Anesthesia Record Keeping (ARK) into a sophisticated modular unit. In 2001, the market portfolio team of Datex-Ohmeda brought to market an even more capable anesthesia delivery device. One member of this team was Tom Haggblom (a former nurse-anesthesiologist and Datex-Ohmeda marketing and product development specialist, and later clinical manager in the Life Support Solutions division of GE) who characterized these new integrated offerings as "a *platform*, as opposed to a product."

The platform idea had arisen as a result of a series of explorations conducted by Haggblom's market portfolio team, which had examined the perioperative (before, during, and after anesthesia) market, exploring the possibilities of broadening the product line from a strictly defined "anesthesia workstation" to a wider range of uses and environments in the hospital.

Essentially, Haggblom's group had created a rudimentary demand landscape and was using it as a springboard for innovation; it was primarily this unique product development methodology that GE found so attractive when targeting Instrumentarium as a potential high-value acquisition.

Instrumentarium's approach relied heavily on systematized clinical and customer input. The anesthesiology delivery effort combined Datex-Ohmeda's five hundred–odd scientists and engineers with several hundred consulting anesthetists and nurse-anesthesiologists from all over the world. Their mandate was to identify and define the specific clinical needs of anesthesiologists working at the leading edge of their field.

And the Customer?

It was a great foundation from which to layer on the elements of the DIG model. And following GE Medical's October 2003 acquisition of Instrumentarium, the marketing transplants from the Instrumentarium side of the fence began that layering by introducing a new factor to Instrumentarium's development equation.

"We were constantly preaching the need to see how the customer sees the equipment," recalls Risto Rossi, a GE manager who had joined Instrumentarium in the late 1980s as a specialist in the integration of patient monitoring solutions and clinical information management. "The clinicians don't see an imaging device, they don't see a monitor, they don't see a delivery system. At 7:00 in the morning walking into the OR, they don't see or think about individual devices, they only see the tools required to do the job with a minimum of frustration and uncertainty. Making correct decisions in such a stressful situation depends upon a clinician's ability to quickly and intuitively construct a complete picture of the patient's status."

In order to inform this new perspective even further (and to jar any static mind-sets), GE enlisted the help of a human factors specialist firm founded by a group of pilots who flew for Finnair. Reaching out to a human factors consultant was a logical step; the immediate connection that GE employees recognized between operating room procedures and piloting an airplane was a valuable bonus.

"For pilots," explained Arto Helovuo, a Finnair pilot and one of the participants in the clinical research project, "takeoff and landing are the most critical phases because they consume the most energy and require the highest degree of concentration. For anesthetists, composing the right mixture of drugs and observing the vital signs before the start of the procedure is like takeoff, while resuscitating the patient, the most critical period, is analogous to landing."

The metaphor of the airplane cockpit provided an appropriate framing device to shift the emphasis in the OR from the demonstration of purely manual skills to a broader—and ultimately more relevant—focus on information management. The airline cockpit–OR analogy also shed light on some of the fundamental issues being raised by rapidly advancing mechanization in the OR, much as the recent introduction of the fly-by-wire family of Airbus aircraft had transformed the pilot's duties and skills from a traditional emphasis on stick-and-rudder skills to one that placed a maximum premium on information management and analytics.

A group of global marketers, with support from engineers and designers, took the next step, forming an observational team composed of engineers and industrial designers to videotape clinicians in twenty-five ORs in a number of countries as they worked with ADUs in a real-world OR environment. Team members painstakingly recorded hours of what clinicians looked at and touched, whom they spoke to and interacted with and why, all without discussing the activity directly with the clinicians. The research was limited to simple, structured, noninvasive, unbiased observation.

Following the filming, the team combed through the videotapes to create a database of the multiple problems, frustrations, and hassles observed, expressed, and inferred from the observational data. They presented four hundred "problem statements" derived from the audio-visual material to fifteen top clinicians—thirteen anesthesiologists and two registered nurse anesthetists—based in Chicago, who were asked to prioritize the problem statements by drawing component configurations on graph paper as a representation of an ideal OR.

Neal Sandy, strategic marketing leader for GE Healthcare, recalls that his primary task was to take the broad learning gleaned from the data and look at the evolving product platform from a customer's perspective. Within the $15 billion GE Healthcare silo, that process involved "looking at the problem horizontally, as opposed to vertically, since a number of the emerging growth opportunities in the medical field span a number of different GE businesses."

The team uncovered problems, frustrations, and hassles to which the clinicians had long since become oblivious, because over the years of working with the same equipment, they had developed compensating behaviors, or work-arounds. Ironically, prior product sets had created many of these problems and hassles, but the customer-clinicians no longer experienced them as problems until they were explicitly pointed out and discussed. For example, before the study, customers were accustomed to stepping over and around a myriad of cables behind and in between workstations and patients. Few clinicians had articulated any frustration with the setup before being impressed by the elegant simplicity of the cable-management setup GE offered as part of the innovation it called *Carestation*—a compact system of "solutions" offered in a single piece of equipment (station) to provide and monitor the delivery and use of anesthesia.

The development of Carestation (whose initial version was introduced in 2005) was fueled by many small but important insights into the ecosystem of customer demand in the OR. But Carestation's big developmental breakthrough occurred also internally to GE, when GE Healthcare was obliged to submit a number of different ideas to the companywide Commercial Council for consideration as Imagination Breakthroughs, a cluster set of "big ideas" that could be credibly considered to carry the potential of generating somewhere in excess of $100 million in revenues. (Imagination Breakthroughs is a global GE initiative. It is a great example of how a company can embed an outside-in approach to innovation, and it is described in greater detail in chapter 9.)

Carestation's formal designation as an Imagination Breakthrough prompted the assembly of a specialized development and marketing team drawn from a variety of GE divisions, disciplines, and specialties, including the information technology business, the anesthesiology subdivision of life support systems, and the monitoring solutions business. The multidisciplinary team's primary task was to make the business case that, first, customers would enjoy better clinical and general work-related results if components were more integrated, and second, driving demand for such an integrated anesthesia solution would, in turn, broaden the market for software and hardware produced by the various P&Ls.

At this point, the significance of the Amersham acquisition as a contributor to GE's growth platforms became clear. Jean-Michel Cossery, a former Amersham executive who became chief marketing officer of GE Healthcare, was also the designated marketing overseer of all of GE Healthcare's

Imagination Breakthroughs. In discussions with the team members, he discovered that while GE had traditionally focused on defining and refining the next generation of medical technology, Amersham's pharmaceutical heritage oriented it toward a greater focus on clinical factors, a result of pharmaceutical companies' need to construct an airtight clinical case for every new product in anticipation of regulatory approval. This outlook was an important addition to GE Medical's new approach to innovation—an approach that resulted in the development of a radically new and capable demand-first growth platform.

From Growth Platforms Toward Organizational Change

GE Carestation's Imagination Breakthrough designation forced the alignment of an organizational structure that pushed the technical non-marketing people on the team to focus their energies beyond achieving and refining a strictly engineering and technical solution. Neither the Instrumentarium, Amersham, or former GE Medical marketing approaches, on their own, could have led to the successful conceptualization and positioning of Carestation as a long-term growth platform for GE. The ethnographic-observation approach brought to GE by Instrumentarium, innovative as it was, would not have been sufficient to create the Imagination Breakthrough. The strictly pharmaceutical approval approach refined at Amersham could not have driven the process forward on its own. The technological approach long perfected at GE Medical required a potent infusion from both Amersham's and Instrumentarium's skills to drive the demand perspective that evolved the product platform into a demand-first growth platform.

Structuring the Opportunity Space and the Relevant Sweet Spot

When companies develop viable demand-first growth platforms, they frame the path to creating customer advantage in one of three ways: (1) by intersecting an existing or new product or service in entirely new ways with customers' everyday lives; (2) by enhancing people's routines around activities, projects, and tasks in ways even customers cannot tell; and (3) by delivering on new or unarticulated needs and wants or by tapping into desires, dreams, fantasies, and urges. These three ways aim to capture a larger share of the ecosystem of demand. In any of these scenarios of creating customer advantage, it is not just an individual product or service, or a collection of products and services, however innovative it may be, that creates customer advantage for the firm. It is the particular combination of capabilities, products, services, tools, and methodologies that captures effectively the demand landscape extracted from the ecosystem of demand that makes the difference. A clear definition and articulation makes it apparent how consumers absorb and assimilate the growth platform into their everyday lives.

An important piece of structuring the opportunity space, then, is to identify the relevant *sweet spot* for a given firm. What is the space or market in which the company should compete—from the customers' perspective? Where does the company have permission to play?

Another important requirement is determining how the opportunities identified in that space should be prioritized. How do these opportunities—alone or in combination—capture the ecosystem of demand, create an integrated and transformative use or consumption or use experience, and ultimately lead to a sustainable customer advantage? Which opportunities comprise the various demand clusters that are in the relevant sweet spot for the firm, and how should this sweet spot be developed? Figure 5-1 illustrates the relationships between demand-first growth platforms and other concepts used in this book.

FIGURE 5-1

From ecosystem of demand to growth platform

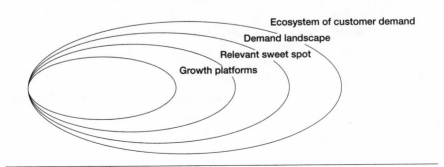

Ecosystem of customer demand
Demand landscape
Relevant sweet spot
Growth platforms

When we drill down deeper, the line of inquiry turns toward consideration of the possible growth platforms that might deliver customer advantage. If Steve Jobs, for example, had viewed the iPod only as an accessory to the company's product line of awfully cool and powerful computers, the iPod might have ended up buried in the accessory section of the iMac product lineup. Considering the iPod simply as one component of a separate demand-first growth platform (that helps consumers manage music) required Jobs to strike deals with music companies for licensing the music downloads, to create iTunes, the iMusic Store, and to cajole some two thousand suppliers (such as Bose, with its SoundDock) to design products around the iPod. Yet it was clearly the option that allowed Apple to create a welcome, game-changing, and, more importantly, transformative use experience and the building of real customer advantage. From a product perspective—given the small price for the iPod, ranging from $199 to $399, relative to a $2,000 computer—the iPod can be considered most naturally a product extension. From a demand-first perspective—namely the tasks of managing music (selecting, choosing, buying, listening, storing, and discarding music) or managing video that the iPod can own in consumers' everyday lives—and the opportunity of the iPod in terms of the size of the ecosystem of demand, Jobs's decision to create a separate growth platform is genius. Consider that it takes about $10,750 to fill the $399 iPod with music from iTunes, while today the average download is about twenty-five songs per iPod. From a product perspective, the huge opportunity for the iPod could have been hidden in plain sight.

What follows is a systematic and simplified guide to structuring an opportunity space.

1. Determining the Logic

A natural starting point for determining the logic of a growth platform is to explore ways of structuring the demand for the product, service, brand, capability, or methodology in question. GE Healthcare structured the demand for Carestation after observing and immersing outsiders and GE executives in dozens of procedures in the OR. Neal Sandy, of GE's strategic marketing group, was explicitly charged with looking at the platform from the customers' (in this case anesthesiologists) perspective horizontally, across the entire GE company, and across businesses for new ideas, technologies, and solutions. Another logical structuring of the demand opportunities is in terms of three critical patient stages: before the patient is taken into anesthesia, during anesthesia, and after. Or, more broadly, the demand landscape can be structured in perioperative and postoperative terms. There is significant value in analyzing the demand landscape to see patterns of meaning that emerge.

Starting the exploration of the logic from this behavioral customer or consumer perspective, from the basis of the underlying processes and patterns of behavior behind needs and wants, ensures that all innovations (products, capabilities, technologies, methodologies, brand-building programs, or other marketing activation activities) are conceived of in terms of how they link precisely to those behaviors that consumers or customers care most about. Thus, growth platforms can transform the very behavior that drives problem solving, consumption, or use in customers' daily lives.

2. Exploring Alternatives

Identifying the logic that will underlie the demand-first growth platforms is a creative process and often requires some trial and error. One useful pressure test is to cross the behavioral pattern of demand clusters with new dimensions, such as the various modules that make up Carestation. From this perspective, GE can learn how the various modules interact with the demand from the customers' perspective. It can identify opportunities where demand is not satisfied and opportunities for leveraging existing technologies across existing and new demand clusters.

Consider, for example, Kodak, which remained trapped for a long time in a limited view of itself defined by its product, the celluloid-based silver halide film developed by its founder, George Eastman. If Kodak executives had evaluated alternatives of structuring the demand landscape early, they would have easily seen the biggest opportunities for the company arising from an integrated view of digital technology rather than relegating it as a mere separate extension of an existing business. From a behavioral and outside-in perspective of the demand, from a customer perspective, it would have become clear that customers' everyday activities and goals were shifting from the purchase of a camera and film to the broader goal of memory management.

From a demand-first perspective, Kodak's opportunity space can be viewed in terms of an activities perspective—what consumers do and care about doing in managing their memories. This is in contrast to the product perspective, which focuses on product attributes such as speed, price, and picture clarity; the brand perspective, which focuses, possibly, on functional, emotional, and self-expressive benefits to consumers; or the consumer perspective, which seeks to divide consumers into targetable segments for a company's products. From a demand-first perspective—consumption behavior, not consumer behavior—the activities of people around memory management are taking pictures, modifying pictures, developing film (through various means from taking the film to the store to ordering film development online), sharing pictures, and storing pictures. Mohanbir Sawhney and his colleagues provide useful alternative structures to this memory management process.[3]

A useful test for validation of the strategic logic of alternative structures is to study the emergence of clear and valuable new growth platforms. For example, a structuring by activities in memory management leads Kodak to think of opportunities in online management of memories. Kodak acted on this opportunity by buying a start-up company called Ofoto and integrated its software technology as a new service, called Kodak EasyShare Gallery, into its offering to customers. The technology can be viewed as far more than simply a product; it could potentially be a comprehensive growth platform for Kodak.

3. Defining the Demand-First Growth Platforms

The power of defining growth platforms is in leveraging the entire business, including R&D, new products, marketing, selling, and distribution, around deepening the relevance of a product or service, brand, or capabilities, thereby increasing the chances for customers to absorb and assimilate the product, service, or solution contained in the growth platform into their everyday lives, and creating a total transformative customer experience.

GE Healthcare needed to decide whether the Carestation concept should focus only on the OR or should extend beyond it into the intensive care unit and the patient recovery room. At the product level, GE needed to define whether the Carestation concept should cover its entire product portfolio or only certain levels—the midrange and high-end offerings but not its lower or entry-level offering. Demand-first growth platforms focus a company's capabilities, products, and services on the relevant demand clusters as a laser beam focuses light in a musical performance.

4. Evaluating the Opportunity Space

If a growth platform is built from a behavioral outside-in demand perspective, some quantification and air approximation of the total opportunity space is possible. Through the quantification of growth platforms, otherwise highly qualitative and subjective findings from ethnographic research are made concrete and a substantive business case for action is developed. As W. Edwards Deming, the quality guru, once observed, "In God we trust. Everyone else bring data."

GE Healthcare was able to determine the component usage of anesthetists and the responsiblities anesthetists had outside the OR. The size and scope of demand for the Carestation growth platform was determined from a customer perspective.

In general, quantification can occur at several levels. First is the level of the demand-first immersion process (the first part of the DIG model). It is extremely important to quantify these highly qualitative interviews. At Frito-Lay, the quantification focused on measuring the prevalence and incidence of a particular moment. As described in chapter 3, the study involved thirty-five consumers from which, on average, twenty food-related activities were recorded over thirty days—a total of about 21,500 food-related activities were collected. Several demand clusters were developed by grouping these activities. In addition, two coders independently rated each of the 21,500 activities according to information in the respondents' diaries and the transcripts from the four-hour confessional discussions with the respondents.

The activities were rated along important dimensions of the ecosystem of demand, such as contextual factors (temporal, social, physical, and cultural), categories of needs and emotions, products and brands in use, and other factors. After the activities were classified into the demand clusters, the data allowed Frito-Lay to describe the demand clusters using the coded dimensions of the ecosystem of demand. After this initial step of describing the demand clusters in a quantitative way, existing research at Frito-Lay was cross-classified with these demand clusters to leverage the information and data from previous studies. Overall, these analyses provided a relatively good approximation of the size of the opportunity.

The second level of quantification can take place at the opportunity space or the growth platform. In this situation, the objectives of quantification changes are different. While we learn from the first level of quantification that there is indeed an opportunity, we do not know to what degree this opportunity varies across consumers or customers, and we do not know exactly who is a target for each growth platform. The second level of quantification has three goals. First is sizing the population that identifies with the relevant opportunity space and the growth platforms. This information helps target the most profitable and viable platforms. Second is segmenting the population by growth platforms. We use descriptors such as demographic profiles, behaviors, and attitudes of those who identify most with each platform. And third is identifying precisely the overlaps across platforms in terms of the populations. This is important because, practically, if common themes emerge across growth platforms and people's values are the same across platforms, an opportunity exists to target several growth platforms at one time by creating a unified offering, brand positioning, and communications architecture. The protocol for this quantification follows standard survey research approaches, including data collection, analysis, and interpretation, often using Internet-based interviewing and record keeping by customers. The linking of demand-first growth platforms to people and segments is important, and this permits quantitatively linking all existing research about markets, products, and brands to the growth platforms and the total opportunity space.

While the quantitative research results provide a key input, other factors also need to be considered in evaluating the opportunity space and growth platforms. These factors include investments required in new capabilities or core competencies, portfolio considerations such as synergies in R&D, marketing, and selling. From a brand perspective, for example, the critical question is whether the opportunities are off-brand and whether consumers give the brand permission in a certain growth platform. A significant consideration is the timing involved in activation of the growth platforms. The impact of the activation of one growth platform and the success in the market can influence the future activation of growth platforms. Additional information may become available after some time that changes the direction. This additional information and other factors can be modeled using a variety of methodologies to quantify the value of growth platform activation and its impact on future growth, such as real options or decision analysis.[4]

Ready, Set . . .

The ecosystem of demand is in focus; the opportunities are in sight; the demand-first growth platforms (defined and honed from all those opportunities) are promising. Everything seems ready, and set. How does a company *go*?

The next chapter discusses the final element in the DIG model: formulating the strategic blueprint. This is the unique set of instructions that a company creates for itself to ensure discipline and to activate its growth platforms and guide the processes that follow. The case of State Street Bank provides a backdrop for our discussion of the strategic blueprint, and the case of Axe—a men's grooming brand—illustrates what activation can look like in practice.

The strategic questions are: Which growth platform should the company focus on initially? Why? What should the timing and sequence of action be? How best can the company achieve customer advantage? What product innovations are necessary? How did GE Healthcare decide to focus on anesthesia delivery in the OR, as opposed to at the doctor's office or in another setting? How did it decide the extent to which it would marry its focus on technology with its focus on pharmacology? These are the kinds of questions a strategic blueprint for action answers.

Chapter Six

Formulating a Strategic Blueprint for Action

COMPANIES that do not explicitly define, structure, analyze, and prioritize their opportunity spaces often chase romantic dreams about big ideas and breakthrough new products or services but fail to realize those dreams. They try to fast-track innovation; they focus on mere improvements of individual products and often waste precious energy and resources because their offerings don't truly hit the mark. And worse, they miss the biggest opportunities of growth that an unbiased demand-first outside-in perspective provides.

Identifying several viable demand-first growth platforms alone, though, doesn't guarantee sustainable success. What matters at this juncture is discipline and action: Which growth platform should we pursue first? Which activation would develop the ecosystem of demand in a profitable way? Should we allocate more resources to another area? If we can see the opportunities, what mix of strategic imperatives and actions will truly bring us customer advantage?

The danger lies in getting this far into the DIG model and then regressing by considering the array of opportunities one at a time, or from a one-dimensional point of view. It's very easy to slip back into a perspective that is driven from the inside of the organization. Improve the design of this product here. Change the user interface of that product over there. Sure, consumers will like it. Let's apply our unique rapid-prototyping process. Quickly, we've got some stuff. Test, and soon we can sell.

It's more difficult to ask the tough questions and push the company to articulate a course of action with a definitive logic that guides the way. That's why the final element of the DIG model is about creating a strategy that *guides the activation of new growth platforms—from thought to action*—from the highest strategic level all the way to the activation in customers' everyday lives. In this stage of the DIG model of innovation, it is also possible to create breakthrough innovations, as we shall see in this chapter.

Reinventing Business-Based On-Demand Opportunities

The case of State Street Bank provides a good look at how one financial services firm has developed a new strategy to reinvent its business by continuously prioritizing and activating demand-first growth platforms in the pursuit of customer advantage.[1]

State Street's Egg Chart

Not long after assuming the CEO's helm at the State Street Boston Corporation (as it was then known), Marshall N. Carter (who had spent the previous fifteen years running the custodial services department at Chase Manhattan, State Street's leading competitor) found himself seated on an airplane, drawing a primitive flow chart by hand. "The simple chart I developed on the plane," Carter later recalled, "had customers along one axis, geography along a second axis, markets along a third axis, and potential products running along a fourth axis." At the dead center of what later became internally known as the "egg chart," he drew a box labeled "customers."

"What I was looking for on the plane," Carter recalled, "was an attempt to depict pictorially what my business was all about." With an undergraduate degree in civil engineering from West Point and graduate degrees in systems analysis and public policy, Carter explained that his "whole background involved using simple little devices to talk to people about where we were, and where we were going." Where State Street was headed, in Carter's estimation, was straight into "a mature stage of the product life cycle."

When Carter assumed the chairmanship of State Street, the venerable financial institution was a highly centralized organization focused primarily on asset custody, a comprehensive service that encompasses the keeping of accounts and the tracking of securities held by institutional investors, including public and private pension funds and mutual fund managers. This former officer in the U.S. Marine Corps knew the terrain he was facing, and much of it looked like a slow uphill slog. "Customer requirements were increasing significantly," Carter recalled, "as the focal point of the industry shifted from transaction processing to information services. Customers were demanding more information every day to do their jobs."

Because of the preponderance of early mutual fund players located in Boston, by the 1920s, State Street—established in 1792 by a consortium of Boston clipper ship captains—had gained an early lead in providing custodial services to the securities industry. Under Carter's predecessor William Edgerly, the diversified firm had solidified its early preeminence in the processing-intensive securities custodial business. By the mid-1990s, State Street had become the largest custodian of mutual fund securities in the United States, servicing 41 percent of registered funds, with total assets under custody having risen annually at the rate of 35 percent over the previous five years. State Street was also the third-ranking foreign exchange (forex or FX) trading services provider worldwide and ranked second in the index fund management business.

By the time Carter arrived at the company in late 1991, he was widely quoted as opining that financial technology was rapidly "transforming financial services by shifting the balance of commercial power from the institution to the customer." Carter's simple hand-drawn egg chart listed "customer requirements" along the top, and used a gently sloping line to illustrate how transactions had dominated those requirements until around 1988. After that year, transactions declined and information services shot up.

Most of the major players in the custodial business continued to view the processing of transactions as the core of their business. Carter's assessment of the opportunities that lay ahead for his firm differed from the industry wisdom in that he was convinced information services was a rich mother lode to be tapped. This conclusion prompted him to start exploring the world from his customers' everyday perspective. He began to systematically break down the everyday investment process of his customers. There were three distinct phases: (1) *pretrade*, in which investors analyze the market, (2) *trade*, in which transactions are initiated and accounts are settled, and 3) *posttrade*, in which records of transactions are maintained. The custodial business, State Street's historical legacy, accounted for 16 percent of the revenue generated by every transaction. Trading generated 60 percent, and pretrade services accounted for 24 percent of revenue. "The hardest question our business was facing," Carter later recalled, "was this momentous shift from *transaction* to *information*. Banks traditionally like crunching transactions, but they don't know what to do with the information they generate." According to research commissioned by Carter, a single stock sale threw off twenty-five distinct pieces of information. Yet for years, State Street had followed its competitors in cautiously "sticking to its knitting" and confining its primary activities to operations associated with tracking the posttrade information flow. But if information was the future, State Street was strong in only posttrade.

What Carter had accomplished in an informal way by drawing his simple flow chart was exploring demand opportunities for the firm in light of the changing landscape of State Street's core customers. He had arrived at this by segmenting his customers not by size, age, wealth, or duration of the relationship—typical banking standards—but by how the everyday activities of all his customers were changing as a result of technology changes—activities those customers pursued in the context of their routine working lives. After he divided the investment process into those three demand clusters (pretrade, trade, posttrade), it became clear to Carter and his management team that they really didn't know as much about their customers' most basic activities as they should.

In light of their obvious interest in moving away from the custodial business into trading and pretrading activities, a formal demand study commissioned by Carter discerned the landscape of customer goals and needs by conducting in-depth interviews with key accounts in more than twenty countries. The framing questions of these interviews were thematically linked:

1. What aspects of your fiduciary responsibilities keep customers up at night?

2. What aspects of your relationships with investment services partners are sources of security and comfort, as opposed to insecurity
   and anxiety?

One strategic question that continued to dog Carter's attempt to refash-
ion the firm from an outside-in perspective was whether State Street was
mainly a bank, a financial services company, a dedicated information services and applied data processor, or possibly a bit of all three. Which of
these core competencies, or a combination thereof, would maximize the
total opportunity space for State Street? During a period of intense competition with a handful of remaining industry players, Carter and his team
attended innumerable customer conferences and sat in on hundreds of
in-depth interviews, all designed to glean information from respondents as
to which specific goals and activities were the most mission critical in getting their urgent jobs and tasks accomplished. As a result of that research,
Carter led his team through a series of structured-thinking discussions
about the role of every business and product and service State Street had to
offer. Each of these demanded scrutiny on one question only: how does
this particular business create value for its customers?

These structured-thinking discussions are excellent examples of strategy formulation in action. In a way, Carter led his team through a process
of deciding which demand clusters were most relevant to State Street. And
only then did he force them to ask which products and services intersected
with each demand cluster, and a host of other questions. How did these
products and services intersect with the activities and goals and daily routines of the institutional investors? Where did State Street add value and
where could it add value in the future?

Carter also raised these questions: What does State Street stand for?
What does it aspire to stand for? These questions clearly addressed the fundamentals of the business, its core, its aspirations, and its vision. From this
discussion, specific strategic objectives could be formulated, the competitive advantage determined, and the specific scope of the business defined—
not just posttrade but with a balanced emphasis on the entire investment
process from pretrade, to trade, to posttrade (see figure 6-1).

FIGURE 6-1

The investment process—State Street's demand opportunities

Pretrade

Goals

- Keep portfolio of investments balanced and perform according to funds objectives

Activities

- Obtain data on investment performance
- Monitor trends

Services/products

- Fundamental data
- News
- Market data
- Analytics
- Performance management software

Pretrade

Goals

- Execute trades quickly, accurately, and cost-effectively

Activities

- Initiate securities
- Authorize related FX transactions
- Borrow or lend securities

Services/products

- Trade management tools
- Order routing
- Trade execution
- Securities lending
- Currency execution
- Cash management

Pretrade

Goals

- Obtain accurate posting and accounting for all transactions and account activities

Activities

- Receive automated trade confirmation
- Access data covering securities under custody

Services/products

- Custody
- Portfolio/fund accounting
- Performance and analytics

An Initiative in Broad, Bold Strokes

No other company in the world was as well positioned as State Street to service the institutional community worldwide. No other company of similar stature or size derived such a high percentage of its earnings from institutional investors. No other company devoted such a high percentage of its total investment dollars, product and technology development efforts, management time, and corporate talent to anticipating and satisfying the needs of institutional investors. What set State Street apart from bank and nonbank competitors alike was its laserlike focus of all available resources on supporting the special needs and processes actively engaged in by institutional investors worldwide. This fact was visible only after State Street cleansed the smoke screen and viewed its business from the outside in.

The most pressing questions were ones of portfolio strategy or scope of activities, of which by far the most vexing was the unresolved issue of whether State Street should retain its two-century-old commercial bank, its sole remaining link to the era of Boston whalers and China clippers. The chief obstacle blocking divestiture was that "we had gotten hooked on the revenue," Carter opined. "Commercial lending represented 8 percent of our asset base, but 19 percent of our revenue base." From the point of view of the institution's key customers, however, the commercial bank had become irrelevant. When the portfolio was analyzed from a demand-first perspective, divestiture of the bank—despite immediate costs to the bottom line and concerns about abandoning cultural links to the firm's past—became inevitable.

The research conducted by Carter's team identified the opportunities for adding value through new products and services. These openings appeared to lie primarily in the areas of technology and information services. These products and services represented integrated growth platforms, tools, methodologies, capabilities, and more. Nearly all the resources of the firm—including a newly unified sales force—were funneled into activating these growth platforms through new products and services that filled the yawning gaps in the firm's current offerings when it came to serving both trade and posttrade activities. Before rolling out FX Direct, one of the firm's most successful new services, State Street closely collaborated with a handful of large customers—IBM, Xerox, and Fidelity—which were not directly competing with each other. "We put them all in one room," Carter recalled, "and got them to talk to each other and talk to us about what they really needed that system to accomplish." FX Direct was the direct result of these conversations.

Several years later, customers began crying out for online, real-time access to State Street's databases. But the firm preferred not to grant them direct access to its mainframe environment. For an alternative, Carter recommended the development of a PC-based tool, ultimately refined by a defense contractor in the Boston area with extensive experience in stress testing systems for the military. "I told them all systems had to be global, scaleable, and to stress test it to ten million hits a day. By the time I walked out the door of the place in January 2001," Carter recalled proudly, "that system was taking up to 300 million hits a day, and was none the worse for wear."

Within nine months of this demand-first-based strategic repositioning, the newly refocused State Street Corporation (sans the name Boston and sans bank) realized not only analysts' revised expectations but Carter's higher aspirations for total return for shareholders. It broke dramatically out of its sluggish bank-PE ratio of 14-to-16 times earnings into the 22-to-30 times earnings ratios more commonly associated with high-performance, high-growth information technology companies like Bloomberg and data processing companies like ADT. Today, State Street is the number-one servicer of U.S. mutual funds, the number-one servicer of U.S. pension plans, the number-one investment manager of U.S. pension assets, and the number-one provider of foreign exchange services worldwide.

The Strategic Blueprint for Action

A strategic blueprint for action is an umbrella tool—defining at the highest levels the strategy that a firm chooses as well as the actions and activities required to move it toward realizing its vision and goals. It provides an essential strategic framework for prioritizing the development of growth platforms and realizing the growth objectives of the firm, but it also defines the activation plan of the growth platforms with customers. The strategy is defined by three main considerations[2]

1. *Objectives.* What we are trying to achieve?

2. *Advantage.* With what resources and capabilities do we achieve this objective?

3. *Scope.* In what domain will we compete?

Objectives define the ends of the strategy. The advantage defines the means. The scope defines the domain from a customer perspective.

Objectives

Objectives are primary goals that motivate the behaviors of the firm and that will be rewarded. These should be simple and measurable. They should be a bit of a stretch but should also be proximate and realistically achievable. Goals should not be confused with visions. Strategic objectives are merely milestones or targets that must be achieved in order to realize this central vision.

Strategic objectives can be chosen from a wide range of targets, including profitability, size of the firm, market or customer share or rank, and shareholder return. They can be defined in absolute terms, as in a state-ment of wanting to be the largest player in the industry, or in relative terms, such as wanting to achieve a certain market share level. Setting a specific time horizon can be critical to achieving a certain market share level within three years or by the end of the decade, for example.

An important set of objectives specifies how the firm's strategic blue-print intends to impact and transform the customer experience and how the firm intends to "own" a greater share of the minutes in the customers' day than it previously did. State Street's specific objectives of achieving deeper penetration in activities not well served by its present product port-folio were ultimately far more meaningful to the future of the firm than more general objectives like market share or profitability. A firm, by con-trast, that defines its objectives in terms of being the *largest* in market share will behave very differently from a firm that defines its objectives accord-ing to its contribution to customers' everyday lives.

Advantage

A second component of the strategic blueprint defines what the firm does differently, better, or uniquely compared with competitors. Defining the ad-vantage and understanding the sources or drivers of the advantage lie at the core of strategy. Traditionally, advantage has been defined in terms of market share and strength in relation to competitors. The classic thinking in strategy is fundamentally about things like "What is our core competency? Let's benchmark that." Traditionally, advantage is obtained by segmenting and tar-geting a subset of customers the firm intends to specifically serve, defining precisely what advantage the firm provides to these customers, and how well the firm's product and service offerings deliver that distinctively to them.

How did State Street define its advantage? The key to its collaboration with the customers was in forging an alliance that created value for both sides: the customers and the firm. The advantage that State Street defined was achieved by the transformations it induced in clients' experiences of their daily activities or processes revolving around the pretrade, trade, and posttrade activities. State Street's advantage lay in how it integrated, bun-dled, and streamlined those processes through integrated platforms in the form of technology solutions, tools, capabilities, and methodologies. One key piece that emerged from the research was that customers were demanding an opportunity to streamline their decision-making process when selecting service providers. By offering not simply a portfolio of products and services or solutions, State Street defined its advantage in terms of customer processes—a customer advantage or customer interaction advantage. So how did the firm intend to deliver this advantage? Defining advantage in terms of low cost, for example, would not be sufficient. The technological solutions innovated by Carter's team were no doubt superior products. However, they evolved the technology around a set of customer needs, based on their observation of customers' behavior and specific daily activities in the investment process.

Carter's strategic objectives focused on expanding State Street's share of customer requirements beyond the activities involved in posttrade. One advantage was entirely defined by the way the firm's products, services, and solutions were seamlessly integrated into the investment process of institutional investors. Another advantage was defined by how these integrated products and services transformed the customer experience. The strategy adopted was an intensive one that broadened and deepened State Street's relevance and connection to customers throughout just about every minute of their working day. The OAS (objective, advantage, and scope) strategic blueprint for action (see table 6-1) shows how strategy considerations change to achieve not only competitive advantage but also customer advantage.

TABLE 6-1

The OAS strategic blueprint for action

	From	To
Objective	Profits	Share of total requirements
	Market share	Transform the total use experience
	Revenues	
Advantage	Competitive	Customer
	Being different from competitors	Absorbed and assimilated into customers' lives
Scope	Category/industry/product boundaries or segments of customers	Context of customers' work processes
		Activities, goals, priorities

Scope

Defining scope answers the question: What sandbox do we want to play in? Classic thinking about scope involves targeting specific segments of customers with specific products and services. Scope can be defined along multiple dimensions: customers, channels, technologies, geographies, products and services, value chain activities, and, here in particular, demand-first growth platforms. An important dimension is the definition of the firm's choice of customers; needs, need states, or behavior clusters the firm intends to serve; and the products and services it offers to them. Seen from the perspective of pursuing customer advantage, scope can define how the offering links into the activities and goals of customers in the context of their everyday lives.

State Street defined its scope by maintaining and even strengthening the comparatively narrow boundaries that defined "institutional investors worldwide." The company did not attempt to broaden its scope by becoming a "financial supermarket." This was a strategy that was pursued by the white-shoe investment bank Morgan Stanley in merging with Discover/ Dean Witter to merge Wall Street and Main Street, offering one-stop shopping to retail customers.

The Details That Get You There

A well-formulated strategy expressed in terms of objectives, advantage, and scope ideally captures the way forward for a firm—how it should grow, where it will grow, through which growth platforms. It defines what job needs to get done by every member or unit of the firm. A strategy is, however, not only lived by the members of the firm. It must be perceived and well received by customers. In other words, the strategy must be able to connect with every relevant touch point in consumers' or customers' everyday lives.

How can a company ensure this connection? By creating an explicit experience and activation plan.

This critical step in creating a strategic blueprint is "where the rubber meets the road" and often is absent in many strategy discussions at great peril. The activation plan brings a company full circle in terms of perspective from the outside in to the inside out. Because now, the company needs to relate the customers' use or consumption experiences (the point of purpose) with the actual transactions or purchase (the point of purchase) *with the company, products, and brands in mind*—how it gets the product or brand to consumers.

Mapping the Customer Purchase Experience

To define a customer purchase experience, a company must map how customers become aware of a specific company, product, or service, how they familiarize themselves with their choices, how they purchase the product, and how they use the product or service and eventually discard or dispose of it.

The company can use the same research studies used in creating a demand landscape from an unbiased demand-first outside-in perspective. These studies can be tailored or embellished to serve the purpose here.

In chapter 3, we illustrated how Frito-Lay developed the consumption and use of snacks in consumers' everyday lives. Day-in-the-life scenarios were used to generate the demand landscape. Such scenarios can also be used to develop consumer purchase cycles with responses from just a few handfuls of consumers. With thirty-five consumers providing diaries over one month, the research generated over one thousand scenarios for where a strategist or marketer could learn how consumers go to buy snacks, what they read, where they shop, and how they shop.

In State Street's case, the use experience concerned how institutional investors experienced State Street's products and services while conducting pretrade, trade, and posttrade activities in their daily work lives. Talking to procurement professionals, IT professionals, and users in its customer base provided key insights.

Analyzing the Transaction

Analyzing the actual point of purchase yields a touch point map that represents a comprehensive enumeration of all touch points where and how customers intersect with the company or product. From a branding perspective, such an assessment helps define the relative importance of the touch points, possibly prioritize touch points, define ideal touch points relative to the brand positioning, and manage touch points from the current toward the desired ideal.[3]

More importantly, it can be the starting point for an exploration of how this purchase cycle itself might be improved or transformed. There may be a variety of ways to simplify the process, reduce the steps to purchase, or transform the process through digital ways of interfacing with a customer. Just think how the potential of the Internet has transformed the purchase of music or how Netflix created a better system of DVD rental using the Internet and basic mail service.

Now the focus turns to what levers or marketing activities the company should deploy to move customers through the purchase cycle and which of these are most effective. This will require a comprehensive analysis and consideration of the customer response to certain marketing activities, competitive strategies, and company's capabilities.

State Street identified three major marketing and business development activities that helped it maintain a connection with clients. First and most important was the sales force. Given the relationship nature of the industry, the complexity of the purchase, and the mission-critical nature of a use experience for institutional investors, State Street's personal selling effort was an important source of customer advantage for the bank. Second was the overall corporate identity and brand strategy of State Street. Carter regarded it as critical to communicate the fundamental repositioning and overall strategy of State Street through a powerful corporate brand and corporate identity program, which touched all internal customers, from employees and executives to customers and other stakeholders, particularly Wall Street.[4] Third was the portfolio of products, capabilities, tools, technologies, and services that were considered important, because many of the new technologies were not in place. Therefore, customers' perceptions of specific products, technologies, and capabilities of State Street strongly influenced consideration and purchase.

The Activation Plan

Armed with a refreshed perspective of customers' purchase and use experiences with existing offerings, a company can finally draw up its blueprint and answer the question What are we going to do?

State Street's plan focused on three important elements:

1. The fundamental reorganization of the sales force and service teams.

2. The unification of the several disparate and separate selling and service teams. Calling with a narrow product range on the same customers was an annoyance for the customers and source of inefficiency for State Street. The new strategy brought the separate sales and service teams together under one umbrella in dedicated client-service teams. This change created a significant shift in focus—from a product-centric to a customer-first selling and service focus.

   A significant brand strategy, corporate identity, and brand change program was led by an outside agency and consulting firm. The program addressed several stakeholders: clients and prospective clients, employees, employee markets, investors and shareholders as well as analysts. The program included a fundamental brand strategy and design development and the launch of a three-month TV advertising campaign, followed by an ongoing print campaign. The change program was guided by comprehensive client and employee touch point maps and included an overhaul and redesign of all marketing and sales literature, a new Web site, new signage, an internal launch for employees including launch kits, video and road show banners, a new corporate profile brochure, redesign of the annual report, changes in pitch material made available to the client-facing team, a significant program of training on team selling called the Sales Calling Program, creation of management speeches and news releases, and PR effort. For investor relations, corporate financial metrics of success were developed. Internally, there was revamping of all employee material and HR policies regarding recruiting and management of personnel, including new performance criteria for sales and service teams.

3. New product and service offerings that expanded State Street's business beyond custody and posttrade services.[5] Significant

investment went into development of the value-added trade and pretrade offerings delivered electronically to users at customer companies. In the pretrade sector, institutional investors had clients whose goal was to gather information about the companies in their portfolios, and they wanted to manage those portfolios efficiently. In order to create an ideal offering, State Street acquired portfolio management software and formed a strategic alliance with Bridge Systems to deliver an alternative distribution channel. In the trade sector, which involves a complex set of actions that need to be executed, it acquired Lattice, a provider of an advanced, event-driven, electronic trading system. This acquisition gave State Street portfolio trade management tools, order routing, and cash management tools. Because different trades were being executed, the portfolio of management tools could be expanded from trading U.S. equities to global equities, U.S. fixed income, and global fixed income. These expansion opportunities created future growth far beyond its traditional foreign exchange capabilities.

Axe: A Strategic Blueprint in Action

The case of the male grooming brand Axe provides a summary-level example of a strategic blueprint in action in a specific context—a mature consumer products category or, better, an activity at the top of mind in the daily lives of a certain male target audience. We offer it here because it provides a major contrast to State Street's business-to-business experience, with an equally effective application of key elements of the DIG model and powerful actions at consumers' point of purpose or consumption and use in the social-cultural context of daily life.[6]

When Anglo-Dutch consumer goods giant Unilever launched Axe (sold under the name Lynx in the United Kingdom, Ireland, and Australia) in France in 1983, even its most ardent internal proponents would have been shocked to learn that two decades later Axe would become the number-one brand worldwide in the freshly conceived male grooming aids category.

Today, Axe boasts a powerful presence in sixty-plus countries and commands an impressive 10–20 percent share of the rapidly expanding market for male grooming products in Europe, Latin America, Asia, and the United States. Narrow that product category down to include just "body spray" (a subset of personal care that Unilever and Axe virtually invented), and the brand controls a whopping 83 percent share of the $180 million market in the United States, with over $150 million in annual sales in 2005. According to a 2005 study by Media Research, Inc., the entire grooming category for Axe's target audience—18- to 24-year-old men—grew 38 percent in the United States in 2004 and leapt an astounding 62 percent from August 2004 to August 2005, amid a remarkable 27 percent rise in sales for the Axe brand for 2005. According to *Advertising Age*, Axe has taken over category leadership from also-growing Old Spice in 2006 (just four years from launch)—a remarkable achievement in a mature U.S. market.[7]

Growth Platforms Create Customer Advantage over Time

The enormous success of Axe has much to do with how Unilever defined the relevant sweet spot in terms of what mattered to the young consumer target: *the mating game*. For several years after the product's launch, Unilever focused on systematically deepening and broadening the conversations about how to "get the girl" and the role of Axe in this activity. The U.S. launch is illustrative.

In August 2002, following two decades of solid success in Europe, Unilever introduced Axe to the North American market with a media spend upwards of $100 million, carefully aimed to persuade its target demographic that Axe could provide them with a decisive edge in their perennially preoccupying pursuit: the mating game. Tongue-in-cheek TV spots depicted bodacious babes fawning over naked store mannequins that had been heavily prespritzed with Axe fragrance at strategically critical body zones. In one particularly spoofy spot, an ardent young woman spraying her male mannequin ended up being caught by her boyfriend, who punched the mannequin's head off while she innocently protested, "Roger! We were just talking!"

The point of the advertising was to be about as blunt and hard edged as network broadcast standards permitted in conveying the message that the product in the sleek black packaging encasing the $3.99–$4.99 4-ounce aerosol spray can had been deliberately designed to be as dramatically different from their grandfather's deodorant stick as a BMW 5 Series is from an Oldsmobile Toronado.

In one sweet-smelling swoop, the global debut of Axe body spray (which uniquely combined, until competitors began crowding its turf, the desiccating properties of a deodorant with the fragrance of a cologne) forced a fundamental shift in male grooming behavior. As the instructions printed on the side of the can sagely advised, "Just hold the can 6 inches from your body and spray all over, including your chest, neck, underarms—anywhere you want to smell great." Fragrance variants launched at regular intervals to keep the brand fresh as a recently scented teen underarm include Apollo, "with a green floral twist," and Orion, "a celebrated hunter in the oldest Greek mythology, after whom the constellation was named . . . aromatic, woody, fruity, energetic and exhilarating."

Three years after Axe's summer 2002 launch, 35 percent of young men aged eleven to twenty-four had grown accustomed to wearing some sort of body spray, according to Unilever. By then, Procter & Gamble had introduced the competing body spray Red Zone, while Gillette's Tag (shortly to fall under the P&G umbrella, with the merger of the two parent companies) complemented P&G's Old Spice, the long-time category leader. By 2005, Axe's share of the antiperspirant and deodorant category had grown to 11.7 percent, according to ACNielsen, while Old Spice's share had contracted to around 10 percent.

Not only had Axe brashly forced a shift in behavior patterns and mating customs among the younger male set, it had dramatically boosted the volume of products sold in its category by strongly suggesting that young men would do better with babes if they sprayed their entire bodies several times a day, thereby increasing *usage* as well as *users*. As *Business 2.0* magazine laid out the brand's unambiguous promise shortly after the U.S. launch, "Men stink. Men want to get laid. To succeed at the latter, they must deal with the former."[8]

Kevin George, vice president and general manager for deodorants at Unilever, insists that the success of the advertising is grounded in a decision to avoid the "functional benefits" approach preferred by competitors.

As opposed to offering a product designed simply to "stop moisture and odor," Axe promises something dramatically different: an edge in the mating game.

Breaking Out of the Attribute Trap

"For years," George explains, "the deodorant market was a highly functional market. Everybody was offering the same package of benefits: stop odor and wetness, stop odor and wetness." Axe's promise and package of benefits included humorous advice and expertise in the dating game. To the *New York Times*, George knowingly observed, "We kind of turned the category on its head. It used to be all about the absence of negatives—not smelling bad. Now it's all about a positive—getting the girl."[9]

One significant factor behind Axe's striking success at capturing the hearts, minds, and bodies of young males worldwide (the brand is a huge hit in India) is its sophisticated strategy of reaching the proverbial "Axe guy" wherever he lives and breathes, whether that be on a college campus, in a Laundromat washing clothes, in a fraternity house, hanging out in a club, online in chat rooms, or feverishly playing macho-edged video games.

One of Axe's more successful forays into the unconventional world of marketing to the Gen Y set has been a series of commercials artfully disguised as home videos, which played exclusively on Axe's Web site (www.theaxeeffect.com). These too-racy-for-prime-time shorts graphically yet whimsically depicted attractive young woman seduced by Axe-wearing footballers. According to George, this was a deliberate spoof on the traditional unique selling proposition of deodorants in the past, which all too frequently depicted "stupid football players sweating and not stinking." In Axe's case, the functional benefits were not product derived (dryness, odorlessness) but contextually inspired, and this became behaviorally transformative: frisky cheerleaders morph into willing sirens with one whiff of magical Axe. "We're not selling 24-hour protection," George explained, "we're selling self-confidence."

Four months into its first campaign, Unilever was thrilled to learn that an estimated 1.7 million young people had logged on to its Web site, at a total cost of less than $1 million, enabling Axe in its first year to capture nearly a 5 percent share of the nearly $2 billion U.S. male deodorant market.

Apart from its adventurous and provocative activities, Axe has effectively leveraged its presence in such alternative media as cell phones, blogs, and video games listed at a dizzying variety of sites (www.theaxeeffect.com, www.gamekillers.com, www.theorderoftheserpentine.com, and www.pimp myfraternityshower.com), reflecting the youth market's restlessness and fickle attention span. Not content to rely solely on alternative media for outreach, Axe devoted extraordinary time and resources to consciously engage with the "Axe guy," including the active recruitment of a cadre of young male "Axe ambassadors" at twenty-five top campuses nationwide. Axe annually hosts a three-day extravaganza at its corporate headquarters in Chicago, where members of the insight team at Unilever "learn all sorts of new things" from its ambassadors about the constantly changing mating game as played at that time in the United States.

"We live and breathe our target consumer," contends Unilever director of Consumer and Market Insights Alison Zelen, who regards her primary task as a definer of insights as "getting the Axe guy" so she and her team can help the Axe guy "get the girl." Deploying a cluster of research techniques that Unilever calls Consumer Connect, Zelen, George, and their fellow members of the Axe North American brand management team spend substantial amounts of time with consumers in their target demographic, both online and in real life. Globally, Axe runs a program called Youth Board, which provides the worldwide marketing teams with frequent opportunities to thoroughly immerse themselves in two or three days in the target segment's life.

Axe divides men's lives into "mind zones," Zelen explains, "ranging from technology to friendship, dating, education, sports, movies, and communications. This is not like ducking for a few hours into a focus group. This is about spending days at a time with your target market. Youth Board is very deliberately not *about* Axe at all. It's not even about *asking* them about Axe." Instead, Axe marketing team members travel to such trendy youth-oriented hot spots as Amsterdam, Los Angeles, and Orange County to immerse themselves in the local culture.

Unilever further maintains a virtual "communispace" online, populated by three hundred young men eighteen and up willing to answer questions "about everything going on in their lives. Axe can expect answers in twenty-four hours. Should we do satellite radio? Ads in movie theaters?" Decoding behavior, Kevin George and Alison Zelen maintain, derived from observation and insight, has been the primary means by which Unilever maintains the relevance of the brand to its customers.

Three Years to Activate the Growth Platforms

Launching a new fragrance variant every year for the last three years has been an integral part of Axe's global brand strategy, Zelen insists. Each one of these new variants—Essence, Touch, and Unlimited—is in its most elementary way simply an annual product launch. Yet behind the effort stands much more—the structuring of the sweet spot, and the activation of a growth platform that seeks to deepen the relevance of Axe in consumers' everyday lives, the engagement of its target customers with Axe through a dialogue between the brand and the consumer on the subject closest to both of their hearts: the mating game.

For Essence, the concept directly evolved from in-depth ethnographic research, which confirmed a central ambiguity about the mating game that has long vexed men and women alike. While women, according to anecdotal evidence, seem frequently to prefer or be sexually titillated by the "bad boys," they also expressed a certain fondness and yearning for chivalry, kindness, and sensitivity in their male partners.

The fragrance variant Essence was created and introduced in the summer of 2003 to directly address this classic postfeminist conundrum. As Zelen puts it, "In every guy there's a good side and a bad side and girls like both. So what do they do?" Apparently, to resolve the contradiction, they spritz themselves with Essence and keep their fingers crossed. As the Unilever Web site sums the variant up, Essence promises to "bring out the sweet, polite, jewelry-buying, 'aw, shucks' side of you that girls *want*, along with the racy, adventurous, expert knot-tying, 'saddle up' side that girls *need*. It's good. It's bad. It's exactly what she's looking for." The launch was supported by a BBH TV ad depicting two young male identical twins who turn up at a young woman's house and take her out on a date. One twin is bad and naughty while the other is nice and good. The girl, not surprisingly, is equally intrigued by both personas. The ad concludes with the three figures all snuggling up on the dance floor at a club, at which point the good twin and the evil twin gradually merge into the same man. The tagline

"The essence of man is both good and evil" expresses a psychological complexity not frequently found in, for example, mass-market beer advertising.

Touch, introduced in the summer of 2004, is styled as "a modern, fresh, watery, woody fragrance" meant to evoke the delicious, yet trembling "butterflies in the stomach" sensation a young man feels the first time he reaches out to touch a girl. But as with Essence, the actual concept expressed by the product was more subtle and complex than simple physical contact. As Zelen explains it, "The concept is *touch without touching*." This variant, too, is based on an insight that emerged from research discussions when young people observed that a specific physical sensation occurs when, for example, a young man and a young woman who are attracted to each other move into proximity for the first time. "A guy watching a girl flip her hair over her shoulder creates a physical act inside him," as Zelen explains it, adding that Touch is—as the name suggests—"less philosophical and more physical than Essence."

Supporting advertising for Touch depicted a young man sitting in a bus station in some exotic tropical locale. A literally and figuratively hot woman, with sweat dripping down her neck, looms near, while another bends over to zip up a long boot. "It's not about touching, but about not touching, a prelude to what *might* happen later." To promote Touch and activate the variant, Axe hosted "dark parties" at bars with no lights on, in which young men and women were physically connected but could only discover each other by touch. Men and women also ate in the dark, served by waiters and waitresses wearing night vision goggles, and danced in the dark, all to build brand buzz around the new variant.

For the summer 2005 launch of the new variant Unlimited, the fragrance and product itself were the direct outgrowth of consumer research in which members of the target segment were asked, "What's going on in the mating game?" As Zelen put it, "Unlimited grew out of a global assessment and study conducted around the world of what it takes to get the girl. We asked men who were successful at the mating game to tell us, quite frankly, what they did that worked. What are your winning strategies and techniques? What is your playbook?"

Of course, Unilever did not confine its research to asking. It also watched, in all the relevant places, what was working and what was not.

"We watched them in action," Zelen said, and discovered such universal customs as the "icebreaker," a man fluent and funny enough to break the ice, possibly in service of a friend's interest in the woman in question; or a "cue ball," a man capable of breaking up a pack of women into smaller groups, which are more easily approached than a herd. A "wing man" approaches one woman on behalf of a friend interested in that woman's friend.

The TV spot supporting Unlimited in the United States varied from the global campaign because the North American team felt that a U.S. flavor was required. "We created our own spot that showed a young man sitting in a sushi restaurant with a hot chick, and behind them is a mermaid swimming in a tank. In the next scene he's with the mermaid *and* the hot chick. Then he's in a casino with a hot female dealer, and he blows on her hand, and then they're all in a hotel suite together. After that, you hear an alarm bell, and of course, he's been dreaming." Unlimited speaks to the common male fantasy that having "all the right moves" will promise unlimited sexual conquests.

The launch of Unlimited was also enhanced by an extensive Web campaign that keeps the conversation with the target audience going, featuring a free-online virtual pickup game called Mojo Master, which posits the "unlimited" potential for conquest of the opposite sex to the young man in command of all the right moves. The male fantasy game enables the young men who play it to test a series of presumably tried-and-true pickup maneuvers on a bevy of virtual vixens, possessed of artificial intelligence as well as artificial physiques, and capable of precisely recalling the efficacy of each move the player makes. Developed by the Redmond, Washington–based online game company WildTangent, the game is configured to reward a gamer with a higher "Mojo" (score) every time he correctly deploys an Axe product as a means to an end: getting the girl.

Mojo Master was further supplemented by a virtual reality show starring two "regular guys" named Evan and Gareth (an improvisational comedy team in civilian life) whom the firm provided with $25,000 in cash to cruise around the country posing as self-styled "seduction crash test dummies," posting their sexual successes and failures on a blog and cameo videos for all the world to see and make fun of.

Buzz

Behind Axe's growth to date has been a very clever and innovative marketing strategy. Unlike other brands in the early launch years, it limits brand extensions to just a few new fragrances and variants, preferring to invest resources in strengthening and deepening customer engagement around key themes of the endless relevance: how to get the girl and to be successful with the opposite sex. Axe positions itself as the expert, the guide, the keeper of the secret.

Unlike other brands in successful launches, Axe also consistently focuses on the same customers and target segments. A typical alternative growth strategy that Unilever might have pursued in expanding the Axe brand is to "trade up" by boosting the price and launching a premium product with higher price points. Such segmentation would not have been unreasonable and is often recommended by experts to capture other demographics: older, young, broader, richer consumers loyal to products from Gillette and Procter & Gamble. Instead, Axe chose to focus on creating customer advantage. It broadened and deepened engagement and dialogue about the mating game with its chosen target segment. New launches created deeper relevance of Axe across a broader set of themes around the endless pursuit of success in the game and created engagement through its very targeted viral and word-of-mouth campaigns. Axe created buzz.

With the DIG model defined and explained, in part III of this book we turn to the issues companies face during implementation of particular brand management, an area where we have spent years intensively developing our expertise. How do issues of new and established brands layer into new growth platforms? How can a company truly embed an outside-in perspective into the culture of the organization? What *can* Manhattan's Times Square tell us about our companies and their potential?

Part III

Strategies for Realizing Customer Advantage

Chapter Seven

Creating Customer Advantage

IN A SENSE, any description we offer of a strategic blueprint—
however detailed—is going to fall short of capturing the full
story and the enormous implications the DIG model has on strategy, marketing, and innovation. That's because even the most straightforward applications contain a myriad of unique consequences and imperatives that
are not possible to touch on, even in the relative luxury of a book-length
manuscript.

It's relatively easy to say, for example, that a company has to decide, for
successful activation, whether it is going to position an innovation as a brand
extension or as a new brand entirely. It is easy to say that a company, upon
completing an analysis of its customers' purchase experiences, might decide
to launch a new brand. It's entirely another kettle of fish to make this decision within the context of a given organizational setting, a challenging business situation, and a complex and comprehensive portfolio and live through
the angst of that decision process, when various brands might be vying for a
limited resource pool, when competitors are adding new levels of "differentiation" attributes that threaten the existing market position, and when the
next quarterly report is due in a week ("Are we meeting our goals?").

That's why this chapter and chapter 8 are devoted to brand strategy and
portfolio issues. Branding comes in almost as an afterthought when a company is beginning to use the DIG model but it isn't. Branding brings with
it a host of established expectations and promises, and therefore can sorely
limit a company's ability to see things in a new light. Brands are also a force

unto themselves: the stronger the brands, the more of an inside-out perspective they instill in the people who manage them over time.

Yet brands are, undoubtedly and ultimately, the principal means of connecting the strategy for innovation of growth of the firm with the ecosystem of consumer demand. Brand portfolios are structures of a company's brands and other brands that are part of a consumers' ecosystem of demand. A brand portfolio strategy defines the position, role, and relationship of each brand in the portfolio. The trick is harnessing their power without allowing their power to limit a company's perspective.

The case of BMW provides the foundation in this chapter to explore how companies can use the power of the brand to connect with consumers, and to engage them and build a profitable business on the back of a strong portfolio and a precise understanding of the ecosystem of demand and the opportunities for the future.

We chose BMW because the company is a study of several key components. First is the development of an increasingly sophisticated brand management system that not only positions the company and its products but also works to connect the dots internally at the BMW Group from consumer insights, marketing, R&D, engineering, and design to sales. Second is the successful evolution of the brand portfolio from a branded house to a house of brands that helped the company achieve the highest volume and profitable growth in the entire automotive industry. Third, but not least, is the emergence of a new branding model that flips the traditional model upside down. This new model is illustrated by BMW Group's MINI launch effort and its integration into BMW's ever-expanding brand portfolio, and demonstrates the power of the DIG model in action.

In chapter 8, we provide five guidelines from the experiences of the BMW Group and other companies to show how your company might integrate these approaches to branding and marketing with the DIG model.

BMW Group

In January 2005, the Munich-based BMW Group announced that for the first time in its history, it had sold more than 1 million vehicles. Specifically, in 2004, 1,208,732 new BMWs, MINIs, and Rolls-Royces—the three "premium" brands currently constituting BMW Group's brand portfolio—had rolled off assembly lines around the world into the capable hands of BMW, MINI and Rolls-Royce dealers worldwide. And BMW's sales had set a volume record, up an impressive 9.4 percent from 2003.

Group revenues climbed 6.8 percent to €44.3 billion in the same period. And profits rose 11 percent over the previous year to a robust €3.5 billion, a particularly strong performance compared with that of U.S. auto giant General Motors, which—despite selling nearly ten times as many cars as BMW Group annually—made a glum announcement of record losses of $1 billion for the first quarter of 2005.

Put another way, in the previous year, BMW Group's automotive operations had more in operating profit than General Motors, Ford, Volkswagen (VW), and Renault combined, leading BMW Group chairman Helmut Panke to proclaim to the press, "Our product portfolio and our international presence are more comprehensive than ever before. We will resolutely continue to utilize further market potential available to us in the future."[1]

It did just that. Several months later, at the close of the first quarter of 2005, Panke announced yet another milestone: the BMW Group's first-quarter sales of 239,387 vehicles had narrowly surpassed the 226,400 units sold by BMW's chief competitor in the luxury car segment, the Stuttgart-headquartered Mercedes-Benz.

"It feels good psychologically for everybody within the organization to beat the perennial rival," Panke modestly opined while basking in the positive public and critical reception that greeted the long-awaited, highly touted introduction of the 1 Series and the top-to-bottom reengineering of the top-of-the-marque 7 Series.

The solidity and stability of BMW's robust financial performance circa 2003–2005 was particularly gratifying to management in the wake of the firm's circa 2000 malaise. Five years before, the company had struggled to sell a mere 700,000 cars globally while suffering from a vicious case of indigestion following the ill-fated 1994 acquisition of faltering British auto legend MG/Rover. The sale of Rover later that year did wonders for BMW's morale and bottom line while permitting new management to focus on refining the marriage of innovative engineering and quality with maturity and luxury that constituted BMW's strong suit going forward.

BMW Brand—Fostering Growth for New Brands in New Opportunity Spaces

Going for profitable growth at BMW brought about new challenges. These included a more complex product portfolio and, more importantly, an urgent need for proactive brand management. Brands needed to be better defined as to what each stood for and aspired to create, with an overall objective of achieving maximum synergy and leverage across brands. Brands needed to be positioned clearly and precisely toward the biggest opportunities in the ever-changing ecosystem of consumer demand for automobiles while leveraging the strengths of the core BMW brand. This is the central challenge of brand portfolio strategy. The BMW Group's most immediate brand challenge would be to engineer a graceful transition from a *branded house* (with the 3 Series, 5 Series and 7 Series model range at its core) to a *house of brands*, one that could provide ample room for the two new arrivals in the group's packed portfolio: Rolls-Royce and MINI.[2]

BMW Group's decision to pluck the long-forsaken original Mini brand from the tatters of the Rover portfolio appeared particularly prescient in light of the rejuvenated premium compact's capacity to capture the imagination of even the most blasé and jaded car buyers. The MINI, produced in a wide range of quirky and creative iterations and launched in 2001 after Land Rover was sold off to Ford, promptly achieved a cult status that easily justified the $3,000 average price premium it enjoyed over a comparably equipped Honda Civic.

The decision to adopt a multi–master brand strategy was prompted by an examination of the opportunity spaces available to the firm beyond the core BMW brand. While the industry categorizes automotive products by price points and divides the market by rear-wheel drive or front-wheel drive, Panke's trenchant analysis of the underlying strength of the BMW brand remained rooted in the fact that while rival manufacturers sought to strategically straddle the upper-end and mass-market segments simultaneously, the BMW Group had deliberately chosen to focus on building up the three premium brands in its stable, with all due emphasis placed on maintaining a premium position at virtually every price point, from a $20,000

MINI to a $250,000 Rolls-Royce Phantom. While the MINI was indisputably a hit on all fronts, the firm continued to struggle with more precisely positioning the most prestigious of all British brands, Rolls-Royce. "Rolls-Royce has to be positioned and re-strengthened as the pinnacle in the automotive market," Panke opined, freely conceding that "over the past 15 to 20 years the brand has lost some of its positioning." As for rumors that the BMW Group was considering launching a "budget" Roller, Panke quashed them with the remark, "If there was a less expensive Rolls-Royce too early, we would not reclaim [the brand's] pinnacle position."

Across every segment, the BMW Group's unwavering commitment to maintaining its premium position across all three brands, price points, and fronts forced BMW to avoid the perils and pitfalls of mass manufacturing. "The two areas are completely different," Panke insisted. "In mass-market manufacturing you have to have the lowest cost base. But in premium you deliver an emotional value to the customer. When a customer decides for BMW or Mercedes, they want to have a specific characteristic. It's about what the vehicle *feels like* to them."

Several decades before, during the heyday of BMW as a branded house in which the flagship models were the only beasts resident in the brand's cozy stable, core customers felt catered to by the stark simplicity of BMW's three model ranges, the 3, 5, and 7 Series, each of which looked so alike (apart from their size) that BMW designers in Munich proudly hailed the "*Eine Wurst, drei Groessen*" ("one sausage, three sizes"). Such stark simplicity was all part of the brand's narrow and stripped-down appeal. But there were problems with maintaining brand strength in only this narrow niche market. How could the BMW brand capture new opportunities?

Renovation Before Innovation

One of the solutions was to focus on renovation by positioning BMW to better respond to the changing context of societal trends, launching new models, and changing the visual expression or raising the design leadership of BMW.[3] The U.S. situation by the end of the 1990s illustrates this effort. As the yuppie boom trailed off and lost cultural steam, the "social strivers" who for years had formed the foundation of BMW's core customers (a positioning precisely conveyed by the immortal tagline "The Ultimate Driving Machine") were growing up. In some cases, the same customers who had lusted after BMWs in their youth had begun looking longingly beyond the "three sausages" to family-sized vehicles like the Volvo station wagon, SUVs, minivans, and luxury marques like those from archrival Mercedes, not to mention the newly introduced Japanese luxury brands, most notably Toyota's Lexus.

But the firm did something deliberately controversial, risking the alienation of core customers, when it rolled out its new SUV X5, X3, and jazzy roadsters Z3 and Z4, all models that sharply departed in style and tone from the prevailing stereotype, as a means of refreshing the entire BMW image. The retro-futuristic, voluptuous, visionary sensibilities of American designer Chris Bangle, while indisputably eye-catching, raised eyebrows among ardent loyalists as too profound a departure from hallowed tradition.[4] "We had to do something different," Panke defensively asserted on the front page of the *Wall Street Journal*, reiterating his conviction that had the group stuck to its design guns, "we [risked] being in a dead end as a brand and as a company."[5] Nonetheless, an initiative to launch a BMW minivan, capable of seating seven passengers (referred to internally as the "*Raumfunktionales Konzept*," or "space functional concept") prompted a few purists to carp, perhaps justifiably, that BMW appeared to be pandering to middle-aged suburbanites and soccer moms, leaving the macho racers in the dust.

Going into the second half of the first decade of the twenty-first century, the overarching brand challenge for a firm first formed as the *Bayerische Motoren Werke* (Bavarian Motor Works), a manufacturer of aircraft engines during World War I, would be to profitably expand its consumer footprint and capture growth opportunities while continuing to foster a level of loyalty virtually unprecedented on the planet.

From Branded House to House of Brands

For nearly eight decades before the acquisitions of Rover and Rolls-Royce (and the resulting inclusion of MINI and Rolls into its brand portfolio),

BMW was a brand and a firm that managed a simple brand architecture. Its product portfolio was organized along the classical lines of a *branded house*, like Sony or Nike. Strategically, this meant that the BMW brand historically stood for both product and firm and that BMW's focus was on building its brand associations around the BMW name. Those three emblematic initials, surrounded by the blue-and-white checkerboard pattern that harkened back to the blue-and-white colors of the Bavarian monarchy, represented everything of value under one roof, from cars to motorcycles to the corporate brand.

Yet by the mid-1990s, when the board elected to grow by acquisition as well as internally, managing a broader portfolio of brands effectively became the number-one management challenge. The group faced the additional pressure associated with retaining a global brand identity for the BMW brand while presenting different facets of that identity in different key markets (in particular, Europe and the United States).

Following the acquisition of MG/Rover, the BMW Group became an overarching umbrella for all three brands within the portfolio, with BMW, Rolls-Royce, and MINI qualifying as the three master brands. The brand leadership challenge involved maximizing the opportunities for growth not only for the BMW brand but also for Rolls-Royce and MINI. To this challenge were added the complexities of managing the same global brand identity across geographic markets. In the United States, for example, BMW's positioning continued to be exemplified by the "Ultimate Driving Machine" tagline. This emphasized an element of the brand identity more closely linked to the product, technology, and driving experience. Meanwhile in Europe, BMW's positioning became broader, exemplified by the tagline "Joy of Driving," which closely linked the myriad cultural expressions of consumers' need for joy in their everyday lives with the ownership and the driving experience of a BMW car.

The complex task of managing the house of brands fell to the group's strategic management team as a way of supporting the growth ambitions of the company as a whole. Indeed, without the stunning success of MINI and the stable performance of Rolls, it is highly unlikely that the firm could have sold close to 1 million BMW vehicles in 2004. Without increasing the sophistication of its brand management system and brand portfolio approach, BMW would likely have suffered serious dilution of its brands.

From Brand Image to Brand Identity

The concepts of brand awareness and brand image are essentially tactical; in contrast, *brand identity* is fundamentally a strategic concept. Brand image is merely the result of a strong brand identity and a measurement device of the health of a brand, much as a thermometer checks body temperature. In contrast, a brand identity system expresses a strategic trade-off and is the starting point of building a strong brand; it clearly defines what a brand is and what it aspires to be. Character is destiny, as Heraclitus, the Greek philosopher, observed. A brand identity system links seamlessly to corporate and business strategy, as discussed in chapter 6—the strategic positioning and the complexities and dynamic nature of the ecosystem of demand.[6]

Brand image as strategy was useful as a tactical tool to guide communications efforts when few products were on the road and positioning was a single point on a product attribute. Volvo, for example, defined itself in terms of the top spot on the attribute of safety and positioned itself in the market. Hertz was number one, and Avis was number two and tried harder. Today, such a strategy of positioning, advocated by the groups of marketers called the "positionistas," may be useful as a communications objective but cannot meaningfully define the strategy with respect to the opportunities in an area of the complex and ever-changing ecosystem of consumer demand. It is simply an approach too narrow and too shallow to position meaningfully a complex portfolio of brands.[7]

Until the 1994 acquisition by BMW of the MG/Rover and affiliated brands, BMW's brand management existed chiefly on the tactical dimension of brand image management. It was strictly product and country-of-origin driven, emphasizing the company's German engineering heritage and the high quality and performance characteristics of the car in the United States. The brand image of BMW had been scrupulously established and codified in 1975 with the launch of the renowned "Ultimate Driving Machine" campaign. This classic campaign was inspired by a decision to impart to the

BMW brand a greater emotional appeal while continuing to lay stress on the performance aspect as the key essence of the brand.

By the 1980s, BMW began to aggressively position its brand, particularly in the United States, as relentlessly upscale, a brand strategy that accentuated a mixture of emotion and function by emphasizing driving excitement and premium value. In so doing, the company explicitly targeted affluent young male drivers who already drove a BMW and who might one day migrate to a Mercedes or a Jaguar as they grew older and their incomes increased. By the early '90s, belatedly conscious that such a blatant and narrow positioning possessed its own inherent dangers—with customers indeed migrating to rival brands as BMW's yuppie image no longer expressed their core values—the company chose to broaden its product portfolio.

With the arrival of Rover in 1994 and the acquisition of Rolls-Royce naming rights in 1998, the company possessed five distinct and strong identities in its stable, each of which would require active management to fully leverage the portfolio's untapped potential. What BMW got from Rover and Rolls-Royce were product platforms, not growth platforms, though. They did not acquire from Rover or Rolls-Royce new ways of thinking to structure the ecosystem of consumer demand or new ways of connecting to consumers. The BMW Group needed to develop strategies for these brands on top of these existing product platforms. What brand could they build from Rover? How should these brands be built, given their new home and context, the BMW brand portfolio? In light of BMW's commitment to building premium brands, the decision to resuscitate the long-dormant MINI was a curious one, given that in Britain it inhabited the same space as the VW Beetle in Germany, and the Citroën 2CV or the Renault R4 in France. BMW could, by self-definition, only build premium brands. BMW elected to take a long-forgotten mass-market marque and build from it a premium product within the context of the BMW Group portfolio.

The BMW Group's increasingly sophisticated brand management approach focused explicitly on managing the three brands using a strategic framework that linked BMW, Rolls-Royce, and MINI to clearly focused positions in major geographic regions of the world, as well as targeting segments within those markets. The genius of the BMW Group was to capture the relevant and new area of the ecosystem of demand, creating a new growth platform that minimized the overlap with the BMW brand. It created a stand-alone business that ensured better development of the brand's values linked to BMW yet intrinsically distinct from the BMW and Rolls-Royce brands. In the portfolio of the BMW Group, MINI became the automotive equivalent of the iPod.

Moving beyond the brand image dimensions that define the brands, BMW, MINI and Rolls-Royce were defined according to a comprehensive brand identity system designed to answer such key questions as:

- What are our core values and the associations we aspire to create?

- What does the brand stand for?

- How does the brand want to be perceived?

- What personality traits does the brand want to project?

- What is the brand relationship with customers?

- How does the new brand identity capture and tap into the evolving and changing ecosystem of demand in the automotive sector?

Answers to these questions were organized into a logical governing system and a brand identity structure. This structure is proprietary to BMW and was developed by the BMW brand management team. The essence of the BMW brand, for example, related to "joy," as conveyed in the famous German tagline "*Freude am Fahren*" ("The Joy of Driving").[8]

The decision was ultimately made to develop the BMW Group as a "shadow endorser" of the three individual brands BMW, MINI, and Rolls-Royce, a strategy that provided a corporate endorsement of credibility and a premium attitude to the individual master brands MINI and Rolls-Royce. In turn, the BMW, MINI and Rolls-Royce brands acted as "second shadow endorsers" of the BMW Group.

Managing Brand Identity Across Global Regions

Globally, the brand identity of BMW was defined around the single and overarching concept of joy.[9] This core of joy has been developed most broadly in Europe, focusing on the elements of "Sheer Driving Pleasure," as articulated along seven dimensions: (1) joy in driving, (2) joy in progress and innovation, (3) joy in beautiful things, (4) joy in life, (5) joy in success, (6) joy in ownership, and (7) joy in real values.

The broad dimensionality of joy is pervaded with a sense of dynamism and speed ("The Joy of Driving"), which bolsters the attribute of performance. In Europe, the brand emphasis revolves around the emotionality of driving itself. In the United States, where BMW enjoys a 1.5 percent share of the total car market, the functional benefits of the legendary German precision and mastery rise to the fore. In Europe, BMW is a far more common sight; the brand enjoys a 7 percent share of the total car market in Germany. Let's look at the distinctions of positioning between the U.S. and European markets.

- "Joy" in Europe possesses a broader and more developed brand identity with virtually universal appeal. It effortlessly combines such disparate functional benefits as high fuel efficiency and power and speed. In the United States, however, this core concept was translated into a position more crisply focused on the notion of "The Ultimate Driving Machine."

- This positioning in the United States is more productcentric and potentially polarizing. The precision of the positioning makes it more appropriate and appealing to a large niche market—the right strategy given the potential in the U.S. market. From an emotional point of view, it satisfies the core market customer's desire for control, driver performance, and the experience of technology.

In Germany, BMW owns a larger share of the ecosystem of demand around a family's total time than in the United States, and its broader positioning reflects that degree of customer advantage. The brand identity system has evolved in different ways to meet the demands and exploit the opportunities of the various markets. In the United States, the primary dimensions of differentiation are high performance and exclusivity. But in Germany, a paradise for performance brands—including Porsche, Mercedes, and Audi—that differentiation along the performance axis can be far harder to achieve. The brand core of joy comes much more sharply into focus as an emotional concept that can exist entirely independently of the car. Joy in the beauty of life, movement, progress, perfection, precision, performance. Joy translates the product into everyday-life terms.

From Brand Identity to Demand-First Brand Strategy

The evolution of the brand management system at BMW is exemplary. Without such an established and evolving system, it is difficult to steward multiple brands across multiple products, markets, and segments and to foster innovation and achieve growth. Without such a system, it is difficult to capture opportunities for growth today while also leveraging the attributes and values of the core brand and reinforcing the positive attributes of the core. The "shadow endorsement" strategy adopted by the BMW Group was the most effective way to break into new markets without suffering dilution of the core BMW brand.

In our experience, a brand management system can also stifle innovation and growth. Just like any other system and process in an organization, the brand management system can define brands too tightly. It can create boundaries, hasten the development of a smoke screen, and lead to efforts and programs that serve the system rather than the overall growth objectives of the firm. This happens when brands are defined around products rather than demand-first growth platforms. Then, brand management is often relegated to the writing of brand guidelines, for example.

When there is a proactive brand management system that works well, it confronts the organization with fundamental questions of its identity in light of its ever-changing ecosystem of customer demand. It mobilizes people. It invokes creativity and funnels imagination. It channels with precision the innovation and growth agenda of the firm. The brand becomes culture, internally and externally. We will discuss this process from two different perspectives in chapters 8 and 9.

From an external perspective, the brand originates from a deep understanding of consumers' everyday lives and a full understanding of the ecosystem of demand, but the brand also becomes part of that external culture.

The addition of the MINI to the BMW Group brand portfolio illustrates this cultural process of brand development.

The BMW MINI

The new MINI has its roots in the original British Mini or Mini Cooper of the early 1960s, an automotive icon and cult brand designed for the volume or mass market of that time. But beyond these roots, the new MINI, as it is also called, is a lot less British and a lot more BMW. The timeless standards of its design have been respected as much as possible inside and outside of the car. It still has the speedometer in the center of the dashboard. Under the skin, though, it is built according to the BMW Group standards. It is larger and more muscular than its predecessor and features the latest automobile technology. In stark contrast to the original, it is a premium car positioned to a very different target group.

The MINI's success lies in its crystal clear brand identity and positioning in the market toward a specific youth culture of today, its role within the portfolio of the BMW Group, and the contextual activation of this positioning.

The MINI is positioned as the embodiment of a small car with an unequaled uniqueness and charm. It is love at first sight. It exudes the irreverence and fun of the original Mini. It stands clearly apart from the BMW brand, which is more synonymous with sportiness and dynamics and the joy of driving. If BMW has an air of exclusivity, the MINI is more integrative.

Apart from this reminiscence of the original Mini and its differentiation from the BMW brand, the MINI seems altogether a very different idea and new concept. It is as if the MINI were designed from the outside in, drawing inspiration much more from the social-cultural context of today and a broadly defined youthful target market of consumers, somewhere between twenty-five and thirty-five years old (although drivers may be significantly older), open minded, and highly educated—a segment of consumers who cherish the premium nature of the BMW car but would reject premium as a form of self-expression.

Consider its visual identity and language. Clearly different from the original Mini and the BMW, it is based on the so-called frame—a black background and colors that are fresh and simple. It uses the codes of the fashionistas of today, where black is cool and a symbol of the technoculture. The simple and straightforward look matters. Its target customers are not just design aware but design forward, and they see substance in style. The latest and most advanced technology is a table stake. Antiestablishment with a world view is in, while establishment (BMW) is out. If the new MINI were simply a retro-design car, like the T-Bird or the new VW Beetle, though, it would be considered lame—even a bit out of place in today's culture. To fit into the lives of today's target, the MINI needed a lot more excitement and power.

The new MINI fits into the cultural context where IKEA is popular and ubiquitous, on the premise that good design is democratic and can be everywhere, and the low-price retailers Zara and H&M solve the contradiction of old that high fashion has to be expensive. The new MINI picks up on this cultural code and climate of today. It says premium does not have to be exclusive.

The launch of the MINI, in a sense the way the brand behaves, was orchestrated consistently to build its brand identity with an audience in mind that is media savvy and rejects being marketed to. Fifteen months before the launch, MINI created a virtual world on the Internet where, curiously, there was no discussion about the new MINI, the product or its specifications. All communication was merely about the ideas, values, and the concept behind the MINI. The frequently changing content focused on issues of music, fashion, art, and design, and served as pure entertainment and dialogue with a specific audience. There were auctions of very cool high-tech products like the world radio. This world was a pure cultural expression of the contexts, lives, myths, archetypes, and cultural codes and symbolism of the target audience. It existed at a time when the terms *viral marketing* and *buzz marketing* were not even coined yet, but the fifteen months of this virtual world had the same effect. The new MINI became a massive topic of conversation with the right people in the right places.

Over time, as this aspiring cultural context grew, communication changed. Slowly, the product was inserted, first virtually and later through numerous events at places where the audience could be found—design exhibitions, art shows, and trendy hangouts anywhere in Milan, Paris, London, or Singapore. Importantly, the MINI was never promoted out of context, because it wasn't just about the car. The MINI was the lead "actor" in the 2003 film *The Italian Job*. It even was inserted innovatively into massive culture events and gatherings. Consider the MINI as a spectator at NBA games. Placing the car into the audience required more than one seat ticket—it took over twenty seats. Compare this clever promotion with an alternative such as appearing on a large billboard or being announced as the proud sponsor during halftime—something that would be more appropriate for the BMW brand, or not.

The New Branding Model

With the MINI brand, the BMW Group illustrates a new branding model, one in which the brand is not simply built around a product. This new model does not simply call for linking functional, emotional, and self-expressive benefits to a high-quality product. Instead, it begins with a concept of culture and the context of consumers' everyday lives. It's not just about messaging from the inside out. It originates outside the company and develops there. It flips the classic model of branding on its head.[10] The lasting success of the MINI over other retro-design cars has to do with the adoption of this new model of branding.

This model is germane to the DIG model and naturally follows from it. When strategists begin with a deep understanding of the ecosystem of consumer demand and develop a demand landscape, they define the rich cultural context in which people live, work, and play. But the DIG model does not stop simply at the level of discovery and understanding of the culture and the processes that create the culture. It further focuses the thinking toward structuring the opportunity space and toward activating the demand-first growth platforms.

Early in his tenure as CEO, A. G. Lafley pushed Procter & Gamble into this sort of radical thinking with the objective to expand the understanding of its brands and their roles in capturing the ecosystem of consumer demand. Should Crest simply be the best toothpaste brand, or should it position itself as an authority on oral care? Conceptualizing Crest as an authority on oral care requires this fundamental shift of looking at the brand from the outside in. It requires an understanding of the context of consumers' everyday lives, the role of health, the role of oral care. Such a rethinking of the opportunity space of its brands has been enormously successful for Procter & Gamble, as described in chapter 2.

Indeed, such thinking can have profound implications for the business. What if Cunard had defined itself not as a shipping company but as a transportation company in the early 1900s—a more transcendent idea across the various cultures from the turn of the century to today. It might have grown into a company bigger than UPS, Lufthansa, and FedEx combined, instead of contracting sharply in the current market to the status of a cruise ship operator. What if UPS had chosen to define itself not just as a shipping company but as a global supply chain manager? For State Street Corporation, the successful transformation of the company was accompanied by a redefinition of the brand not around the profitable transaction business but around an information business. When Richard Harrington, CEO of the Canadian media conglomerate Thomson, inherited a several-billion-dollar newspaper business, he charted it into new waters, selling its significant newspaper assets while building through a series of acquisitions and spending over $8 billion to create Thomson, an integrated information provider to financial, legal, scientific, and health and educational markets. Does Steve Jobs think of Apple as a computer company?

A demand-first and outside-in perspective nearly always challenges the current business definition, the brand strategy, and what a company stands for. A demand perspective can serve a meaningful purpose for a business's innovation and growth agenda. And it should. But when it does, it does so from the perspective of the context or culture of consumers' everyday lives. From the outside in, the question becomes how to develop the opportunities in plain sight that are presented to a company or business.

We'll close this chapter with a short recap of the Intel story, to emphasize the significance of viewing the brand challenge from multiple perspectives—the typical perspective as well as the demand-first perspective. Intel illustrates how the outside-in perspective can lead to a change of not just the brand, as the face of the business strategy, but the business itself.

Ideas in the Lead at Intel

In 1985, the seventeen-year-old Intel Corporation was deeply engaged in the memory business. Intel and its customers stored their digital memories on silicon chips—the wafer-thin, finely etched integrated circuits invented by Intel cofounder Robert Noyce in 1959. Intel's first product was a 64-bit memory chip.[11] Over time and in accordance with Moore's Law—as set forth in a landmark 1965 paper by Intel cofounder Gordon Moore, who famously and accurately predicted that computer memories would double in density every eighteen months—the company developed chip memories with increasing numbers of transistors packed closer together. For a time, they were the best in the world.

As the undisputed originator of the memory chip business, Intel enjoyed all the typical first-mover advantages, including an almost 100 percent share of the market for nearly a decade. By the early 1970s, however, a handful of U.S. competitors (including the long-since-forgotten Unisem and Mostek) had entered the fray, only to be quickly dispatched by overwhelmingly dominant industry leader Intel, as a result of its superior technological edge. By the 1980s, Japanese chip makers were aggressively whittling away at Intel's lead by offering products superior to Intel's in both quality and price. As Intel president Andrew S. Grove later recalled, "In the 1980s, the competition became better than us." Intel's competitive response, once again according to Grove, was to boost its production quality status from "okay" to "superb."

Yet the Japanese just kept on coming and getting better and better. "Their principal weapon," Grove later ruefully recalled, "was the availability of high-quality product priced astonishingly low." By 1985, Grove found himself sitting in his office with a grim-faced Moore, facing "a crisis of mammoth proportions":

> Our mood was downbeat. I looked out the window at the Ferris wheel of the Great America amusement park revolving in the distance, then I turned back to Gordon and I asked, "If we got kicked out and the board brought in a new CEO, what do you think he would do?" Gordon

answered without hesitation, "he would get us out of memories." I stared at him, numb, then said, "Why shouldn't you and I walk out the door, come back, and do it ourselves?"

Grove and Moore's symbolic decision to fire—and then, being equal opportunity employers, to rehire—themselves is a tale of gritty, hardy survivors who, after years of stoic denial, face the harsh reality of their situation and do something radical and dramatic about it. Yet it is also possible to see this as a story fundamentally about *seeing*: about having the courage to step outside the blinkered and narrow confines of one's perceptions, of lifting the smoke screen, of cleansing the doors of perception to see the infinite opportunities in plain sight.

In his mind's eye, Grove, past master of the "strategic inflection point," *saw* himself walking (with Moore) out the door of Intel, *saw* himself looking back at Intel, and *saw* himself *seeing* something new about Intel from the outside in. That something new was an Intel that was no longer in the memory business, but was flourishing in the newer, higher-margin microprocessor business. He envisioned—correctly—the future of Intel. He had, in the parlance of this book, expanded or recalibrated the opportunity space for his firm and his brand so that it could reposition itself not just to survive, but to thrive, in the coming decades.

Chapter Eight

Connecting with and Engaging Customers

G ROWING IN NEW MARKETS, reinventing the business model and transforming the company, expanding into adjacent markets, and building new demand-first growth platforms create enormous brand challenges. An important brand challenge is to connect with and engage consumers. Without doing it, a company cannot create customer advantage. There are five major guidelines.

1. Challenging Assumptions and Held Beliefs

The toughest challenge for the strategist is to recognize that the current well-thought-out business and brand strategy needs to evolve or be changed. Management has invested so much to develop and implement the positioning, to write a clear and concise statement of what the business and brand stand for. A vision statement has been written and a mission statement published. The brand identity system and structure have been developed. A brand strategy manual has been written. Documents show exactly how the brand should be expressed across consumer touch points. The positioning has most likely been implemented and results displayed in consumer research studies. The communications partners have been educated, and they understand how to support the execution against the brand positioning. Good branding principles laud consistency.

Nevertheless, it is precisely at this point, when everything important seems to have been accomplished, that it becomes so vitally necessary to confront the business and brand with the realities found in the ever-changing ecosystem of demand—a cold and unbiased demand-first view from the outside in—and to *challenge the assumptions and beliefs that underlie the positioning.*

Look at Electronics Arts (EA), the gaming company that has grown nicely and dominates the top spot among like companies. If you are the strategist for such a company with such a strong gaming heritage and a record of success in producing blockbuster video games like *Monday Night Football* and *Madden NFL Football*, it would be precisely the right thing to do to focus on what you do best, to strengthen your core competencies, and to watch the marvel of consistent strategy take its course. Precisely not! The ecosystem of demand that this company faces is changing rapidly (gaming is becoming mainstream, for example). Positioning becomes not a one-off exercise every five years but a dynamic and continuous process based on a strong and clear brand identity system. It would require challenging the dominant view of EA as a gaming company in response to the ever-increasing balkanization of its industry borders. A more appropriate view of the company, a way to reframe the opportunity space, would be to see it as a sports management, media, and production company, a sports company like Nike, or an entertainment company like Fox, MySpace.com, or any combination.[1]

The focus of brand strategy must inevitably shift toward a greater emphasis on how the brand and the business contribute to the total transformative experience of consumers as people living, working, and playing, in addition to defining how emotional benefits link to tangible proof points and reasons to believe in the product. This represents a shift from product to consumers, or people in the social-cultural context. Procter & Gamble must define the dish detergent Dawn Direct Foam no longer simply around its grease-cutting power but around the challenge of getting kids involved in the household chores. If you are Kodak, are you really in the silver halide film business? Should you really position yourself as the company that can give people the best film roll or digital camera, or are you in the business of managing the memories of people's lives?

Such "reframing" creates new perspectives about the business and brand and can lead to exciting new and different ways of building the brand—not only through communicating it but through creating new and interactive experiences. The experience creates the brand. If this experience is an authentic part of culture, it builds the brand through a natural cultural process. Brand building here is particularly effective if channeled within the confines of a company's well-defined demand-first growth platforms. Creating such experiences and processes will require more than communications and creativity; it will require the mobilization of a full spectrum of new capabilities to contextualize the brand in culture and daily life. Media will be the new creative tools. The grand prize is that the brand ultimately engages consumers and ensures that customers assimilate and absorb the product or service or innovation and make it part of their lives and cultural context.

2. Making the Brand Part of Culture

Another essential step in achieving customer advantage is to mobilize the organization around the strategy of the firm and the role of the brands and the portfolio in capturing a larger share of the ecosystem of demand. The BMW Group provides an excellent case study. The company deploys a comprehensive and continuous process to ensure that all efforts, all activities of the firm, the entire innovation and growth agenda are aligned with its vision of a multi–master brand strategy.

When the BMW Group develops a new car, it assigns several hundred people from engineering, design, production, marketing, purchasing, and finance to its Research and Innovation Center, called FIZ, for several years.[2] This effort fully immerses a group of people into a virtual world of the ecosystem of demand of consumers for some time.

Equally, from a brand perspective, the BMW Group uses immersion to ensure that there is a deep and comprehensive understanding among BMW Group employees of how its master brands integrate into its new house-of-brands architecture and how it is experienced by consumers. The role of the Brand Academy is illustrative of the diligence and care with which this company operates. In 2002 the BMW Group created its own Brand Academy, a state-of-the-art learning sanctuary positioned adjacent to the group's distinctive multicylinder-shaped headquarters in Munich today. The Brand Academy was premised on the notion that employees are generally skeptical toward any kind of internal branding approach and that the company's approach had to exceed everything thus far created in its industry.[3]

During a typical one-day event, participants at the Brand Academy—typically senior executives and managers, dealers, and other key employees—are provided with a unique opportunity not only to passively learn about their brands but also to actively experience them in specially appointed brand rooms. Before the day is over, participants have engaged in diverse and intellectually challenging events ranging from classic classroom work to the making of brand movies to the hands-on creation of an automobile.

The Brand Academy is, quite literally, a house of brands, in which a distinctive suite of rooms and all-enveloping sensory environments have been designed to exemplify from a multisensory perspective the most salient attitudes and attributes of the brand. The company's multiple premium brand strategy is executed with precision as a fully immersive brand environment. Over twenty-five hundred people spend a day in the Brand Academy each year, building the foundation for a successful brand orientation of the BMW Group and hence a splendid future for its premium brand portfolio.

From a management perspective, the issue of transforming the organization as a whole from a branded house to a house of brands required the institution and implementation of a change management process within the culture, in which all brand values are coherently communicated across the organization to employees. The evolution of the Brand Academy began with a determination of the key messages to be communicated across the organization. Based on questions such as "What modules need to be developed in order to best internally communicate these key messages?" the messages were focused on two characteristics: the importance of brand in general to the BMW Group and the importance of the multiple premium brand portfolio strategy to the overall strength of the BMW Group. The notion was to make BMW's people more sensitive to the importance of the brand, to get people excited about the possibilities of the brand, and above all, to understand and experience the brand.

The learning experience imparted at the academy was designed to provide answers to the following questions:

- What makes a brand strong?

- What do the various brands and the BMW Group stand for?

- How do the different brands within the BMW Group differentiate from each other and from the competition?

- How does the BMW Group manage the brand portfolio?

The training facility enables participants to experience and immerse themselves in a multisensory environment, or "psychological learning path," that conveys mainly in tactile fashion the core values of the three brands within the larger branded house. The brand values are conveyed along multiple dimensions: sensibility/inspiration, understanding, anchoring, and realization/implementation.

What is truly unique about BMW's Brand Academy is that it is a permanent institution and not a transitory experience, which companies often create at a dealership, at a trade show, or by means of an industrial film or video. This is a place to go back to and reflect on a brand as an experience. This is the core, the center, even a shrine, if you will, which can be visited again and again, for the group's internal marketing program. Above all, it is a place where one can have a serious discussion about the brand strategy. And a place to persuade even the most hard-core engineers that there is something more than designing that drive train, than the technology and the product and their attributes. This center provides a continuous platform for learning and enhancing the sense of differentiation between brand and product and the context of the ecosystem of life. This is internal marketing on steroids.

Even after the training program, the contact to the brand and brand content is not lost. The participants are accompanied through an Internet platform in order to support the transfer of the brand work into the daily business through active brand knowledge.

"In premium you deliver an emotional value to the customer," BMW chairman Helmut Panke recalled. "When a customer decides for BMW or Mercedes, they want to have a specific characteristic. It's about what the vehicle *feels like* to them."[4] At the Brand Academy, this emotionality is tactilely experienced.

3: Find Customers Where They Are

After making the brand part of the culture inside the firm, the firm needs to communicate, to connect the brand with consumers, and to engage them. The strategist can guide this process through activating demand-first growth platforms. Ultimately, the challenge is to have consumers absorb and assimilate the brand into their lives, to make the brand part of their culture.

To make a brand part of the culture requires that the brand *fit in* the cultural context and daily life rather than *stand out*. Relevance, connection, and engagement within a demand cluster take center stage over differentiation and messaging to "cutting through the clutter."

Effectively, the classic communications model inverts.[5] What is that classic model? It implies a funnel-shaped downward progression of consumers from awareness to interest, to desire, and, ultimately, to purchase and loyalty. At the top of the funnel is the entire population of potential buyers who become aware of the product through communications; at the bottom is the far smaller number of those who actually purchase the product. At each downward stage, advertising and other marketing tools bombard consumers with product and brand messages to push the dwindling number of potential consumers along toward the point of purchase, culminating in a sales transaction.

In the new and inverted communications model, greater resources need to be directed to the points nearest to consumption and usage as defined in the demand clusters. This requires activating a broad array of programs that address the activities and touch points in each cluster in which a narrow set of passionate consumers engage in the context of consumers' everyday lives.

There is a much smaller role for and lower value of the simplistic messaging of a single word or one-sentence positioning through expensive classic media channels. If you want to position Pampers, for example, instead of communicating the unique selling proposition of superior dryness through maximum reach (to as many people as possible) and frequency (as often as possible), you engage consumers around how to enhance a child's development. This would include specific programs—daily, weekly or monthly—for the various stages of development—from pregnancy to new baby to toddler to the preschooler stage when the child is twenty-four months old or more. The programs are designed to create a transformative experience for the parent and child that includes the role of Pampers and its superior brand promise. The goal is to capture influencers who transmit to others, and to capture the dynamics and complexities of the evolving ecosystem of demand directly and intimately by orchestrating the "influencer" consumer experience through embedding the product, service, or brand in core or passionate consumers' everyday lives, the cultural context and myths, archetypes, and mental models of everyday life. Communications synchronizes in lockstep with the consumption and use experience rather than with the consumer learning model of the past.

Activating a broad array of programs does not simply imply playing the integrated marketing communications piano with ten keys, starting with advertising, print, sponsorship, events, and other promotions. It means fully taking advantage of the current and emerging possibilities to strike up conversations with core or passionate consumers as the individuals they are, and leveraging the current advances in technology, marketing, entertainment, and media. This takes us from video and audio that used to be available exclusively on TV or radio, to iPods, PCs, mobile phones, and even outdoor billboards. It ranges from interruption marketing to permission and viral marketing not only that consumers invite in but also that makes them producers of media in the form of so-called user-generated media—blogs, videoblogs (or vlogs), photologs, or videologs.

The entire effort needs to be managed much more proactively in a media-agnostic or media-neutral way, a creative form of combining alternatives within the context of demand-first growth platforms. It is no longer a let's-spend-it-and-hope-they-will-see-us approach. We liken this new approach to the effective drilling of an oil well, where maximum pressure is applied to the subsurface stone encasing the oil, not to where the drill enters the ground. Likewise, our inverted funnel (which is no longer a funnel at all) devotes resources at each stage of the consumption and use cycle and process with the goal of optimizing the impact on customers at the end stage. This makes the product or brand contextually relevant, and culturally fit in specific and tangible ways. The classic communications model may be called the mass market awareness model because its goal is to maximize reach and frequency. The new model may be called the 1,440-minute model because it seeks to maximize the amount of time—its share of time—in the customer's life. If you are Starbucks, you want have more of the 1,440 minutes all of us live every day. If you are Pampers, you want not only to be recognized for superior dryness but also for being relevant from the months before birth through the child's early development.

Reviving Volkswagen

Inverting the funnel and spending along the entire consumption or use process works differently and makes brand building a cultural process that is more natural and authentic. An excellent application of this new model of communications comes from the effort of reviving the Volkswagen GTI brand in America. The effort began with the launch of the new GTI in the spring of 2006, that original "pocket rocket" that appeals to primarily young males, the tuner crowd, and longtime VW devotees. These auto enthusiasts have a need for speed, and the GTI was historically the car that gave more speed per dollar than any other car in the hot hatch segment. The genius in this new and gutsy effort lies in branding of not just the car—touting product features and handling attributes—but in branding around a cultural myth and belief system particularly strongly held by the passionate GTI target customer. The effort picks up on the well-known and pervasive myth of the rebel—a streak of defiance, bucking the norm, and refusal to accept authority—that is so central to the American male culture. The modern-day expression of rebellion makes James Dean look too extreme, too far out. It manifests itself in daily life in a set of milder and "undesirable" behaviors that we all know too well. Research showed the hot hatch enthusiast target market is more likely to dislike observing the speed limit, is more likely to drive faster than traffic, and will pay a premium for an engine with more horsepower. They love tuning and customization, but some enthusiasts think that some tuning, particularly in Japanese cars, is overdone and too showy.

VW picked up on this rebel myth of American culture and developed symbolism, iconography, designs, and expressions around the GTI launch that fit the culture of the target audience like a glove. As Kerri Martin, the executive in charge of brand innovation at VW, remarks, "We want to create culture and become part of culture."[6] One key symbol became the "Fast," a quirky, mischievous-looking brand icon that expressed in a tangible way the rebellious myth. The Fast was launched by inviting five thousand GTI enthusiasts to visit a Web site called ProjectFAST.com and participate in a nationwide research experiment exploring the psychological and social concept of *fast*. By answering a series of questions, the visitors designed their "own" brand icon. One question, for example was, If Fast had eyes, which shape would they be? The Web site journey concluded with the creation of the Fast, and the text read, "Inside most, but not all of us, there is a Fast. And according to data we collected from thousands of respondents it looks a little something like this. Maybe you've never thought about what your Fast looks like. But when we designed the GTI MK V, we did. We thought about what Fast smells like and how much it weighs and what it eats for breakfast. It's all we thought about. Because we wanted this GTI to make your fast happy." Visitors then see the mischievous-looking brand icon they created that represents the need for speed. Not coincidentally, the features of this rabbit-inspired icon shared several key design features with the GTI. For example, the mouth of the icon had the same shape and red-on-black color of the GTI front grille, and it had interchangeable tails inspired by the golf ball shifter from the original GTI MK I. Long before the GTI was even available, the Web site became a huge topic of conversation on the Internet. Traffic picked up to over a hundred thousand on the site, and the Fast soon was traded on eBay at prices up to $600. You could also get it for free with a purchase of a GTI. Auto dealers reported significant increase in traffic to showrooms for test drives. Conversations among the target customers were further stirred up through invitations to take a quiz: "How well do you know your Fast? Take the quiz inside and find out." The quiz was distributed in a very innovative brochure that departed significantly from the typical automotive collateral and material.

Another key feature of the GTI launch effort was the *configurator*. This is a Web site where enthusiasts could configure their GTI and in conclusion take a test drive with Helga, a dominatrix who also starred in the subsequent TV commercials together with Wolfgang, a fictitious German engineer who loves to "unpimp the auto." The configurator Web site became a huge traffic generator; the three main TV commercials were downloaded in huge numbers and distributed over YouTube, generating over 2 million hits. Billboard advertising supported the effort with unique headlines; three examples are, "Auf Wiedersehen, sucka," "German engineering in da haus," and "Fast as schnell." A massive number of blogs have been written generating discussions about every aspect of the GTI launch effort, and some enthusiasts created their own Web sites.

The effort drew the consumer into the story of the launch and engaged the target audience with the GTI, starting with a narrow but passionate consumer base. The various launch activities were carefully orchestrated to steer the process for potential buyers, to get into conversations with them, and to encourage and facilitate a cultural process. The effort began even before the GTI was available. The sales results and showroom traffic generated were extremely positive for VW.

This emphasis on experience, usage, and behavior in context changes communications in a radical way. In comparison, the mass-market awareness approach to get consumers through the purchase funnel or brand funnel is far less effective. It becomes far more important to work with the right iconography, the right contextual codes, the mood of the times, and cultural expression. It is far more important to work in a context-specific way and to steer and become part of the cultural process. This approach is valuable for branding and communicating a new product but can work particularly well in building and communicating the brand of an institution, like the United Nations; a leading hospital, like the M. D. Anderson Cancer Center; a university; or even a country.

Building a Country Brand

Consider, for example, the case of Germany. Image campaigns abound that try to communicate about Germany and its modernity, but none of these efforts are as powerful as the brand-building efforts during 2006, when Germany hosted the 2006 FIFA World Cup, the most important competition in soccer. It is well known that soccer plays an enormously important role of identity in German culture. It is a significant part of everyday life. The following story provides a showcase for how the new brand-building and communications model works.

The German team was coached by Juergen Klinsmann, a former German star who, as a player, had helped Germany win the 1990 event and the UEFA European Championship in 1996 and who had retired from soccer in California. When Klinsmann became the German national team coach in 2004, he inherited a relatively young group of players and a team that had lost in the first round of the 2004 European Championship, an unthinkable failure for Germany. Germany's fans were divided about the prospects of their team for the upcoming 2006 competition, with public opinion primarily ranging from negative to extremely pessimistic. A major disappointment for Germany was looming.

Against this background or social-situational context, the performance of the German national team in the World Cup was a huge success—it finished in third place. Most significantly, Germans in Germany and everywhere else united as a country to embrace the team's success. They turned the entire World Cup hosting opportunity into a positive and memorable experience and a display of German values, culture, and the brand.

Several factors came together to create a perfect context for building and reinforcing the brand of Germany, many of which have to do with some key leadership decisions of Klinsmann, the new head coach. First, he built the team for the World Cup from the same players who lost in the 2004 UEFA European Championship competition. Despite their failure in the competition, the inexperience of many of his players at the international level, and the naysayers in the media and the public, Klinsmann made the team the center of his effort, instilled a positive esprit de corps, and gave them an unbelievable stretch goal: win the World Cup! Klinsmann thought that this was the only acceptable goal because of German culture and the successful history of Germany's national team (*Die Mannschaft*) in international competitions.

Klinsmann then selected Joachim Loew, Andy Koepke, and Oliver Bierhoff to be the management team within the German national team. Each of these assistants had his own successful football career, each was considered smart and very successful, and each had a physical presence that radiated confidence and a can-do attitude. They stood for the best in German football—and they represented the mythical model of success in Germany. Individually and collectively, they helped convey Klinsmann's message to the German players and the German public—that Germany was ready to succeed in the World Cup.

The combination of a new head coach who had come back from semiretirement in America and the appointment of three former but popular and successful German players to the management team instilled an optimistic outlook in the national team, and created an underdog persona and a sympathetic, likeable, and friendly character for a team with nothing to lose and the will to pursue the only goal worthy of commitment: to win against the best.

Klinsmann found a way to take the spirit in the team to the people, engage them in the process long before the first World Cup game, and build a campaign of support for the team. First was the style of play, an important element of success in the game. Klinsmann developed a style that was built on historical German strengths but also supported the capabilities and interests of his younger-generation players. This reinforced the team as an authentic German selection with the will to succeed. In stark contrast to extant practice in soccer, where coaches or spokespersons broadcast messages on TV, Klinsmann then made the team openly available to the German public. Rather than having the team train in seclusion, hidden from cameras and the press, Klinsmann encouraged its exposure. He even located the team's World Cup headquarters in the nation's capital, Berlin, so the team was training in the "heart" of Germany. Klinsmann even allowed the players to go out in public during their free time. He repeatedly explained through the media and demonstrated with activities such as open training sessions that the team was Germany's team, a team of the people. Prechampionship exposure in the media of every effort and movement of the national team or the coach was at an all-time high, including press coverage, intensive discussions, and word-of-mouth communications on the Internet and live.

Klinsmann's own soft-spoken personality and style of leadership of hard work, focus, and confidence reinforced some essential core values. His style became a catalyst for the entire team and mobilized the German public and fans around the world. When the team placed third in the competition, its performance far exceeded expectations. The nation celebrated. Over a million German fans came out to say thank you to their team the day after the third-place match. Since Germany was the host of the World Cup, the third place finish was an ideal time for the German team to bow out of the competition as the perfect host.

The coach had led the way in making the team and its effort a symbol of the important values of Germany, a work ethic and a belief system that drew in first soccer fans, then the German public, and then many other nations, both participating and not participating in the World Cup. Klinsmann himself personified these values as the leader who builds a team that wins against the odds, and who unites his players and succeeds in the face of adversity by going against convention. This model of leadership is a myth in many cultures, including Germany's, that becomes a story of the brand that draws people in and engages them. While Klinsmann could not plan the magnitude of the success for Germany stemming from the World Cup competition, as the coach, he set high goals, practiced inclusion, and championed German culture, to become a powerful builder of the brand of Germany. The story of his leadership and the success of the team on the FIFA World Cup stage became a story of the fans and people in Germany, a cultural process that was magnified through all possible forms of communications anywhere.[7]

At the other end of the spectrum are niche brands that benefit from this new form of brand building—special-interest brands in areas such as eco-travel or athletics with a narrow customer base. A brand like Tauck World

Tours, for example, which orchestrates some of the most exquisite discovery and travel experiences, would benefit from drawing in a very select clientele using the inverted brand-building model rather than marketing to a general audience. Here, branding is not a conquest or marketing warfare, with positioning and targeting, but a form of attraction, of creating pull toward a powerful idea. Many brands in the so-called long tail will benefit from this model of communications. These brands benefit far less from branded entertainment, or product placement on steroids, where products and brands are integrated seamlessly into films, television, music, gaming, and theater performances as a way to showcase the brands' relevance in context because they are too passive. Such context-neutral communication often promotes brand image, big ideas, and new advertising slogans in clever or grandiose ways: the Energizer Bunny promoting battery life, for one example, or whiter clothes creating happier marriages, for another.

Context-relevant and culturally sensitive communication that fits into the cultural process, as shown in the story of the World Cup in Germany, by contrast engages the audience and cuts the distance, or even reverses the sequence from learning to point of purpose of product usage and consumption, making communications personal, interactive, direct, and ubiquitous. In a way, it is not about communication but about creating conversations. It tries to connect in the most relevant way by determining when, where, and how to reach consumers in their everyday lives, and connecting with and engaging people when and where they are living, playing, working, and consuming—not interrupting them to gain their attention, but enhancing their experience of everyday life. For companies to achieve this, planning has to become media agnostic and media neutral.

Procter & Gamble illustrates the commercial means of working in the new form of brand building and the paradigm of relevance, connection, and engagement in still another form. Procter & Gamble strikes up conversations with people taking care of the home by using massive word-of-mouth communications. It's called Vocalpoint, a database of six hundred thousand women who have large social networks and chat with a lot of other mothers.[8] Gone is the marketing messaging and razor-sharp focus of product messages and benefits to targeted consumers.

Procter & Gamble begins with the clustering or segmenting of consumers not only through optimal media buying of TV time but by building powerful "connectors" through recruiting on social networking sites like iVillage or MySpace.com or through monitoring podcasting, blogging, and photo-sharing sites. These sites are virtual worlds where consumers share and voluntarily express their opinions, feelings, and everyday lives with others—even strangers. Photo-sharing sites, for example, allow people to upload photos for everyone to see. Some keep diaries in the form of blogs—there are over 14 million today. Podcasting, in which consumers create short segments of audio or video clips that can be downloaded on iPods—hence the name *podcasting*—like blogs or photo-sharing sites, is a way for consumers to express to others what bothers them and what is happening in their lives, here and now.

4: Leverage the Contextual and Cultural Code

Textbook recommendations for marketers from time immemorial have revolved around emotionalizing the product message to consumers. Another tack has been to define the brand beyond the product and express emotional or personal benefits. Harley-Davidson created a fervent cult and a great business by emphasizing strong personality, the polarizing emotion of owning a hog, and powerful attributes like patriotism and independence, deep-seated cultural values of society. Driving a Harley became more than just riding a bike from point A to point B. As a Harley executive was quoted as saying in *Results-Based Leadership*, "What we sell is the ability of a 43-year-old accountant to dress in black leather, ride through small towns, and have people be afraid of him."[9] In effect, the product itself, whether it was the bike or the merchandise associated with it, provided the starting point for expressing a powerful emotional connection, affiliation, and message that resonated with riders around the United States. Harley became a branded community of people who wished to express their self-identity through ownership.

American Express and Visa built their brands in precisely the same way. The classic American Express campaign, "Membership has its privileges," positioned the brand as the upscale credit card, or the choice of payment for an elite group or whoever wanted to belong to the class. Visa developed a positioning around the luxury of global travel and the sheer ubiquity of its card—"It's everywhere you want to be." Visa is the "it" that you should always have with you because it is accepted worldwide. Visa essentially emotionalized the product or a particular feature, namely global acceptance of the card—an incredible and amazing achievement. These approaches worked for both cards. American Express and Visa took market share from the leader, MasterCard. MasterCard was de-positioned in the trilogy of competitors as the "people's card," the card for everyone and no one. Master-Card suffered losses in market share to the low twenties.

However, MasterCard followed a very different recipe to success. Instead of emotionalizing the card (which was, in any event, a commodity and something consumers cared little for—they already had Visa or American Express in their wallets anyway) or emotionalizing a feature, Master-Card leveraged the emotional context and cultural codes of a particular moment and episode that really mattered in consumers' everyday lives and strongly linked MasterCard to these emotional moments.

MasterCard

By October 1996, when Larry Flanagan joined MasterCard International as senior vice president of advertising for the United States, the most popular credit card company in the world was in deep trouble. Flanagan, a former marketing director for the beauty-care division of P&G, with a stint at L'Oréal before joining MasterCard, had been brought aboard to help stem the tide threatening to swamp onetime industry leader MasterCard from longtime competitors Visa and American Express, lately aided and abetted by Sears's brash newcomer, Discover. In a climate of brutal "economic Darwinism," MasterCard faced potential extinction. As Flanagan recalled the typical mind-set of bankers at the time, "Just as nobody ever got fired for buying IBM years ago, no banker ever got fired for choosing Visa over MasterCard."[10] Some MasterCard executives sincerely believed it was merely a matter of time before MasterCard was "pushed into the sea."

MasterCard Incorporated, now a publicly traded company, was originally created by United California Bank, Wells Fargo, Crocker Bank, and the Bank of California as a competitor to the BankAmericard issued by the Bank of America, which over time morphed into the Visa card now issued by Visa International. In 1967, the name "Master Charge" was licensed by this consortium of California banks from the First National Bank of Louisville, Kentucky, and with the help of New York's Marine Midland Bank (now HSBC), the California consortium joined forces with the Interbank Card Association (ICA) to create "Master Charge: The Interbank Card." In 1980, Master Charge was rebranded and shortened to "MasterCard."

Despite its smaller market share, American Express enjoyed a far more secure position in the industry than MasterCard leading into the mid-'90s. Yet, it too had gone through a rough patch a few years before in 1991, when a group of disgruntled Boston restaurant owners and longtime AmEx customers had staged what they called a "Boston Fee Party," a vehement protest to underscore their distress at being obliged to pay far higher fees to American Express than to either Visa or MasterCard. Newly appointed Travel and Related Services Division president Kenneth Chenault went to great lengths to repair relations with American Express's dissatisfied merchants. But by 1994, following a 7 percent revenue decline in 1993, American Express was back on track, pressing its advantage in 1995 by releasing the Delta SkyMiles Optima Card, the first of many co-branded products.

Yet even as American Express aggressively expanded its reach, it continued to enjoy—unlike its bourgeois competitors—great success by expertly segmenting and targeting only the most affluent consumers. The American Express card was not just a way to purchase goods, it was an exclusive club reserved for the truly elite, as was ably reflected in its tagline, "Membership has its privileges." Visa, for its part, had also strengthened its brand image by positioning itself against American Express and ignoring MasterCard in its advertising altogether. Visa commercials featured consumers in exotic locations buying goods and services better suited to the champagne-and-caviar than Joe Six-pack crowd. By latching onto American Express, Visa was able to project a high-class image onto its card for the masses while simultaneously promising the ubiquity, low cost, and convenience that American Express so conspicuously lacked. It was a powerful unique selling proposition (USP).

MasterCard, for its part, faced an increasingly challenging marketing environment. While two tough competitors had staked a claim on the high end of the market, and even though MasterCard's global reach and merchant network were now every bit as extensive as Visa's, the brand could not shake customer perceptions that it was, on the one hand, low end and, on the other, less expedient and functional than Visa.

With MasterCard's two main competitors fighting tooth and nail to dominate customer associations with luxury and global acceptance as key differentiators, it seemed inadvisable for the company to adopt a "me too" positioning and brand-building campaign. Yet, for a while, that is precisely what MasterCard did. Over ten years, it changed its direction several times, launching five major advertising campaigns, sowing little more than chaos and confusion in the minds of its customers and potential customers.

Between 1990 and 1996, MasterCard had gained market share in just two of the six years leading up to Flanagan's appointment in 1996. Over the same period, the brand's market share slipped from 37.6 percent of bank cards to 35.9 percent, despite several hundred million dollars in advertising. Both Visa and American Express stole market share from MasterCard.

Yet even as Visa and American Express were pushing in on MasterCard from above, the newly arrived Discover Card was aggressively pressuring MasterCard from below. Discover was especially appealing to price-sensitive consumers because of its "cash back" feature, which provided Discover Card holders with a few cents back on every dollar they spent on credit. While Discover had an edge in terms of day-to-day functionality, Visa maintained its perceived edge in functionality for luxury, travel, and global acceptance. MasterCard was in danger of losing everything: market share, credibility with customers, merchant relationships, and brand equity. And because Visa spent more than twice as much as MasterCard annually on marketing, and American Express and Discover each outspent MasterCard by tens of millions of dollars each year, MasterCard was rapidly losing its voice.

In 1997, Flanagan's newly installed marketing team decided to make its move. According to research conducted by Yankelovich Partners, a megashift was taking place in what consumers regarded as "signs of success." While the '80s had been a decade of abject materialism, epitomized by the Masters of the Universe lampooned in Tom Wolfe's *Bonfire of the Vanities*, by the mid-'90s, Yankelovich research revealed that abject materialism was fast falling out of fashion. Success was no longer measured by the quality of a person's *stuff* but by the quality of their life.

Success meant something other than conspicuous consumption and a capacity to show off a flashy car, a lavish hotel, ostentatious jewelry, or expensive designer clothing. While American Express and Visa had both fared well in this environment with advertisements glorifying acts of self-indulgence, MasterCard spied an opportunity to target not so much rich people, as people determined to lead a rich life.

The company's marketing executives under the direction of Flanagan began by exploring not how well its brand positioned relative to American Express and Visa, but how its brand fit into customers' daily lives and how the brand captured the shifting ecosystem of consumer needs, wants, desires, fantasies, and pleasures. The question became, What really mattered to them? What were the activities, projects, and things they wanted to accomplish in life and that created deep meaning? What were their everyday goals and life expectations? What did people do, not just what did they say they wanted to do? What were their priorities? And how could a mere credit card transform itself into an integral and prominent component in their everyday lives?

The research MasterCard commissioned drew marketers' attention to four basic truths:

- People care deeply about love and relationships.

- They value the freedom to do what they want and go where they please.

- They want more time to spend on things they want to do and less time wasted on activities they have to do.

- People desire security and physical, emotional, and financial freedom.

The research asked the question How can one build a brand in a world where people don't care about the differences of one commodity over the other? The functional differences and benefits between MasterCard and its competitors were and are, after all, rather trivial. The answer that Master-Card came up with was to leverage the contextual code of memorable moments in consumers' everyday lives with the link to the MasterCard brand.

This recognition, this epiphany, led to the creation of MasterCard's award-winning "Priceless" campaign, which was brilliantly conceptualized with the aid of now longtime agency partner McCann-Erickson/New York. Yet a popular misconception that "Priceless" is nothing more than an advertising story is belied by the facts. While MasterCard CMO Flanagan unhesitatingly credits McCann-Erickson for developing the "Priceless" concept and executing it brilliantly, the agency based its work on a detailed creative brief supplied by MasterCard, which had already established a clear set of strategic hurdles that a revitalized brand positioning needed to clear in order to ensure success.

Few people realize that the "Priceless" campaign very nearly never happened. MasterCard engaged five advertising agencies to flesh out its marketing strategy and craft an appropriate advertising message. Thirty-five concepts were presented to MasterCard's marketing team. Of these, two stood out above all others. "Priceless" was one of them. Extensive consumer research was conducted, and the results were tabulated: "Priceless" came in a far second. The board of directors, comprising executives from many of the world's largest financial institutions, was composed of bankers, not marketers, and they reacted to "Priceless" and the rival advertising concepts just as the research predicted they would. They preferred the other campaign very slightly to "Priceless." Fortunately, MasterCard's marketing executives knew the stakes were much higher than a single commercial. The next ad campaign was to form the basis of an entirely new positioning for the brand and guide the strategy of the company. The message would need to withstand the test of time and evolve to meet the challenges of an uncertain future. Marketing executives believed that the other advertising concept was too limiting. While it did not test quite as well, "Priceless" seemed to offer more range. Marketing executives eventually managed to persuade the board to go with "Priceless."

The final decision was based on selecting a stronger strategic platform with long-term prospects—a large cluster of moments, each with an emotional code that could be leveraged for the MasterCard brand and that captured a relevant and important part of the evolving ecosystem of consumer demand—over an exceptionally powerful single ad that scored extraordinarily well.

MasterCard's new integrated marketing materials—of which the advertising campaign was merely the most visible part—emphasized *memorable moments*. Rather than shouting from the rooftops ever more loudly about the same product-focused functional attributes, MasterCard's new campaign and branding efforts emphasized the role played by precious and "priceless" moments in cardholders' lives. The campaign explored a new brand positioning, meant to convey MasterCard's deep understanding of the fact that there are moments—many moments—that no amount of money can buy.

Ironically, this theme of "pricelessness" was artfully integrated in the campaign to connect with various "payment moments" associated with the use of the card. MasterCard intuitively grasped the essential difference between buying goods and leading a good life, between being rich and leading a rich life. This emphasis on intangibles and relationships, from reading a book to your child to watching your children playing with the cardboard boxes that packaged the toy instead of the toy itself, established MasterCard as a brand to be trusted and to display the right "family values."

From its first launch in October 1997, the MasterCard "Priceless" campaign, now seen in 105 countries in 48 languages around the globe, has brilliantly positioned the MasterCard brand as "the best way to pay for everything that matters." After nearly a decade of creative iteration, the campaign has earned more than one hundred individual awards and was still capable of winning awards as recently as August 2005, when "Home—Broken Window" won an award. *Adweek* commented, "The 'Priceless' campaign, after many years, still has the ability to tug at our heartstrings."[11]

The spot highlighted kids around the world playing baseball, with makeshift equipment, merely for the love of the game. "First base (old tire): $58. Second base (folding lawn chair): 630 pesos. Third base (car parked on the street): 300,000 yen. Home (the sound of glass breaking, then the kids scattering): priceless."

Upon being appointed chief marketing officer for MasterCard International in November 2000, Flanagan observed to *Brandweek*, "Being at ground zero for the development of MasterCard's highly successful Priceless advertising campaign provided an excellent perspective on where the brand was and where we wanted to take it. The success of the campaign has allowed us the opportunity to dramatically build awareness and preference for MasterCard globally. Priceless has evolved beyond an advertising campaign [to become] integrated throughout our marketing programs."[12]

While the "Priceless" campaign is still going strong nearly eight years after it first aired, it united, integrated, and rationalized the firm's diverse brand-building programs. Most specifically, it conveyed the message in whimsical, ironic, and knowing terms that customers and MasterCard both understand that what "really matters" is family time, relationships, and memorable moments. Such brand-building programs as a "Weekends Matter" sweepstakes artfully and simply reinforce the brand message. Inspired by research indicating that 40 percent of card purchases occur on Fridays and Saturdays, MasterCard gave sweepstakes winners a weekend home for a full year, providing them with ample quality family time. MasterCard developed a whole weekend-themed program to capitalize on these "Priceless" moments.

Developing and implementing these globally integrated brand-building programs has not been easy. According to Flanagan, "The executional part of integrated marketing may look simple on paper, but the execution and strategic integration can be tough" and need to be seen in the context of other major strategic initiatives that were implemented at the same time. There was a significant upgrade of the customer-facing/sales organization and a rebuilding of its processing capabilities. The fixing of the brand by leveraging the contextual code of important memorable moments through the "Priceless" campaign restored the banks' confidence in MasterCard and began the slow process of reversing years of decline.

MasterCard's success with its "Priceless" campaign demonstrates that product and benefit differentiation does not matter nearly so much as tapping into a relevant and important aspect of the ecosystem of consumer demand—here the emotional and memorable moments that we all share in our lives—and leveraging the contextual and cultural code. "Turning up the volume" and "cutting through the clutter" don't matter nearly as much—and are therefore not nearly as effective marketing tools—as indications and assurances that the brand understands that what matters to consumers and what they want is to live life—particularly those deeply empathetic, emotional, and humanistic moments that we call simply: priceless.

5: Activate a Driving Idea Around Growth Platforms

What happened at MasterCard can be put in clearer focus by looking at the key success factors that MasterCard shares with the efforts of other brands, such as Apple. Apple, like MasterCard, had identified platforms for growth to activate the brand. At MasterCard, the growth platform is about the clusters of priceless and memorable moments in consumers' lives. They were activated through its media advertising campaign and other forms of communications. At Apple, the growth platform is about the consumer music cycle: how you search for and learn about music, how you buy music, how you listen to music, how you store music, and how you discard music. The driving idea is that Apple helps "manage" this cycle, the entire music experience.

Managing music for a consumer is much bigger than just selling them a well-designed and functioning MP3 listening device. Adding a video to an iPod can be much more than simply watching video clips of artists. It can be the beginning of managing your entire video or visual library—an entirely new growth platform for Apple. Even managing music or video may be viewed as limiting because these are just components of managing a much bigger world from a consumer's perspective: the entire digital home or personal communications. With deals between Pixar, Disney, and AT&T, the possibilities are not this far out.

The iPod alone did not change how consumers live, work, and play around music. However, the iPod, together with its entire system of over two thousand accessories, did. It has captured a significant part of the ecosystem of consumer demand and hence changed how we live, work, and play. Such a system communicates, engages, and connects consumers. *Engagement* is the key search word. Consumers talk about the brand not simply in terms of a desired feature, such as the cool design, but in terms of how the brand helps them manage a certain activity in their lives. They become "hired" ambassadors to spread the word via word-of-mouth communications to others, explaining the value of the product in their own terms and language. The brand actually becomes an active word, as in "managing" this or that, not a paragraph describing the brand in a brand book or an elaboration in a graphics standards manual. Consumers engage, figure out how to make use of the "system," and share their thoughts, feelings, and opinions with others naturally, intentionally, and deliberately. Brand building becomes a massive open-source movement.

What works for Apple also does for those brands that were built precisely the traditional way of yesteryear. Think Marlboro, and one conjures up images of freedom and cool personified by the rugged, horse-riding, Stetson-wearing cowboy of the past.[13] Today, Marlboro is a big social networking affair for many. The driving idea here is not the activity in the cultural context, as at Apple, but the myth that Marlboro taps into and how it activates it in today's youth culture. Working from a database of 26 million smokers, Marlboro applies viral marketing, buzz marketing, and permission marketing text artfully. There are all the usual suspects: promotional giveaways, events, and weekend outings. But unlike serving as a supplemental marketing activity to traditional mass marketing, those efforts are the efforts—period. This is so in part because of severe restrictions on advertising but also in part because of self-imposed restrictions—for example, avoiding magazine advertising.

Nevertheless, Marlboro has built a vibrant community of people—people who chat, connect, text message, and meet in cool places. And this strategy is working: the parties are bigger than ever before, and market share is up. Marlboro events are not designed to promote the brand. This is not about having half-naked girls walking down Fifth Avenue in a fur coat—a recent event by another brand marketer. Marketing and brand building here is about activating a driving idea of people wanting to have fun, meeting, hanging out, socializing, and more. For those who care, Marlboro is part and parcel of the fabric of their lives, just as the iPod is for those managing their music.

In this situation, marketers are no longer the marketing department. The marketing department has democratized and is everywhere, inside and outside. It has left the building. Your customers are your marketing department! Inside and outside Apple, there are product developers who are equally a part of marketing as they develop new products, extensions, and functionalities that enhance the system and contribute to more buzz and engagement among consumers. Their efforts enable the stuff that really matters in life—going about activities, projects, tasks, and daily routines—living, working, and playing. The brand is built not only by emphasizing features through marketing messages that grease the purchase but by showcasing the brand in consumption and use situations.

In a way, the brand becomes the activity. If Kodak wants to really manage the memories of consumers, as it says in the long-running and successful campaign "Managing Memories," it needs to activate the brand around the major steps in the cycle from capturing to archiving photos: taking photos, editing photos, ordering prints, creating an album, archiving the photos. It needs to review its marketing, branding, and communications program in terms of how it engages consumers along these activities in consumers' everyday lives. It needs to define how it creates the consumption and use experience through Kodak products and services. In order to build the Kodak brand, this is far more important than evaluating how the "Managing Memories" campaign is consistently communicated across brand touch points in the spirit of an integrated marketing communications campaign. In fact, to build Kodak, consistency and communications matter far less, while transforming consumer experiences along the changing memory management cycle in the digital world matters far more. Ultimately, if Kodak is successful, it will be not because it has communicated its brand but, more importantly, because consumers have deeply embedded Kodak technologies, products, and services into their everyday lives. They will have assimilated and absorbed Kodak seamlessly into their everyday activities and behaviors, ultimately creating advantage over competitors—namely consumer advantage.

The final chapter discusses how companies can embed an innovation and growth agenda in real time so that the pursuit of customer advantage never goes stale.

Chapter Nine

Internalizing the Innovation and Growth Agenda

O NCE A COMPANY HAS GRASPED the essentials of pursuing consumer advantage, and after its leadership begins to see the possibilities that such an approach reveals, the task becomes implementation.

Creating the strategic blueprint so that the company can capitalize on its newly discovered potential is the immediate goal. But what happens down the road? The thrill of building on new demand-first growth platforms is intoxicating, but equally important for the long term, however, is ensuring that the smoke screen does not reappear. Enjoying the success that a well-placed offering can produce, a company can easily allow its new success to inadvertently foster blind spots that hide future strongholds of consumer advantage.

What's needed is a way for companies to embed the DIG model so that the approach remains, even after the initial discoveries (and the courses of action they demanded) are long past.

This chapter focuses on two long-established companies with widely different DNA that have transformed themselves into companies and cultures that are constantly seeking either to lift the smoke screen or to ensure that it does not appear. It is a difficult challenge. When there is a lack of fit between strategy and culture, it is usually the culture that wins. In the process, these organizations have created systems, processes, and tools that have changed the way they go about identifying opportunities and executing breakthrough innovations and growth.

The first company is GE. In chapter 5, we discussed how GE Healthcare acquired Instrumentarium and Amersham to develop vital growth platforms for GE Carestation. We mentioned the parent company's Imagination Breakthroughs initiative but did not go into detail. Here is the story of that important initiative. It describes how Jeffrey R. Immelt, the CEO, along with then-CMO Elizabeth Comstock (who has since moved on to broader responsibilities within GE's NBC Universal business) sought to transform an otherwise hugely successful company with discipline, results orientation, and Six Sigma efficiency into a company that also emphasizes creativity, imagination, and innovation and focuses on customercentric innovation and organic top-line growth.

Deutsche Telekom (DT) is the second story. It is the number-one European telecom company and one of the largest in the world with a complex portfolio of brands and businesses. The chief marketing officer, Jens Gutsche, provides the details here of how under the aegis of two CEOs—Kai-Uwe Ricke, who served from 2002 until 2006, and Renee Obermann, who has filled the position since November 2006—the company established a set of metrics and demandcentric accountability measures that are essential and form an analytical framework and basis for finding and executing a service-focused innovation and growth strategy.

The stories of GE and Deutsche Telekom are very different; together, however, they illustrate well how companies can embed a powerful new demand-first perspective toward profitable growth and innovation.

General Electric

Jeffrey Immelt's first day on the job as CEO of GE was September 7, 2001. Shortly after his appointment, Immelt—who had launched his career at GE in 1982 and held a series of global leadership roles in GE's plastics, appliance, and medical businesses in his twenty-two years at the company—delivered a speech at MIT laying out his long-term vision for the company. The speech made it plain that 120 years after its founding by the legendary inventor and entrepreneur Thomas Alva Edison, GE is in many ways as strong as ever. It remains the one firm on financial journalist Charles Dow's 1904 list of a dozen industrial stocks, published as the Dow Jones Industrial Average, that still retains its place in the Dow Average of thirty public companies today. But if GE were to possess an equally golden future, Immelt stressed, it would need to productively cope with a number of fresh threats not known to firms in Thomas Edison's or Charles Dow's day. "No matter what business you are in," Immelt maintained, "four huge forces, the equivalent of Hurricane Isabelle, will shape your future."

1. The emergence of a world of slower growth, defined by the presence of greater volatility and geopolitical risk—this in the wake of 9/11—in which the excess capacity suffered by nearly every industry potentially verged on 74 percent.

2. The emergence of "the most dominant global competitors of our lifetime" in China and India, nations where the establishment of solid technical foundations combined with ample human and material resources to create a level of global competition with non-Asia-based industrial powers unprecedented in the modern era.

3. The emergence of a global communications revolution, in which the Internet and the World Wide Web have created conditions in which "perfect information and pricing transparency" conspire to put producers and manufacturers at a distinct disadvantage in relation to customers.

4. The increasing consolidation of channels that control value—including Wal-Mart and Dell—producing a situation in which a small handful of players "set prices for everybody."

The inevitable outgrowth of this powerful convergence of global market forces, Immelt contended, presented companies like GE with a monumental challenge. They could either successfully fend off the impending horror of "commodity damnation" or relinquish their long-standing status as global leaders. The stark solution Immelt proposed to forestall this depressing fate, the only reliable and genuine source of profit advantage, "exists in our ability to differentiate through innovation." Fostering organic growth through innovation at GE was not a luxury, Immelt insisted, but a necessity for the company's survival in the coming decades.[1]

But doesn't every CEO on earth talk about fostering organic growth and innovation? Actively embedding such a process and a posture at a multibillion-dollar diversified firm the size of GE was obviously easier said than done. Immelt took immediate steps to get the innovation ball rolling by boosting the firm's target organic growth rate—tracking increases in revenue from existing operations, as opposed to acquisitions and currency fluctuations—to 8 percent from the average of 5 percent achieved over the past decade. He further insisted that to meet these aggressive growth targets, the product development and marketing functions at the company would need to begin working much closer together than heretofore imaginable.

Vowing to "make marketing a leadership function," after twenty months on the job Immelt announced the appointment of Comstock (who had led the company's corporate communications department for the previous two years) to the newly revived post of chief marketing officer for GE Corporate, a position that had gone unfilled for nearly two decades under Immelt's predecessor, Jack Welch. In a series of remarks delivered at a conference convened by the *Economist* in the fall of 2004, Comstock reflected on her mandate of marrying marketing, product development, and customer service in organizational terms. "The point of marketing," she said, quoting Immelt, "is to grow the company. Growth is not just about *making* our numbers, or even *beating* our numbers, or getting the costs out— something we've been remarkably good at at GE—but about taking risks and developing a pipeline of great breakthrough products, and marketing the hell out of them. Jeff wants marketing to become part of our bloodstream. He wants marketing to become as critical a component of our overall cultural process as Six Sigma."

One of the first concrete efforts to embed an innovation and growth agenda into the DNA at GE was the October 2003 launch of a high-profile initiative known as Imagination Breakthroughs. At the outset of this process, all business unit leaders at GE were asked to generate five breakthrough ideas, each of which could be credibly supposed to pack a potential of generating $100 million in new organic revenue for the firm. This mandate, for obvious reasons, caused considerable consternation among GE's executive ranks. According to Comstock, "The traditional view of marketing at GE had been that the product development people are the owners of innovation. The product development people create a product then the marketing people figure out how to persuade customers they need it. But at GE today," she emphasized, "we need to anticipate customers' needs before they can articulate them. Our marketing people need to work hand-in-hand with our technical people to develop a product that meets this emerging demand."

For twenty years, GE had generated new ideas by means of a brainstorming process known as TTT, an acronym for "Time to Think" and an integral part of the intellectual legacy of Alex Osborn, GE's legendary ad man as chief of BBDO. One concrete manifestation of this recent effort to reorganize the firm around innovation, as opposed to operations, was the enhancement of the responsibilities of GE's Commercial Council, a diversified group of about a dozen senior executives drawn from the ranks of senior sales and marketing executives, senior technologists, strategists, and product development staff. Council members meet by phone monthly and in person quarterly to ponder growth strategies and value creation for the customer. The "customer focus" mandate laid out by Immelt specified that every new initiative at GE be strictly evaluated through a critical lens that poses the broader question: How does this particular product or service improve the competitive position of the customer?

The next step Immelt took to deeply embed the new growth agenda into the GE organizational structure was to tie senior executives' compensation to their ability to generate these new breakthrough ideas. "Everyone thought, 'I've got to get into sales and marketing to be relevant in this company?'" Comstock recalled, before answering the question with an unequivocal yes. "People asked, What is this crazy stuff about marketing? *Isn't innovation about technology?*" To which she invariably responded with an equally unequivocal no.

"What we were proposing to construct was a fundamentally different model for the company," Comstock insisted. "We were still in the learning process of how to think about customers first. How do we develop this passion for the customer? How do we get closer to the customer? This being GE, we were inclined to do it partly by brute force, by introducing a flurry of new initiatives, and by freeing the sales folks to get closer to the customer. We talk about coming out from the back room into the front room. It's all about bridging the gap between producer and customer." What marketing was being held accountable for at the end of the day was *commercial innovation*, a term intended to stress the fact that true innovation is not always about sparkling new technology but about creating customer value. "Our marketing team had to be the voice of the future and the Voice of the Customer at GE."

Key to embedding this demand-first growth agenda at GE was the evolving concept of "One GE," a notion intended to unite the disparate elements of the far-flung firm into a unified customer-facing enterprise. Primarily, "One GE" became a means of ensuring that the customer was not confused by being approached by multiple GEs, representing different business units. To address the health-care customer, for example, multifunctional teams drawn from different parts of the company integrated with the health-care business customer, as was done with the evolution of GE Carestation. "The Emir of Qatar wants to do business with one GE, not five GE's," Comstock maintained. The 2005 ecomagination initiative provides a case in point, as it pulled five different businesses—water, energy, transportation (rail and engine), advanced, materials, and finance—into a single platform with which to approach customers interested in infrastructural projects differentiated by an energy-saving, "green," and sustainable twist.

In GE's case, close collaboration with customers provided the key to providing them with a series of new long-range value propositions. The process begins with "dreaming sessions" conducted at GE's executive center at Crotonville, where executives drawn from multiple constituencies within the company strategize about an uncertain future. "It's all a part of keeping the effort focused externally as opposed to internally," Comstock insisted. "It's all part of figuring out where we should place our long-term bets on where the needs of the customers will be ten years out." Ecomagination came about after GE energy customers openly expressed frustration at the lack of policy guidance emerging at the federal level in the United States with regard to energy policy. "There's nobody who knows their business quite so well as the customer," Comstock observed. "It was a big part of our job just to listen."

Deutsche Telekom

In 1990, amid a wave of deregulation sweeping the telecommunications industry worldwide, the German state-owned monopoly Deutsche Bundespost announced the impending privatization of Deutsche Telekom, its telecommunications arm, in what was slated to become the largest sale of private shares to the public in European history. For decades, telephony in Germany had been regulated as a public utility, as an adjunct to the far larger postal service. Yet as the iron curtain fell in 1989, the last remnants of socialism, the great lumbering "national champions" of Western Europe, were also falling by the wayside throughout the capitalist countries of the globe. Among the most potentially valuable of the assets destined to go on the auction block were the telephone monopolies and quasi monopolies that nearly every European government had created at the beginning of the twentieth century. Those same governments were now hungry to divest themselves of these white elephants, hoping to revitalize them, improve customer service, create wealth for private shareholders, and, not incidentally, cash in on the future revenue streams for the long-term benefit of many frustrated citizens.

On January 1, 1995, Deutsche Telekom was transformed into a joint stock company, one of whose most critical tasks became to persuade the great mass of German citizens (a notoriously risk-averse group) that purchasing shares on the open market of a quasi-moribund former government monopoly was placing a good bet on the future. Deutsche Telekom faced an uphill challenge in making the business case for itself as a going private concern, since for many Germans the sprawling organization had come to symbolize everything they despised about government monopolies: poor service, high rates, and a frustrating lack of accountability to the public. Yet for the first time in its history, as it prepared for its first public offering, executives at Deutsche Telekom were for the first time obliged to talk directly to consumers. This was the beginning of a profound institutional sea change at the firm.

In the fall of 1996, DT geared up to saturate the German media with an endless barrage of billboard, print, and TV advertising, all intended to generate public enthusiasm for acquiring the "T-shares" (*T-Aktien*) due to be sold on the Frankfurt Stock Exchange starting on November 18, 1996. Out of fear that the floated offering might sink like the *Bismarck*, the firm (backed by a consortium of Germany's behemoth banks) offered as a hedge against risk a tranche of so-called Safe-T shares. These were guaranteed to protect prospective Deutsche Telekom stockholders against any loss of capital from their purchase. The *Christian Science Monitor* memorably referred to this expedient as "capitalism with training wheels."[2]

In what would provide a stiff shock to the smart money, the German public responded to Deutsche Telekom's ardent pitch with feverish enthusiasm, hungrily devouring 713.7 million T-shares worth nearly $12 billion—100 million shares more than previously anticipated—in a single gluttonous gulp, with barely time for digestion, let alone indigestion. Even after the sale, the government retained a sizable 74 percent share of the public company, which has since been reduced in a succession of public offerings to around 45 percent.

Deutsche Telekom's victory in the marketplace was momentous. It not only had succeeded in selling its own shares, it had succeeded in selling itself and its vision of a rosy future to the German public. Investors who bought in on the ground floor quickly saw their shares fluctuate (as measured by the American Depositary Receipts, or ADRs, sold on the New York Stock Exchange) between $25 and $20. By January 1999, two years after the public offering, Deutsche Telekom shares had experienced a more than 200 percent increase, to nearly $42. By March 2000, Deutsche Telekom had risen amid a global telecom boom—fueled primarily by the rise of mobile telecom and public furor over the Internet—to an all-time high of $95 per share. Because of that rapid appreciation, holders of T-shares in Germany and abroad became swept up in the "irrational exuberance" of the time, and began furiously cashing in on the appreciated value of these shares (if they were lucky, savvy, or both) to fund exotic vacations, second homes, flashy new cars, and other luxuries and indulgences. Soberer souls who held on to their shares were in fact the ones who received the worst dunking.

By mid-August 2001, Deutsche Telekom's share value had sagged back to barely over its opening price of €14, even as Deutsche Telekom's costly purchase of VoiceStream Wireless (soon to be rebranded T-Mobile) further depressed disenchanted investors. On July 16, 2002, CEO Ron Sommer, who had presided over the privatization, stepped down. On November 15, 2002, Kai-Uwe Ricke, the former chief of T-Mobile, the fastest-growing and most consumer-facing piece of DT's portfolio, became Deutsche Telekom's new CEO.

Despite its slumping share price and public perception of long-term growth problems, Deutsche Telekom had grown into the largest integrated telecommunications company in Europe. It had successfully branched into the lucrative U.S. wireless market as the parent company of T-Mobile, a nationwide wireless service provider of digital voice, messaging, and high-speed wireless data services to more than 17.3 million customers in the United States. T-Mobile stood out in the competitive U.S. market as low priced, hip, and youth oriented, a service that offered Global System for Mobile Communications (GSM) phones, an enormous incentive and customer advantage to those accustomed to traveling abroad. With nearly 250,000 employees worldwide, Deutsche Telekom had boldly forged ahead with an expansion plan to build up its continental presence, acquiring the British cell phone company One2One and the French landline company Siris, in addition to increasing to 100 percent its control of Austrian mobile telephony firm max.mobil. Deutsche Telekom was particularly proud of the fact that as of 2004, more than a third of its $70 billion in revenues was generated outside of Germany.

Leading the Organization from the Outside In

In early 2003, Deutsche Telekom's CEO Kai-Uwe Ricke hired a senior executive to fill a position that had gone unfilled throughout the firm's existence: that of chief marketing officer.[3] Jens Gutsche, the former vice president of marketing at Lufthansa, had also served a senior stint at AOL

Germany, a joint venture with publisher Bertelsmann. Armed with a wealth of experience in the marketing ranks of two of Germany's most prestigious and customer-focused firms—Lufthansa, a model for service quality and operational excellence, and Bertelsmann, a model of a decentralized company with a vast portfolio of media and entertainment companies, brands, and assets—Gutsche promised to bring a strong balance of creative, operational, and service capabilities, all leavened with a broad global vision, to what would turn out to be a daunting task of engineering a cultural shift at DT toward a more consumercentric focus.

From a business perspective, the need for deepening connections with customers and opportunities for growth across the entire portfolio of Deutsche Telekom businesses appeared fairly obvious. For more than ten years, the company had been organized into four business units with different business models and maximum independence. Each of these businesses (T-Mobile, T-Online, T-Systems, and T-Com) was structured according to the major technologies of mobile communications, online, systems integration, and fixed line. The four businesses were branded using a common and powerful visual identity: the familiar magenta colors and the *T* reflecting their shared heritage and common future.

From an outside-in perspective, however, this seemingly logical separation into businesses by technologies did not effectively communicate to the customer the strength of DT's comprehensive portfolio. The successful 1996 launch of Deutsche Telekom, the highly publicized floating of the company on the DAX (the German stock index), and the significant and constant media and advertising presence of the (occasionally called) Telekom sisters, created strong awareness and familiarity for the corporate name Deutsche Telekom and its strongly linked house of brands. Research showed that consumers saw themselves primarily as customers of "Telekom" more than customers of T-Mobile, T-Com, or T-Systems. The division by technologies was further blurred by the fact that telecommunications services were provided by several divisions. For example, in order to get fast Internet access, a consumer gained access through T-Com, but the online services were provided by T-Online. Some of the same services were provided by the different Telekom sisters. On the horizon were dual-phone services, triple-play services (combination offers of TV, Internet, and telephony), and VoIP—new services that made the oft-talked-about convergence of telecommunications a reality. (A dual phone is a mobile phone that converts into a fixed-line home phone. VoIP would bring low-price fixed-line telephony services over the Internet rather than the network.)

Consumers increasingly saw the need to have all their communications solutions provided by a single source. Some consumers preferred to visit conveniently located retail storefronts, *T-Punkt*, or call into a call center to take care of all their communications needs. T-Punkt stores provide all the communications solutions offered by Deutsche Telekom and offer a convenient way to buy prepaid cards, pay a telephone bill, shop for a better calling plan, or take care of other necessary telephony chores.

In response to the changing telecommunications requirements of consumers, Deutsche Telekom adjusted its organizational structure into three strategic business units (SBUs):

- A broadband–fixed network area focused on consumers and small to medium-sized businesses and comprising the T-Com and T-Online businesses and brand names. This unit also handled the wholesale business with resellers and the entire basic infrastructure in the fixed-network field—the backbone of the company.

- A mobile services area and wireless services comprising the T-Mobile business.

- A third unit focused on business customers, divided into T-Systems Enterprise Services, focused on large multinational clients, and T-Systems Business Services, focused on the 160,000 large and medium-sized companies in Germany.

While these shifts in alignment of the organization toward consumer segments were important, many of the challenges facing Deutsche Telekom in adapting to the rapidly evolving European telecommunications landscape remained. Consumer demand had become more fragmented, while large telecommunications providers like Deutsche Telekom suffered from heavy losses in the fixed-line business, coupled with a decline in mobile telephony and enterprises. Historically, consumers rated the incumbent leaders' customer services as deficient and overall service quality in need of improvement. New and aggressive competitors lacking the "old government" baggage benefited from market liberalization and entered niches with focused offerings targeted to, for example, the low-price segments of consumers. At the enterprise level, competition intensified because of the convergence of mobile and fixed line as well as information technology and telecommunications. Customers also demanded integrated solutions (IP-VPN, mobile solutions, and LAN) and outsourcing deals, particularly major T-Systems customers.

Gutsche's first day on the job—Friday, January 2, 2004—was an unusually cold morning in Bonn, the former capital of West Germany. After spending a few minutes shivering outside the locked entrance to DT's imposing headquarters, Gutsche began knocking at office windows, hoping to find someone in their office during that holiday week. At last, he succeeded in attracting the attention of a lonely coworker camped out inside one of the first-floor offices, who let him into the hushed building, as deserted as a tomb. Even by the following Monday morning, by which time most of the enterprise had trickled back into work, he found that the corporate marketing department of the largest company in Germany by market capitalization, the largest phone company in Europe, was not really a department at all. Under previous management, the marketing functions, as well as product development and innovation, had all been decentralized and pushed out to the business units. As he sat down at his desk on his first day, Gutsche decided to define for himself the task ahead.

As he saw it, his task was nothing more or less than to transform Deutsche Telekom from a stolid and staid former monopoly into a company that deeply understood consumers. One of the first concerns he explored during this period was the intense competition in both domestic and foreign markets coming from number-two telecom player Vodafone, as well as the large number of feisty new start-ups such as O2 and Arcor. Gutsche's self-defined agenda became to figure out a way "to see the world from the perspective of a consumer and customer of the various services of Deutsche Telekom." From this vantage point, Gutsche sought to develop a strategy "to connect the consumer to how DT delivers its services."

One of the primary tasks that ranked high on Gutsche's agenda was to determine how the various Deutsche Telekom brands might be more precisely aligned with specific market opportunities, and to identify in which market opportunities the DT businesses and brands could be leveraged. It was only natural that each business unit would focus on its own products. Even the business divisions—between mobile and broadband, business systems and fixed line—encouraged such a product orientation. Each division booked revenue and achieved profit improvements strictly within its own core line of business. "Only in those few countries where Deutsche Telekom services were integrated, as in the US—where T-Systems and T-Mobile work closely together—did any incentive exist to think *beyond* the product," Gutsche recalled.

Gutsche divided his responsibility into four distinct areas: (1) advertising, (2) sponsorships, (3) brand portfolio management, and (4) customer relationship management (CRM). As he took inventory of the processes and systems in place to accomplish the task ahead, he noted some major gaps. Although Deutsche Telekom was one of the largest buyers of media in Europe, Gutsche lamented that there existed no rational system of evaluating marketing spend with regard to its impact on consumer purchase consideration or preference across Deutsche Telekom's brands. Advertising was largely evaluated on the basis of measuring campaign impact via several image trackers or postcampaign evaluations of effectiveness by the advertising agencies. There was no reliable system of measuring brand equity or of measuring the impact on purchase and repeat purchase of services from knowing the brand. There was little to no understanding of the impact of the relationships among the different Telecom sister brands and how they contributed to purchase and repeat purchase and ultimately overall top-line growth. Equally, there was little to no understanding of the lifetime value of customers, or customer equity, or which segments provided the highest and best opportunities for the T-brands.

Gutsche did have access to an abundance of market research studies on satisfaction, loyalty, customer retention, and brand image across the various divisions of Deutsche Telekom. An audit of this research revealed that the studies lacked comparability across businesses and consistency across time; also some were of questionable reliability and validity. The most important finding was that not one piece of research conducted with consumers could be applied to the question of exploring total demand-side opportunities across the entire Deutsche Telekom company and interdependencies among and between the T-brands.

A few weeks into the job, Gutsche commissioned a study to examine the business drivers of telephony in Germany, the United Kingdom, and Croatia from a consumer or customer perspective. This study entailed culling all existing research, working closely with each division to isolate those factors that drive purchase and repurchase of telephony in Europe. The exploration began with the identification of a list of problems and hassles with telephony that consumers experience in their everyday lives—solved either by some providers or by no providers. Several hypotheses were developed using one-on-one in-depth discussions in which consumers were asked to describe an everyday-life experience—a procedure to dissect the activities of a particular routine task, such as making a telephone call. The initial hypotheses were translated into a questionnaire used to interview seventeen thousand consumers by telephone. The result of these various analyses was a series of foundation maps—for each division and major segments of consumers—that clearly described the factors and drivers of business performance. One of the major and most welcome findings was that there were pronounced similarities across the different businesses and divisions of Deutsche Telekom. In addition, the foundation maps clearly defined the business drivers for each business in terms of purchase and repeat purchase of consumers, which provided the input for a comprehensive customer-based brand equity measurement study.[4]

Measuring Brand Equity

Measuring brand equity at Deutsche Telekom became a complex undertaking for a number of reasons. Gutsche and his strategic team were required to gain a clear understanding not merely of the equity of the Deutsche Telekom brand but of the entire portfolio of brands, including T-Com, T-Mobile, T-Systems (B2B), and T-Online. These brands shared a common and powerful visual identity—in a way, they were stapled to each at the hip; hence it became critical to more accurately measure not just the equity of each brand but also the *interdependencies* among the brands. How did T-Mobile influence the corporate brand Deutsche Telekom? How, in turn, did the Deutsche Telekom brand influence the mobile telephony brand T-Mobile?

In contrast to standard and off-the-shelf approaches to measuring brand strength, Gutsche was particularly interested in studying, measuring, and isolating those aspects or elements of the brand that drove each business's top-line growth. His key questions were:

- What drives purchase and repeat purchase of telephony services? In other words, what are the business drivers?

- How well does the current brand strategy support purchase and re-peat purchase? That is, how does the current positioning impact the business drivers?

This was obviously a different approach from the standard measurement of brand equity management, in which a brand's positioning is translated into a set of attributes or associations and the attributes are measured after taking measures of awareness and familiarity across a set of competing brands.

The single outstanding fact and insight that emerged from the consumer research related to brand equity was that consumers cared most about the performance of their provider on some fundamental business drivers and far less on positioning and claims delivering emotional benefits. Creative advertising campaigns, a standard practice in the European telephony market, full of warmth and emotions were perceived as far less effective in driving purchase and repeat purchase intentions than were improvements in service quality factors, such as the experience when calling the call center or visiting the T-Punkt retail stores.

This insight was deemed important and game changing for marketing at Deutsche Telekom particularly because there was a general and mistaken belief that younger target consumers—the so-called M-Gen, or mobile generation, of consumers—preferred to do business with a provider that was perceived as cool, that aspired to do new things with telephony, and that mirrored their self-perceptions.

This comprehensive study of brand equity was then used to develop a portfolio of metrics and measures to frame discussions about positioning, advertising effectiveness, and, most importantly, the relative contributions of the T-brands to each other and the role of the corporate brand Deutsche Telekom in the portfolio. An important development was the establishment of key performance indicators (KPIs) and targets that in the future were expected to become part of the annual performance bonus plans of key executives. These KPIs were established across major themes of brand equity that influenced four specific business drivers. Targets were established after various sensitivity analyses that showed the potential impact on purchase and repeat purchase that can be expected from a change in the levels of the four specific business drivers.

Customercentric Marketing

Gutsche then took up the issue of managing the entire marketing effort from a customercentric perspective. He introduced notions of customer equity, or lifetime value of the customer, a concept intimately related to brand equity but one that should be, in his view, the ultimate goal of all the disparate activities of the firm. "In those countries where we offer an integrated package of services," Gutsche maintained, "the sheer volume of data on customer behavior is extraordinary. We know what products they buy, what usage they have, what services they rely on, what price points they take. We can segment the customers by value—how much revenue that customer can be expected to generate, over time. A customer who is more valuable to us is obviously going to be addressed differently than a customer who generates virtually no revenue." Yet all of this data desperately needed to be sorted and culled through with regard to one overarching question: *What truly matters to the customer?* How could this information and new consumer insight be translated into how Deutsche Telekom and its brands managed customer interactions? How could the information and insights be used to enhance or optimize the offering to customers?

In early 2005, DT launched a customercentric profitable marketing initiative across all business units in Germany. At the core of this initiative was a segmentation of customers based on behavioral data (customer equity/value) as opposed to more traditional criteria for segmentation. Corporate marketing at DT assembled a cross-functional team of senior marketing executives, financial controllers, and IT staff who convened every Friday for a product development meeting for up to four hours at a stretch. DT's first behaviorally based segmentation was designed to address each segment with a specific range of products and services.

The key insight gleaned by Gutsche's team from this new segmentation was that achieving quality in telecommunications had little to do with such conventional measures of success as technology superiority compared with competitors', brand awareness, peer referrals, or other metrics so dear to the marketing community. "What is quality really about?" Gutsche asked rhetorically. "It is about how the SBUs deal with customers." Of course, the tricky part, organizationally speaking, is that "the corporate marketing function can't bring that much value to the table. Only the people inside the SBUs are capable of providing this advantage." At the corporate level, the framework provided to the units, labeled Customer Promise, came complete with a new set of metrics that were entirely customercentric: How many contacts does a customer have to have with a customer care center to get the product she needs? How much time does the customer wait at the shops? How many contacts does the customer have to make in order to obtain a repair or a replacement? Even the advertising messages were revised to reflect this customer-driven behavioral bias. "If you're looking for a new phone, we guarantee that you won't have to wait for more than five minutes in one of our shops to be waited on." As for e-mail exchanges, effective responses were guaranteed to take place within twenty-four hours.

Both brand equity and customer equity measurement KPIs provided Deutsche Telekom with a set of new metrics required to drive the business from a product to a customer- or consumercentric perspective, as a means of measuring business performance against the demand landscape of each of the businesses and brands and a means to provide a framework for the individual businesses to thrive and to seek their own points of difference and positioning. Often, companies make decisions without such valuable information at hand.[5] An obvious next step was not simply to determine actions for current-day management of the portfolio of brands and customer assets toward the goals of profitable growth but to develop broader, longer-term growth opportunities, or customercentric or demandcentric growth platforms that would leverage the advantage of Deutsche Telekom across all its brands and businesses and deliver new ways of meeting and solving the needs and wants of consumers.

Gutsche's goal at DT, strikingly similar to the goal at GE, became "to introduce customers and marketing as a leading discipline at the company." All companies have controllers, producers, and marketing people, Gutsche pointed out. Yet under the rubric of marketing typically are put sales and other forms of customer care. The people in charge of production are purely operational. Financial controls promote efficiencies and maximize profit. But whose job is it to care about the customer, to listen to the customer, to think, if possible, like the customer? The answer is obvious and has been the basis of a substantial organizational shift at both DT and GE.

Just as GE people ask, "What does marketing have to do with innovation and top-line growth?" and the answer is, of course, "Everything," so is Gutsche frequently asked at Deutsche Telekom, "What does marketing have to do with quality?" To which he invariably replies, "Because it's so critical to the brand."

The success of a company will not be determined by technology, but by the customer's perception of the added value generated by its services. At Deutsche Telekom, we don't just create products, we create products that *customers want*. We don't sell performance as an abstract concept, we embody it in our culture . . . We are also gearing our structures to the new era. They, too, will no longer be set in stone. In the future, they will develop continuously in line with market requirements. As a company of the future, we think and act with our customers in mind. And we are applying this mindset today—at all levels.[6]

Gutsche's task continues to be to ensure that this fine language forms a basis for action, as opposed to mere rhetoric.

In November 2006, Rene Obermann was appointed CEO of Deutsche Telekom. One of the many challenges facing the new CEO was to strengthen the company consistent with its leadership position. Obermann's new strategy consisted of initiatives, under the name of "Save for Service," to significantly improve service quality, enhance customer responsiveness, and save to improve competitiveness and value proposition to customers.

As Deutsche Telekom enters 2007, it is confronted with the unique opportunity to finally create the transformative customer experience and service quality that discerning telecom customers demand today. The opportunity is in plain sight. The new Save to Service strategy aims squarely at creating customer advantage through strengthening the key assets of the company, namely its customer relationships. This strategy is supported by the new demand perspective that includes the Gutsche work on brand equity, customer relationship processes, and quality initiatives. This work provides an analytical framework and underpinning for making decisions on how to win (what service improvement initiatives will return the maximum gains in terms of customer acquisition and retention?), where to win (which segments of consumers will most value the new DT, its broad portfolio of products and service, and its new service quality promise?), and what will win (what new innovations, products, services, business models, marketing programs, and revenue models will deepen the relationships and create true customer advantage?).

Embedding the Demand-First Perspective

The two case studies illustrate the challenges of embedding the demand-first perspective in two large, global and multinational firms. There are several key take-away lessons. The first is that it is important for a company to have a "champion" function leading the effort. In both cases, marketing, in its interaction with the CEO and particularly the establishment of a chief marketing officer position, has created an important impulse for the organization. At GE, the key structural change goes even beyond the marketing function. There, the establishment of the Commercial Council and the boundary-spanning market leader positions contributed enormously. Success at both companies required the person or group in charge of the innovation and growth agenda to reach far beyond the typical boundaries of just a single function like marketing.

The second take-away lesson is that there seems to be no simple recipe for embedding the process. This is critical; there is no silver bullet—and as a result, attempting to "cut and paste" verbatim what any of the companies featured in this book have done will not work. The starting point of the process toward achieving a demand-first perspective seems different depending on where the organization is. Deutsche Telekom is clearly at a very different vantage point than GE. As noted, GE is a very efficient company, already having launched one strategic initiative after another to streamline the organization. Deutsche Telekom is a much younger company that has emerged from a previous institutional character and organizational structure. Gutsche at Deutsche Telekom needed to build the tracks first before he could get the train of demand-first and customercentric development going in the right direction. GE was in a different place and required a different approach.

Having said that, however, these cases and the others in this book do suggest several "parting guidelines."

1. Clearly Identify the Key Demand-Relevant Assets and Make Use of Them

Much of GE's success can be attributed to the company's legendary discipline and productivity and process orientation. GE is well known for its ability to develop managers along these lines on the job and at Crotonville to deliver results and to manage a business efficiently. The higher challenge for Immelt and Comstock became how to harness this major asset of the firm and turn this asset around toward the customer. Creating value for customers from this asset required a new capability to unleash its value. This new capability became the innovation process—Imagination Breakthroughs married with a sophisticated marketing function, creativity, and imagination of the future.

Similarly, when Gutsche joined Deutsche Telekom, he observed that one of the incumbent telecommunications provider's major assets was its customer relationships—80 million of them—and the various brand relationships these consumers had with Deutsche Telekom or its business units. These various relationships were predicated on a long history of delivering new technologies and telecommunications services to consumers and the quality of services provided. The strength of the relationships with customers rises and falls with the quality of the services delivered by DT. The overriding task for Gutsche became not to leverage the discipline and processes and point them in a new way toward these key assets but rather to create the discipline and processes around these assets first. For Gutsche and Deutsche Telekom, this involved developing a companywide understanding of the brand equity and establishing the customer relationship management processes. In a way, Gutsche needed first to lay the tracks on which the train could move forward. Then he could focus on the important business driver that built, maintained, and nurtured these assets: service quality.

Both Gutsche and Comstock needed to expand their habitual domain and develop a deep understanding of functions and processes typically not connected to marketing. The functional silo is a killer for the DIG model, as this next story illustrates. Marketing professor Philip Kotler once had a conversation with the vice president of marketing for a major airline. Kotler asked him what he did in this job. Did he control pricing? "Not really," the marketing vice president replied. "That's the yield management department." Did he control where and how often the airline flies or the classes of services it offers? "Not really—that's the flight scheduling department." Did he control the services that the airline provided on the ground? "Not really—that's the operations department." So what exactly did he control? "Well," he told Kotler. "I run advertising and the frequent flier program."[7] Much like the hapless vice president of the airline, Comstock and Gutsche did not control much of the context they needed to become effective. The resources and profit-and-loss responsibilities were with the businesses,

SBUs, or divisions. Both marketers commanded through influence, using a staff of several dozen managers. However, the larger organizations of marketers and market leaders to be influenced were in the divisions or SBUs. At GE, Comstock had over five thousand professionals to work with.

2. Critically Evaluate and Develop the Distinctive Capabilities Deployed to Manage Key Assets

At GE, the issue was not whether the company was good at innovation—it is world class at innovation. GE, however, resembles many other large technology-based companies—3M, Boeing, or Siemens in Europe, to take just a few examples—that either enjoyed or suffered a long history of favoring strictly technical innovation over nontechnical innovation. Immelt and Comstock defined *commercial innovation* as the type of innovation most likely to be a driver of organic growth. The way GE established the commercial innovation capability—driven by the demand-first perspective—can be illustrated through some major new and old initiatives:

- *Setting up Imagination Breakthrough projects.* There are as many as eighty projects now. True to GE fashion, all business leaders must play; there is no choice. Each project is expected to deliver $50 million to $100 million in incremental revenues and support the company's $25 billion organic growth target. The objective of the program is to show what marketing can do and to seed innovation across all businesses and functions of GE.

- *Organizing dreaming sessions.* These day-or-more sessions with key customer groups focus on big issues in sectors like health care, energy, and rail and the future five to ten years out. In these sessions, the CEO of GE and several CEOs and top executives of customer companies think about broad solutions to challenges and new trends that change the boundaries of the industries, and frame major new opportunities for aligning GE's interests with those of its customers.

- *Leading a three-and-a-half-week creativity course at Crotonville, its executive education facility.* Every year since the program started, sixty of the most senior marketers from GE's businesses have gone on "an odyssey of creativity," with the objective to strike a balance between a culture and a company known for discipline, process and productivity, and imagination, creativity, and innovation, and driving specific innovations across the businesses.

Another important leadership challenge is to clearly communicate how the distinctive capability links to strengthening the assets of the firm and how this capability impacts customer-facing processes and hence profitable top-line growth. Capabilities alone do not create value. They must influence the major customer-facing processes of the firm.

At Deutsche Telekom, Gutsche's mandate became to clarify the role of brand and customer asset management in driving the company's growth agenda. Brand equity and customer equity initiatives demonstrated where value creation was, and development of these assets would impact the major business drivers for each SBU. Rather than merely relying on measuring brand strength, he focused brand management efforts on those aspects of the brand that created a differential response in customer behavior. In this way, he could demonstrate how changes in brand equity and any investments in brand-building efforts or improvements of service quality along major customer touch points directly impacted the top line through improved customer acquisition, increasing customer retention, or lower churn. Customer equity efforts further clarified the impact of service quality and other customer requirements at the segment level.

3. Choose Major Strategic Initiatives That Force the Integration of All Demand-Facing Processes

Stephen Shapiro, author of *24/7 Innovation*, contends that "regardless of what they say, many companies are, organizationally speaking, still focused on products, not on the customer or the market place."[8] Not so at GE. Its Imagination Breakthroughs initiative pushes change toward commercial innovation across the entire organization through a process called CENCOR.[9] The acronym stands for calibrate, explore, create, organize, and realize. Behind these words are a set of tools and concepts that help managers bring innovation to everything they do, from how to define the business or how to formulate a going-to-market plan to how they evaluate their performance with customers—for example, its well-known voice-of-the-customer process.

A distinctive capability must impact demand-facing processes of the firm from product development to customer relationship management or the going-to-market process. CENCOR integrates the innovation process with the commercialization process. In service-oriented companies, this usually involves employee management as well. At Deutsche Telekom, brand equity and customer relationship processes are brought together in quality initiatives that define service quality standards and behaviors for the entire employee base, from frontline call-center personnel to management.

4. Build the Culture

The DIG model creates value when it becomes part of the culture—the way things are done around here. Making it part of the culture goes far beyond a set of sequential steps and giving managers a toolbox. It often requires hiring from the outside in. GE, for example, brought in over two thousand marketers in just two years and hired five thousand new salespeople. It also changed the structure of the organization. GE created a Commercial Council that meets monthly over the phone and every quarter physically. It created new positions, called market leaders, that looked at GE from an outside-in demand-first perspective. Neal Sandy of GE Healthcare does not have a primary line but horizontal responsibility and brings the broad capabilities of all of GE to bear on behalf of customers of GE's Carestation anesthesia delivery system.

Samsung's advantage over Sony is often attributed to culture. Samsung operates more hierarchically and forces marketing, design, and R&D to work together. New ideas from outside—changes in consumer tastes in Berlin, Mumbai, or Singapore—travel very fast to engineers in Seoul rather than at Sony, where fractionalism still rules.[10] The separation between R&D, design and marketing can be found in many industries. Automotive companies, for example, are notoriously functionally organized in this respect and are responding. Ford Motor Company recently reorganized its Lincoln division to give less breadth and more depth to marketers. Rather than being in charge of multiple brands, marketers henceforth are in charge of just one brand but reach deeper and earlier into new product development.[11]

The culture-building process should not be confused with establishing a position in the organization that is in charge of the DIG process. While champions are important, the concepts and tools and processes that become part and parcel of the everyday work are equally so. Federal Express and UPS have developed a logistic capability with flawless execution not because of the presence of a single champion for quality but because quality has become an integral part of the culture of these companies. Capability has become culture.

The Tumult of Times Square—Epilogue

Does the outside-in approach, the focus on customer advantage, and the DIG model to achieve innovation and growth advocated in this book have staying power? One has only to consider Manhattan's Times Square to know that the answer is both "yes" and "increasingly so."

Tourists visiting New York City from every point on the globe have for decades included Times Square high on their itineraries. Marveling at the neon kaleidoscope of advertising imagery, bombarded by seemingly limitless options in shopping, dining, movies, plays, and tourist paraphernalia, these visitors walked, eyes to the neon sky, amid honking taxis and cars, barely conversing with friends and family, engrossed in the surrounding tumult. Uniquely vivacious, Times Square offered a concentrated dose of commercial energy unlike any other spot on the globe.

Today, however, almost all of us live in Times Square or a place quite like it. Tokyo's Shinjuku, London's Bond Street, Paris's Champs-Elysées, Shanghai's Nanjing Road, and other commercial thoroughfares broadcast at similarly powerful frequencies to visitors and residents alike. And even if you don't happen to live in proximity to one of the world's major Times Square equivalents, you are frequently, if not constantly, exposed to new products, marketing messages, and advertising ammunition of comparable complexity and intensity.

So intense is the onslaught, so loud is the din, in fact, and so dazzling the imagery, that the once-awe-inspiring mecca known as Times Square has lost much of its unique luster.

Even global villagers in towns thousands of miles from the nearest metropolis are being bombarded by a multitude of competing brands, products, pitches, services, offers, and promotions every time they visit a mall, turn on a computer or television, or open a magazine or mailbox. In the realm of advertising, the average American is exposed to over six hundred advertising messages in a single twenty-four-hour period. By one count, there are over forty thousand stock-keeping units (SKUs) in the average supermarket. Yet the average American family covers 80 to 85 percent of its needs from just one hundred fifty SKUs. Nor are American families unique in either regard.

Mathematically speaking, the world's business output is tending ever closer to infinity. Yet as infinity beckons, the limited absorption capacity of potential customers only becomes more precious, discerning, and selective. A record number of new product launches are announced every quarter and every year. Most fail. Marketers' efforts in touting these new products are not helpful either. A survey by Yankelovich Partners found that consumer resistance to advertising is at record levels. Sixty-five percent of Americans feel "constantly bombarded" by advertising. Fifty-nine percent claim that ads have no effect on their consumption. Likewise, nearly 70 percent of the American public expressed interest in goods or services that help block out marketing messages.[12]

Even more challenging for businesses is the fact that a significant number of consumers turn off. They multitask when using media, they time-shift consumption of media using technology like TiVo and zap commercials, or they opt for not being a cable or TV subscriber at all, thus avoiding marketing messages altogether.[13]

In this world, the desire for personal peace of mind has become increasingly urgent. People no longer want to satisfy a need or want. They want their Saturdays back. In this world, the fundamental premises of business over the last fifty years are changing. The notions of finding a need and filling it, or building it and they will come, are being replaced with new ones that are sensitive to the new behaviors, desires, and motivations of consumers. The consumer is in control.

This book's premise is that we cannot understand these new realities for businesses by looking from the inside out at the world of consumers. We must understand the behaviors of people and their daily experiences without our products and services or solutions tucked under our arms. We must immerse ourselves in their world in an unbiased way.

We also must not rely on what consumers tell us. Consumers cannot know what they have not experienced. If we want to see the hidden opportunities in plain sight, we must first cleanse the doors of perception and then some. We must expand our perspective in seeing what consumers want. We must explore the deep recesses of this ecosystem of consumer demand. We must challenge ourselves and reframe and expand the opportunity space to really see what cannot be seen in plain sight. And we must develop strategies and actions that capture a share of this evolving ecosystem of consumer demand. This will require not more radical innovations, more new products or services, but the activation of demand-first growth platforms by whatever means, and help customers absorb or assimilate an innovation, or retool old ways of doing new things, into their daily life or work experiences.

Ultimately, that is what the pursuit of customer advantage is about.

Notes

Chapter One

1. Saul Hansel, "New Man at Top Crossing Oceans to Confront Internal Borders," *New York Times*, March 8, 2005.

2. We make the distinction between customer and consumer to acknowledge that some companies view *customers* as the immediate buyers of their products—for example, retailers in the consumer goods business or other business partners in industrial markets— and view *consumers* as the end users. Hereafter, however, we intend to employ the terms pretty much interchangeably. The important distinction of our work is the unbiased study of the behavior of people first—the consumption or use behavior in consumer settings or work processes in an industrial or B2B setting rather than (or followed by) the study of individual differences across customers or consumers or characteristics or differences along such dimensions as demographics or lifestyles.

3. There is a rich foundation of studying these motivational forces, and we draw extensively on this work. See, for example, Grant McCracken, *Culture and Consumption II: Markets, Meaning, and Brand Management* (Bloomington, IN: Indiana University Press, 2005); and, specifically, on passionate consumption: Russell W. Belk, Güliz Ger, and Søren Askegaard, "The Fire of Desire: A Multisited Inquiry into Consumer Passion," *Journal of Consumer Research* 30 (December 2003); on seduction: John Deighton and Kent Grayson, "Marketing and Seduction: Building Exchange Relationships by Managing Social Consensus," *Journal of Consumer Research* 21 (March 1995): 660–676; and on hope: Gustavo E. de Mello and Deborah J. MacInnis, "Why and How Consumers Hope: Motivated Reasoning and the Marketplace," in *Inside Consumption*, eds. S. Ratneshwar and David Glen Mick (New York: Routledge, 2005), 44–66.

4. Dennis Kneale, "iPod Nano $250," *Forbes*, November 14, 2005.

5. The line continues with "for man has closed himself up, till he sees all things thro' narrow chinks of his cavern," from William Blake's most influential book, *The Marriage of Heaven and Hell*, composed in London between 1790 and 1793.

6. Jane Goodall, interview by the National Education Association, March 2004, on the occasion of its upcoming seventieth birthday.

7. David H. Maister, Charles H. Green, and Rob M. Galford, *The Trusted Advisor* (New York: Touchstone, 2000).

8. Michael E. Porter, "What Is Strategy?" *Harvard Business Review*, November–December 1996, 64. Some authors—like Milind M. Lele, *Monopoly Rules: How to Find, Capture, and Control the World's Most Lucrative Markets in Any Business* (New York: Crown Business, 2005)—believe that competitive advantage is to help improve profits in a market, but competitive advantage is not helpful to create the profits in the first place and to find new growth markets.

9. Clayton M. Christensen and Michael E. Raynor, *The Innovator's Solution: Creating and Sustaining Successful Growth* (Boston: Harvard Business School Press, 2003), 79–88. See also Clayton M. Christensen, Scott Cook, and Taddy Hall, "Marketing Malpractice: The Cause and the Cure," *Harvard Business Review*, December 2005, 74.

10. Richard Miniter, *The Myth of Market Share: Why Market Share Is the Fool's Gold of Business* (New York: Crown Business, 2002), 82–102; and Tom Osenton, *The Death of Demand: Finding Growth in a Saturated Global Economy* (Upper Saddle River, NJ: Financial Times Prentice Hall, 2004), 88–98.

11. David A. Aaker, *Brand Portfolio Strategy: Creating Relevance, Differentiation, Energy, Leverage, and Clarity* (New York: Free Press, 2004).

12. Kurt Badenhausen, "Brands Branching Out," *Forbes*, June 16, 2005, based on a research study conducted by Vivaldi Partners; and Chris Koestring, "Brand-Driven Growth and Radical Innovations: Leveraging Brands Beyond Conventional Wisdom" (PhD diss., Bocconi University, 2005), which describes five empirical studies conducted during 2005.

13. From a speech by Bill Ford, Chairman of the Ford Motor Company, delivered in 2000 at a conference organized by Greenpeace.

14. Theodore Levitt, *The Marketing Imagination* (New York: Free Press, 1983).

15. This story was written on the basis of several sources: Timothy J. Mullaney, "The Mail-Order Movie House That Clobbered Blockbuster," *BusinessWeek*, June 5, 2006, 56–57; Jena McGregor, "At Netflix, the Secret Sauce Is Software," *Fast Company*, October 2005, 48–51; and "Netflix Makes It Big in Hollywood," *Fortune*, June 13, 2005, 34.

16. Christensen and Raynor, *The Innovator's Solution*.

17. Gary Hamel, *Leading the Revolution* (Boston: Harvard Business School Press, 2000), 8–9.

18. W. Chan Kim and Renée Mauborgne, *Blue Ocean Strategy: How to Create Uncontested Market Space and Make the Competition Irrelevant* (Boston: Harvard Business School Press, 2005), 74.

19. David A. Aaker and Erich Joachimsthaler, *Brand Leadership: The Next Level of the Brand Revolution* (New York: Free Press, 2000), 153.

20. Gary Hamel, interview by Joel Kurtzman, http://www.strategia.com.br, 2001.

Chapter Two

1. According to Information Resources, Inc. (IRI) data reported in a *BusinessWeek* article, seven of Procter & Gamble's top nine brands lost market share in food, drug, and mass discount stores in 2000. Robert Berner, "Can Procter & Gamble Clean Up Its Act?" *BusinessWeek*, March 21, 2001, 80–83.

2. David A. Aaker and Erich Joachimsthaler, *Brand Leadership: The Next Level of the Brand Revolution* (New York: Free Press, 2000), 3.

3. Patricia Sellers, "P&G: Teaching an Old Dog New Tricks," *Fortune*, May 31, 2004, 59–63.

4. Kenneth Klee, "Rewriting the Rules in R&D," *Corporate Dealmaker*, December 13, 2004.

5. Patricia Sellers, "P&G."

6. Bruce Nussbaum, "Get Creative! How to Build Innovative Companies," *BusinessWeek*, August 1, 2005, 60.

7. Gilbert Cloyd, "At P&G It's '360-Degree Innovation,'" *BusinessWeek Online*, October 11, 2004, www.businessweek.com/magazine/content/04_41/63903493.htm.

8. Nancy Byrnes and Robert Berner, "Branding: Five New Lessons," *BusinessWeek*, February 14, 2005, 26.

9. Todd Wasserman, "Where Will Genie Go Next?" *Brandweek*, October 17, 2005, 23–24.

10. "Procter's Creative Gamble," *Campaign*, March 18, 2005.

11. Todd Wasserman, "Moment of Truth," *Brandweek*, October 10, 2005, M9–M18.

12. A. G. Lafley, "Procter & Gamble's A. G. Lafley on Design," interview by Peter Lawrence, Corporate Design Foundation (September 2001).

13. Patricia Sellers, "P&G: Teaching an Old Dog New Tricks," *Fortune*, May 31, 2004, 59–63.

14. Cannondale 2004 Power Rankings of the best manufacturers, mentioned in Kenneth Klee, "Grand Opening," *IP Law & Business*, February 2005.

15. Nathaniel J. Mass, "The Relative Value of Growth," *Harvard Business Review*, April 2001, 102.

16. This conceptualization of understanding the ecosystem of consumer demand has a strong academic and empirical basis in consumption behavior research. Cynthia Huffman, S. Ratneshwar, and David Glen Mick provide a thorough review ("Consumer Goal Structures and Goal-Determination Processes: An Integrative Framework") in *The Why of Consumption: Contemporary Perspectives on Consumer Motives, Goals and Desires,* eds. S. Ratneshwar, David Glen Mick, and Cynthia Huffman (London: Routledge, 2000), 9–31. In this book, these authors present an extended framework that focuses on goal structures and goal-determination processes of consumers and that explores more deeply how consumers set goals in their everyday lives. The role of the social-situational context to drive consumer behavior can be found in the extensive work of Russ Belk. In his recent work, he focuses on passionate consumption over the linear discourse of fulfilling consumer needs. This theoretical and empirical research has been a rich source for our work over the last twenty years. See, for example, Russell W. Belk, Güliz Ger, and Søren Askegaard, "The Fire of Desire: A Multisited Inquiry into Consumer Passion," *Journal of Consumer Research* 30 (December 2003): 327. Another source is Douglas Holt, who studied the cultural processes that create brand meaning; see Douglas B. Holt, *How Brands Become Icons: The Principles of Cultural Branding* (Boston: Harvard Business School Press, 2004). In the early 1980s, we studied passionate consumption processes and how context caused changes in behaviors of consumers. See Erich Joachimsthaler and John Lastovicka, "Optimal Stimulation Level, Exploratory Behavior Models," *Journal of Consumer Research* 11 (1984): 830–835.

17. We use the term *demand landscape* in reference to the work of sociologist Sharon Zukin, who uses the term *landscape of consumption*; see Sharon Zukin, *Landscape of Power: From Detroit to Disney World* (Berkeley: University of California Press, 1991). The term *demand* clearly details the opportunity for a company that results from consumption.

18. In fact, research has shown that, when asked, customers recall more often features they have experienced in another product. By pursuing these types of customer insights, companies actually may pursue an innovation strategy that leads to commoditization across product features.

19. Richard Bagozzi and U. Dholakia, "Goal Setting and Goal Striving in Customer Behavior," *Journal of Marketing* 63 (Special Issue 1999): 19–32.

20. There are rich sources of conceptual and empirical developments to understand context—specifically, how culture, cultural codes, and processes impact the ecosystem of demand and how consumers ascribe meaning to brands. For example, see Holt, *How Brands Become Icons*; or more recently, Jonathan E. Schroeder and Miriam Salzer-Moerling, "Introduction: The Cultural Codes of Branding," in *Brand Culture*, eds. Jonathan E. Schroeder and Miriam Salzer-Moerling (London: Routledge, 2006), 85.

21. Rick Kash, *The New Law of Demand and Supply: The Revolutionary New Demand Strategy for Faster Growth and Higher Profits* (New York: Currency Doubleday, 2001).

22. Gian Luigi Longinotti-Buitoni, *Selling Dreams: How to Make Any Product Irresistible* (New York: Simon & Schuster, 1999), 15.

23. Virginia Postrel, *The Substance of Style: How the Rise of Aesthetic Value Is Remaking Commerce, Culture, and Consciousness* (New York: HarperCollins, 2003).

24. In contrast to our concentration, Clayton Christensen focuses more narrowly on the "jobs to be done" of the consumer's ecosystem of demand. See Clayton M. Christensen and Michael E. Raynor, *The Innovator's Solution: Creating and Sustaining Successful Growth* (Boston: Harvard Business School Press, 2003), 79–88. See also Clayton M. Christensen, Scott Cook, and Taddy Hall, "Marketing Malpractice: The Cause and the Cure," *Harvard Business Review*, December 2005, 74.

25. "Press '1' If You're Steamed," *New York Times*, July 7, 2002.

26. Gary Hamel referred to this aphorism in Gary Hamel, *Leading the Revolution* (Boston: Harvard Business School Press, 2000), 121.

27. Sellers, "P&G."

28. Jeffrey R. Immelt and Thomas A. Stewart, "Growth as a Process: The HBR Interview," *Harvard Business Review*, June 2006, 60.

29. W. Chan Kim and Renée Mauborgne, *Blue Ocean Strategy: How to Create Uncontested Market Space and Make the Competition Irrelevant* (Boston: Harvard Business School Press, 2005).

30. For further discussion, see Stephen Brown, who explores these issues in depth and distinguishes between the one-world-one-brand world of the past and the "ambi-brand" culture of today. Stephen Brown, "Ambi-brand Culture," in *Brand Culture*, eds. Schroeder and Salzer-Moerling.

31. An excellent description of these traditional notions of market segmentation can be found in Daniel Yankelovich and David Meer, "Rediscovering Market Segmentation," *Harvard Business Review*, February 2006, 122.

32. Simply studying customers in context by defining the environment in which people consume improves significantly the prediction of brand preference. This has been shown in extant academic research; for example, Sha Yang, Greg M. Allenby, and Geraldine Fennell, "Modeling Variation in Brand Preference: The Roles of Objective Environment and Motivating Conditions," *Marketing Science* 21, no. 1 (Winter 2002): 14–31.

33. Jennifer Reingold, "What P&G Knows About the Power of Design," *Fast Company*, June 2005, 57.

34. Anthony W. Ulwick, "Turn Customer Input into Innovation," *Harvard Business Review*, January 2002, 5–11.

35. Professor Mohan Sawhney of Northwestern University pointed out to me this simple contrast of searching for products and services for customers versus the traditional marketing paradigm's way of finding customers for products or services, during a visit for an alumni meeting at Kellogg in 2002. See also Paul Nunes and Frank Cespedes, "The Customer Has Escaped," *Harvard Business Review*, November 2003, 31.

Chapter Three

1. PepsiCo 10-K Annual Report, 2005.

2. See www.smartspot.com for more information.

3. PepsiCo case-study quotations in this chapter come from interviews conducted by Erich Joachimsthaler and Steve Fenichell in February 2005 with Carlos Veraza unless otherwise noted.

4. The team of consultants was led by Nick O. Hahn, a managing director of Vivaldi Partners.

5. Susan Fournier, "Customers and Their Brands: Developing Relationship Theory in Customer Research," *Journal of Customer Research* 24, 1998, 343–373.

6. This figure was developed by a team of researchers, Georgina Miller, Andrea Wolf, Silke Meixner, and Agathe Blanchon-Ersham, according to a framework created by Georgina Miller, "Analysis of New Customer Understanding Methods as a Supplement to Traditional Customer Research Methods to Facilitate Opportunity Identification for Innovation in High Tech Companies" (thesis research, ESADE, Barcelona, 2004). Full references can be obtained from the author upon request.

Chapter Four

1. Allianz case-study quotations in this chapter come from interviews conducted by Erich Joachimsthaler and Steve Fenichell between February and August 2005 with Michael Maskus, Joe Gross, Erik Heusel and Thomas Summer, unless otherwise noted.

2. The methodology is called the Day Reconstruction Method (DRM), whose objective is to solicit from participants the social-cultural context in which they live and the primary activities, projects, and goals they pursue in their everyday lives. In this specific research, participants were encouraged to think deeply and clearly about key moments in their lives when they experienced fear, frustration, anxiety, happiness, and grace, all feelings and emotions oriented toward particular episodes or moments that might bear some relationship to the purchase and consumption of insurance products. Daniel Kahneman et al., "A Survey Method for Characterizing Daily Life Experience: The Day Reconstruction Method," *Science*, December 3, 2004, 1776–1780.

3. The exploration of goal adjacencies differs from exploring adjacencies typically done today where adjacencies focus on the product, or category, or brand. For example, a product adjacency of a car is the area of *telematics*, or technologies or services that could be used in vehicles. Examples are global positioning systems.

4. Philip Kotler and Fernando Trias de Bes, *Lateral Marketing* (Hoboken, NJ: John Wiley & Sons, 2003), 62–63.

5. There is recent and very deep discussion of the role of complementors in strategy by Nicholas G. Carr, "Complementary Genius," *Strategy + Business* 43, (2006): 26–30; and David B. Yoffie and Mary Kwak, "With Friends Like These: The Art of Managing Complementors," *Harvard Business Review*, September 2006, 88–98.

6. C. K. Ranganathan, conversation with author, February 2005.

7. Allianz AG, *Kundenmonitor Assekuranz* 2003, Psychonomics (internal document).

8. There has been extensive discussion about challenging industry conventions by authors in related fields. For example, from a strategy perspective, Gary Hamel, *Leading the Revolution* (Boston: Harvard Business School Press, 2000), 117, 144. From a perspective of advertising, Jean-Marie Dru, *Disruption: Overturning Conventions and Shaking Up the Marketplace* (New York: John Wiley & Sons, 1996); and Jean-Marie Dru, *Beyond Disruption: Changing the Rules in the Marketplace* (New York: John Wiley & Sons, 2002). Here, we focus on challenging industry conventions from the specific perspective of their relationship and impact on consumers' everyday lives as reflected in the demand landscape.

9. Kevin Werbach, "Using VoIP to Compete," *Harvard Business Review*, September 2005, 140.

10. Aline van Duyn, "Internet Causes 'Fundamental Shift' in Advertising," *Financial Times*, August 15, 2005, 21.

11. "Paying to Avoid Ads," *Economist*, August 7, 2004, 52.

12. Exploring new business models has been extensively discussed in Adrian Slywotzky, *Profit Patterns: 30 Ways to Anticipate and Profit from Strategic Forces Reshaping Your*

Business (New York: Crown Business, 1999); Hamel, *Leading the Revolution*; and many other sources.

13. See, for example, Jacob Goldenberg, Roni Horowitz, Amnon Levav, and David Mazursky, "Finding Your Innovation Sweet Spot," *Harvard Business Review*, March 2003, 120–129; and Reena Jana, "The World According to TRIZ," *BusinessWeek*, May 2006, 31.

14. Barry Nalebuff and Ian Ayres, *Why Not? How to Use Everyday Ingenuity to Solve Problems Big and Small* (Boston: Harvard Business School Press, 2003), 45.

15. Donald L. Laurie, Yves L. Doz, and Claude P. Sheer, "Creating New Growth Platforms," *Harvard Business Review*, May 2006, 80–91.

Chapter Five

1. Carestation case-study quotations in this chapter come from interviews conducted by Erich Joachimsthaler and Steve Fenichell from March to July 2005 with the following executives: Sandy Brandmeier, Joean-Michel Crossery, Tom Haggblom, Arto Helovuo, Risto Rossi, Neal Sandy, Deb Schaling, Marijean Trew, unless otherwise noted. A big thanks to Neal Sandy who significantly helped develop the case study.

2. See, for example, Donald L. Laurie, Yves L. Doz, and Claude P. Sheer, "Creating New Growth Platforms," *Harvard Business Review*, May 2006, 80–91. These authors focus primarily on the organizational challenges of growth platforms (how to manage growth platforms inside an organization) and less on identification and execution of growth platforms that emerge from a demand-first, unbiased, outside-in process to achieve customer advantage, which we are focusing on in this chapter and this book. We turn to the organizational challenges in more detail in chapter 9.

3. See Mohanbir Sawhney, Sridhar Balasubramanian, and Vish V. Krishnan, "Creating Growth in Services," *MIT Sloan Management Review* 45, no. 2 (Winter 2004): 34–43; and Mohanbir Sawhney, Sridhar Balasubramanian, and Vish V. Krishnan, "Finding Growth Through Product-Service Linkages" (Kellogg School of Management, Northwestern University, Evanston, IL, October 2004) and an article based on an interview of Antonio Perez, the CEO of Kodak, for a comprehensive discussion of these points of view (Steve Hamm and William C. Symonds, "Mistakes Made on the Road to Innovation," *BusinessWeek*, November 27, 2006, 26).

4. There are several sources for quantifying and evaluating the future value of financial valuation methodologies (Mark Esser, Tharek Murad Aga, Sandro Principe, "Valuation of Strategic Growth Options," Vivaldi Partners Working Paper, New York/Düsseldorf/Zurich, 2006) as well as decision analysis methodologies (Sam Dias, and Lynette Ryals, "Options Theory and Options Thinking in Valuing Returns on Brand Investments and Brand Extensions," *Journal of Product & Brand Management* 11, no. 2 (2002): 115–128.)

Chapter Six

1. State Street case-study quotations in this chapter come from interviews conducted by Erich Joachimsthaler from July and August of 2005 with State Street executives, particularly Marsh N. Carter, unless otherwise noted.

2. The formulation of the strategy statement along the dimensions of OAS—objective, advantage, scope—was developed by the late Michael Rukstad, formerly senior lecturer in the strategy area of the Harvard Business School. Since 1997, Professors Rukstad and David Collis and I have developed action learning tools and facilitated workshop methodologies to formulate strategic blueprints for action and applied them in a large number of companies.

3. There are a number of excellent reviews for conducting such an analysis. For example, Lisa Fortini-Campbell, "Integrated Marketing and the Consumer Experience," in

Kellogg on Integrated Marketing, eds. Dawn Iacobucci and Bobby Calder (Hoboken, NJ: John Wiley & Sons, 2003).

4. The strategic repositioning also included a comprehensive brand strategy and corporate identity program that changed the identity from State Street Bank to State Street. This program was led by James Cerruti of Vivaldi Partners while he was chief strategy officer of the corporate identity firm FutureBrand.

5. The evolution of State Street's product and service offerings is well described in Kelley A. Porter and Stephen P. Bradley, "State Street Corporation: Leading with Information Technology (B)," Case 9-799-034 (Boston: Harvard Business School, 1999).

6. Unilever case-study quotations in this chapter come from interviews conducted by Erich Joachimsthaler and Steve Fenichell from July and August of 2005 with Unilever executives, particularly Kevin George and Alison Zelen, unless otherwise noted.

7. "The Real Axe Effect," *Advertising Age*, May 15, 2006, 1, 45.

8. Thomas Mucha, "Spray Here. Get Girl. Young Men Have Just One Thing on Their Minds. The Trick Is to Convince Them They Can Get It If They Wear the Right Deodorant," *Business 2.0*, June 1, 2003, 13.

9. Julie Bosman, "How to Sell Body Sprays to Teenagers? Hint: It's Not Just Cleanliness," *New York Times*, October 28, 2005, 5.

Chapter Seven

1. BMW Annual Report 2004, Preface by the Chairman of the Board of Management.

2. See chapter 4 of David A. Aaker and Erich Joachimsthaler, *Brand Leadership: The Next Level of the Brand Revolution* (New York: Free Press, 2000); David Aaker and Erich Joachimsthaler, "The Brand Relationship Spectrum: The Key to the Brand Architecture Challenge," *California Management Review* (Summer 2000): 8–23; and Erich Joachimsthaler and Markus Pfeiffer, "Strategie und Architektur von Markenportfolios," in *Handbuch Markenfuehrung*, ed. Manfred Bruhn (Wiesbaden, Germany: Gabler Verlag, 2004), 723–746.

3. Sergio Zyman discusses extensively the need for renovation strategies over innovation strategies; see Sergio Zyman, *Renovate Before You Innovate* (New York: Portfolio, 2004).

4. Chris Bangle, "The Ultimate Creativity Machine: How BMW Turns Art into Profit," *Harvard Business Review*, January 2001, 47.

5. Neil E. Boudette, "BMW's Push to Broaden Line Hits Some Bumps in the Road," *Wall Street Journal*, January 10, 2005, A1.

6. The brand identity system is an essential component to articulate the strategy of business unit or firm or product; see David J. Collis and Cynthia A. Montgomery, *Corporate Strategy: A Resource-Based Approach*, 2nd ed. (New York: McGraw-Hill/Irwin, 2004). Two additional elements of the strategy are the formulation of the objective, advantage, scope (OAS) strategic statement and the strategic positioning that links corporate strategy or business strategy and the brand identity system. A comprehensive framework and model of strategic positioning is the customer-based brand equity (CBBE) management model by Kevin L. Keller; see Kevin Lane Keller, *Strategic Brand Management: Building, Measuring, and Managing Brand Equity*, 2nd ed. (Upper Saddle River, NJ: Prentice Hall, 2003); and Kevin Lane Keller, Brian Sternthal, and Alice Tybout, "Three Questions You Need to Ask About Your Brand," *Harvard Business Review*, September 2002, 3–8. These approaches comprehensively define a brand strategy from a demand-first perspective. This includes, at a minimum, answers to the following questions: In what business *are* we and in what we are not, and in what businesses do we *want* to be? What segments do we want to address? What segments do we choose to ignore? What do we stand for and aspire to create in the minds of consumers and other stakeholders? How do we fit into the context of consumers' everyday lives?

7. See further discussions on this topic in: Heribert Meffert, Christoph Burmann, Martin Koers, *Markenmanagement* (Wiesbaden, Germany: Gabler Verlag, 2005), 19–32; Franz-Rudolf Esch, *Moderne Markenfuehrung* (Wiesbaden, Germany: Gabler Verlag, 2005, 3); Franz-Rudolf Esch, Andreas Herrmann, and Henrik Sattler, eds., *Marketing* (Wiesbaden, Germany: Gabler Verlag, 2006); and Manfred Bruhn, *Integrierte Unternehmens- und Markenkommunikation* (Stuttgart, Germany: Schaeffer-Poeschel Verlag, 2006).

8. From the speech "What Makes BMW a Strong Brand?" by Jürgen Pawlik, director, Group Brand & Product Portfolio, Market Research, BMW Group (Corporate Identity Optimizing Brand Strategies Forum, Amsterdam, May 24–25, 2005).

9. Ibid.

10. See a much more comprehensive and complete discussion of this new form of branding in Jonathan E. Schroeder and Miriam Salzer-Moerling, eds., *Brand Culture* (London: Routledge, 2006); Douglas B. Holt, *How Brands Become Icons: The Principles of Cultural Branding* (Boston: Harvard Business School Press, 2003); or Rob Walker, "The Brand Underground," *New York Times Magazine*, July 30, 2006, 28–55.

11. This section draws on several books and articles about Intel, particularly Jeffrey Brown, Sandeep Junnarkar, Mukul Pandya, Robbie Shell, and Susan Warner, *Lasting Leadership: What You Can Learn from the Top 25 Business People of Our Times* (Upper Saddle River, NJ: Wharton School Publishing, 2004).

Chapter Eight

1. David Whelan, "Name Recognition," *Forbes*, June 20, 2005, 113.

2. Jena McGregor, "The World's Most Innovative Companies," *BusinessWeek*, April 24, 2006, 62.

3. This section was written by Joachim H. Blickhäuser, general manager, BMW Group Brand Academy. The Brand Academy's role in creating a brand culture that understands the three master brands at BMW is an important effort in light of research that shows how few employees generally believe that a company has a strong culture. Spherion Corporation found in a study that only 44 percent of adult workers said they believed their company "has a widely embraced and understood corporate culture." See Paul Michelman, "Value Perceptions by the Numbers," *Harvard Management Update* 11, no. 1 (January 2006), 10. These results are generally lower in companies with a house-of-brands portfolio structure.

4. Gail Edmondson, "BMW's Dream Factory," *BusinessWeek*, October 16, 2006, 70.

5. The notion of inverting the funnel of the communications mix was first expressed by Jean-Noel Kapferer, *Reinventing the Brand* (London: Kogan Page, 2001); and Markus Pfeiffer, *Interactive Branding—Eine interaktions- und wissensorientierte Perspektive, Schriftenreihe Global Branding, Bd. 2, Eds. v. FGM Fördergesellschaft Marketing e.V.*, Munich, 2001.

6. Personal conversation with the author, June 2006.

7. Mick Hoban and Warren Mersereau, two world-class sports marketers, helped with their insights on branding and the role of sports in building a brand.

8. Robert Berner, "I Sold It Through the Grapevine," *BusinessWeek*, May 29, 2006, 32–34.

9. Dave Ulrich, Jack Zenger, and Norm Smallwood, *Results-Based Leadership* (Boston: Harvard Business School Press, 1999).

10. MasterCard case-study quotations in this chapter come from interviews conducted by Erich Joachimsthaler in 2004 with MasterCard executives, particularly Larry Flanagan and Charles Unger, unless otherwise noted.

11. Best Spots, *Adweek*, August 15, 2005.

12. Chuck Stogel, "Priceless Promotion for MasterCard's Flanagan," *Brandweek*, November 20, 2000.

13. Nanette Byrnes, "Leader of the Packs," *BusinessWeek*, October 31, 2005, 38–39.

Chapter Nine

1. GE case-study quotations from interviews with various executives at GE, particularly Beth Comstock, during August 2005. Since we interviewed and wrote the story for this book, an excellent interview that further details the GE story has been published; see Jeffrey R. Immelt and Thomas A. Stewart, "Growth as a Process: The HBR Interview," *Harvard Business Review*, June 2006, 60–70.

2. A more extensive discussion about Deutsche Telekom's initial public offering of T-Shares and the *Christian Science Monitor* quote of "capitalism with training wheels," can be found in the online supplement (www.german-way.com) to the books by Hyde Flippo, *When in Germany* (New York, McGraw-Hill, 2002); and Hyde Flippo, *The German Way* (New York: McGraw-Hill, 1996).

3. Deutsche Telekom case-study quotations in this chapter come from interviews conducted by Erich Joachimsthaler and Steve Fenichell in August of 2005 with Deutsche Telekom executives, particularly Dr. Jens Gutsche, unless otherwise noted.

4. Conceptually, the framework and model of brand equity management was that of Kevin Lane Keller, *Strategic Brand Management: Building, Measuring, and Managing Brand Equity*, 2nd ed. (Upper Saddle River, NJ: Prentice Hall, 2003); Kevin L. Keller and Donald Lehman, "The Brand Value Chain: Optimizing Strategic and Financial Brand Performance," *Marketing Management*, May–June 2003; and Markus Pfeiffer and Joel Rubinson, "Brand Key Performance Indicators as a Force for Brand Equity Management," *Journal of Advertising Research* 6 (2005): 187–197.

5. A survey by Strativity Group on customer experience management showed that only 12.9% of those surveyed knew the average annual value of a customer to their business, only 9.7% knew the cost of a customer complaint to their business, and only 8.6% knew the cost of acquiring a new customer; see "Do You Know What Your Customers Are Worth?" *Fast Company*, September 2006, 68.

6. Deutsche Telekom Annual Report 2004.

7. Mohanbir Sawhney, "A Manifesto for Marketing: What Ails the Profession and How to Fix It," *CMO Magazine*, Summer 2004.

8. Stephen M. Shapiro, *24/7 Innovation: A Blueprint for Surviving and Thriving in an Age of Change* (New York: McGraw-Hill, 2002).

9. Bruce Nussbaum, "Get Creative: How to Build Innovative Companies," *BusinessWeek*, August 1, 2005.

10. Cliff Edwards, "The Lessons for Sony at Samsung," *BusinessWeek*, October 10, 2005, 37.

11. Karl Greenberg, "New Grill Adorns Lincoln Effort," *Brandweek*, October 17, 2005.

12. "A Farewell to Ads?" *Economist*, April 17, 2004, 61–62.

13. A 2005 study conducted at Ball State University in Indiana that observed four hundred people—across a broad age range—for a day found that 96% of them were media multitasking about a third of the time they were using media. A study conducted by MTV Networks using an online sample of 4,213 people found that respondents engaged in 15.6 hours of leisure activity a day, which included nonmedia activities like shopping, socializing, or eating. About a third of that time was spent multitasking, often involving consuming more than one medium at a time; see Sharon Waxman, "A Laboratory Eye's View of

Multitasking," *New York Times*, May 15, 2006. Time-shifting devices (DVR or TiVo) will be in over 18 percent of all American households by the end of 2006 and in nearly 40 percent by 2010; see David Kiley, "Learning to Love the Dreaded TiVo," *BusinessWeek*, April 17, 2006, 88. According to Nielsen Media Research, while only about 11 percent of U.S. homes have DVRs so far, 87 percent of those households zap commercials; see Roland Grover, "The Sound of Many Hands Zapping," *BusinessWeek*, May 22, 2006, 38.

Index

About the Author

DR. ERICH JOACHIMSTHALER is one of the world's leading authorities on brand strategy and marketing, and is the founder and CEO of Vivaldi Partners, a global strategy, innovation, and marketing firm. He works inside leading companies around the world and across industries to build strong brands, formulate new growth strategies, reinvent business strategies and models, and establish capabilities in innovation and marketing to help his clients succeed.

Dr. Joachimsthaler is the author of more than sixty articles on strategy, branding, and marketing in leading academic and business journals including *Harvard Business Review, Sloan Management Review* and *California Management Review*. His previous book, *Brand Leadership: The Next Level of Brand Revolution*, coauthored with David A. Aaker, was published by The Free Press in 2000.

Early in his career, Joachimsthaler held academic positions at various institutions in the United States and Europe. He taught at the University of Southern California, and after finishing his post-doctoral fellowship at Harvard Business School, he joined IESE Business School in Barcelona and later the University of Virginia, Darden School of Business. Joachimsthaler has maintained his ties to many executive programs around the world and continues to teach classes when time permits. He is also a sought-after speaker and consultant.

Dr. Joachimsthaler resides in New York City. He can be contacted by e-mail: ej@vivaldipartners.com.